INSIDE THE | **CUBAN REVOLUTION**

INSIDE THE

CUBAN
REVOLUTION

FIDEL CASTRO AND THE
URBAN UNDERGROUND

JULIA E. SWEIG

HARVARD UNIVERSITY PRESS

CAMBRIDGE, MASSACHUSETTS

LONDON, ENGLAND

First Harvard University Press paperback edition, 2004

Library of Congress Cataloging-in-Publication Data

Sweig, Julia.
Inside the Cuban revolution :
Fidel Castro and the urban underground /
Julia E. Sweig.
p. cm.
Includes bibliographical references and index.
ISBN 0-674-00848-0 (cloth)
ISBN 0-674-01612-2 (pbk.)
1. Cuba—History—1933–1959.   2. Cuba—History—
Revolution, 1959—Underground movements.
3. Movimento Revolucionario 26 de Julio.   4. Castro,
Fidel, 1927– —Relations with revolutionaries.
5. Revolutionaries—Cuba—Attitudes.   6. Guerrillas—
Cuba—Attitudes.   I. Title.

F1787.5 .S96 2002
972.9106'3—dc21   2002017151

Designed by Gwen Nefsky Frankfeldt

FOR REED, ISABEL, AND ALEXANDER

Contents

Illustrations

Acknowledgments

This project began as graduate research, continued as a dissertation, and ended, to my great fortune, as a bona fide published book. I have accumulated many debts during that process and wish to extend my thanks to all of those individuals and institutions that have encouraged me to complete this endeavor.

The Council on Foreign Relations, where I work as senior fellow and deputy director of the Latin America program, graciously—in fact, insistently—allowed me to clear my desk of day-to-day duties in order to transform the text into a readable manuscript. Leslie H. Gelb, president of the Council, has been a true champion, demonstrating his commitment to nurturing young foreign policy scholars, giving me generous advice and, most important, the time and encouragement to finish this project. It is more than a dream come true to have been able to focus first on Cuba and now more broadly on Latin America at an institution of the Council's prestige, under Les Gelb's magnanimous leadership.

I am profoundly grateful for the advice and example of Kenneth Maxwell, distinguished senior Latin America scholar at the Council, who has enthusiastically encouraged me since the day I showed up at his door by reading portions of the manuscript and generously providing crucial advice and guidance. Larry Korb, the Council's vice president and director of Studies, deserves sincere thanks for nurturing my work. He, along with my close friend and adviser Walter Russell Mead, paved the way for my meeting Les Gelb and joining the Council. Mike Peters, Alton Frye, and Paula Dobriansky each provided much crucial advice along the way, as have Janice Murray, David Kellogg, and Patricia Dorff.

My research associate, Jessica Duda, worked far beyond the call of duty in providing last-minute research, reading and rereading, editing, and proofreading the final manuscript. She posed challenging questions throughout that forced me to clarify my argument and made this a far more coherent book than it could have been otherwise. I am truly fortunate to have had such a spirited aide-de-camp during the final round of work. We were blessed this summer by the appearance of an intern, Margaret Myers, then an undergraduate at the University of Virginia. Her energy and wizardry in fact-checking and research came as an unexpected boon, for which we thank her. Tomás Amorím, Charlie Day, Theo Gemelas, Linda Harsh, Chris Sierra, Deepak Trivedi, Lorena Cohan, and Michael Marx McCarthy have my special thanks.

This work would not have been possible without the support of many individuals at the Johns Hopkins University School of Advanced International Studies (SAIS). The director of the Latin America program, Riordan Roett, opened many, many doors for me—and kept me from walking through some others. It wasn't exactly fashionable to wear one's motherhood on one's sleeve in my particular field, but Dr. Roett had several working mothers in his graduate program whom he avidly supported as we raised babies, produced books, and built careers. Moreover, his intellectual and institutional guidance was consistently of great value. My thesis adviser, Piero Gleijeses, gave me the confidence and support I needed to launch this project. I am grateful to him for the many hours he spent reading chapters, talking over my research, and helping me navigate through the often choppy waters of politics and bureaucracy that a project of this nature inevitably confronts. I say more about the value of his guidance in "About the Research." Wayne Smith deserves my heartfelt gratitude for trusting me with one of his projects, *CubaINFO*, and for his guidance, friendship, and time since I moved to Washington, D.C. in 1987. Franklin Knight's comments on my chapters and insights into Cuban history were indispensable, as was his camaraderie and support when we met on research trips in Cuba. Cynthia McClintock of George Washington University read the manuscript and volunteered to sit on my committee, and I thank her for her valuable comments and generosity with her time. At the Bologna program, I was fortunate that John Harper encouraged me to begin pursuing some of the ideas herein. My thanks go as well to Steven Szabo, academic dean at SAIS, Peter Promen, Linda Carlson and the entire staff of the SAIS library, and finally Diane Monash, for her support to all of us in the Latin America program.

I also benefited along the way from research assistance by Jon Elliston, Lourdes Prado, Ben Smith, and Carol Sweig. My best friend, Jaimie Sanford, spent a week with me at the Eisenhower Library in Abilene, Kansas, sifting through government records. David Haight, senior archivist at the Eisenhower Library, provided energetic assistance during my research there. Three friends who are also accomplished writers, William Arkin,

Robin Broad, and Marianne Szegedy Maszak, gave me desperately needed advice in organizing the material and structuring the story. Gail Reed, Virginia Schofield, and Janet Shenk are true friends and great critics. Consuelo García also deserves many thanks, as do June Erlich, Steven Goldstein, Bunny Kolodner, Martin Poblete, Stephen Schlesinger, Victor Wallis, and Cora Weiss. The novelist Barbara Raskin treated me like a writer long before this project came close to resembling a book. Her vote of confidence and the friendship of her family have stayed with me long since her untimely passing.

Though they are in no way responsible for the work at hand, I want to acknowledge the intellectual debts I have to several accomplished scholars and observers of Cuban history and politics: in the United States, María de los Angeles Torres, Fulton Armstrong, Philip Brenner, Jorge Domínguez, Peter Kornbluh, William LeoGrande, Marifeli Pérez-Stable, and Louis A. Pérez, Jr.; and in Cuba, Pablo Armando Fernández, Soraya Castro Mariño, Rafael Hernández, Gladys Marel García Pérez, and Oscar Zanetti. I wish also to thank the two anonymous readers during Harvard's review process, whose extensive comments helped me enormously to convert the text from thesis to book.

There is one individual who merits his own category of thanks: Saul Landau, documentary filmmaker, journalist, scholar, teacher, poet, and friend. I met Saul in 1983 when he came to teach at the University of California, Santa Cruz. Since then, he has encouraged me to write and think, especially about Cuba but about so many other things, first as a mentor, then as a boss, and now as a colleague and friend. He introduced me to Cuba almost twenty years ago. In ways too numerous to list, this project would simply not have been possible without him.

For financial support, I wish to thank the Dwight D. Eisenhower Foundation, the Johns Hopkins University Graduate Fellowship program at SAIS, the Cuba Exchange Program also of Johns Hopkins, the Latin America Studies Fellowship Program at SAIS, Hobart Spalding and the Wellspring Foundation, the Ford Foundation, the John D. and Catherine T. MacArthur Foundation, the Arca Foundation, and the General Services Foundation. Carol Bernstein Ferry and Ping Ferry, two legendary Americans and dear friends, provided support, financial and otherwise, and I am saddened that neither is here now to consider the final product.

In Cuba, my thanks go first to Dr. Pedro Álvarez Tabío, director of the Council of State's Office of Historic Affairs (OAH), the archive that contains the Cuban primary source documents that form the basis for this book. Over a three-year period, Tabío and his superb deputy, Elsa Montero Maldonado, graciously put the staff and records of the archive at my disposal and helped arrange many of the interviews I conducted in Cuba. They willingly answered my questions and helped me locate materials even as my requests for material seemed to increase exponentially. My thanks go as well to Manuel López Díaz, director of the Institute of History, whose able staff facilitated my work there with generosity and patience. Also in Cuba, many individuals spent long hours with me talking through different aspects of this project, helped open doors I could not have otherwise pushed through myself, or simply offered friendship and warmth to me and my family during research trips to the island: Ramon Sánchez Parodi, Juan Escalona Reguera, José Antonio Arbesú, and Fernando García Bielsa helped me gain access to the OHA archives; Manuel Fraga, Hugo Yedra, Fernando Remírez, Patricia Semidet, Dagoberto Rodríguez, Josefina Vidal, Milagros Martínez, José Barrios, and Miguel Alvarez facilitated communications at crucial moments; José and María Josefa Fernandez and their family helped me with interviews; Rafael Hernández, Marisel Caraballo, Isabel Jaramillo, as well as Soraya Castro and Fernando García Yip and their family have shared many years of friendship; Gloria Leon Rojas, Antonio Lopez Lopez, and their family welcomed my own into their home and supported my research immeasurably; Elsa Montero Maldonado and José Gómez Abad championed this project; and Pablo Armando Fernández and Maruja Fernández opened their home and talked with me about the research on many occasions. Roberto González and Edelberto Lopez Blanche offered friendship and help at critical moments.

The forty-year-old friendship between Saul Landau in the United States and Pablo Armando Fernández in Cuba has spawned children and grandchildren in a vast extended family that connects many of us in the two countries. Despite the continued enmity between our two governments, these two are in many ways the godfathers of this book and of numerous other cultural and scholarly projects involving the United States and Cuba.

My grandparents Eli and Naomi Blumberg and my parents, Carol Sweig and James Lawry, made graduate school and summer research trips to Cuba possible with their love, support, and enthusiasm. My parents read many drafts of the manuscript, bless their hearts. Heidi Bourne and Michael Sweig, book lovers both, will, I hope, have fun with this one. Sam and Dorothy Sweig would have been wholeheartedly behind this project, had they lived long enough. And I hope that Howard Sweig will one day enjoy reading it.

My husband, Reed Thompson, is the true hero of all of this. In addition to being the über-Dad to our then toddler daughter during a sweltering summer in Havana, he manned the fort at home during my many subsequent research trips, including the last, to select photos for the book, which meant I was in Cuba and not with my family on September 11, 2001. He read many drafts of the manuscript, listened to me talk about it endlessly, and gave me love and support that only the two of us can truly understand. My daughter, Isabel, now seven, already has her own sense of Cuban history—from direct experience and from following the twists and turns of what she once called "Mommy's long story," which I hope she will soon read to her younger brother, Alexander. And I am grateful to their grandmother, Mary Thompson, for her love and support along the way.

Finally, let me extend my sincere thanks to those at Harvard University Press who have dedicated themselves to publishing this book: Aida Donald, now retired, who first accepted this manuscript while it was still a dissertation; Kathleen McDermott, the History and Social Sciences acquisitions editor, who inherited the manuscript and enthusiastically shepherded it through to publication; and Julie Carlson, whose gentle, intelligent edits polished the manuscript.

Abbreviations

AAA	Friends of Aureliano Arango
ARO	Oriente Revolutionary Action
BRAC	Bureau of Anti-Communist Repression
CNOC	National Confederation of Cuban Workers
CTC	Confederation of Cuban Workers
DRE	Student Revolutionary Directorate
FCR	Civic Revolutionary Front
FEN	National Student Front
FEU	Federation of University Students
FON	National Workers Front
FONU	United National Workers Front
M267	26th of July Movement
MNR	National Revolutionary Movement
OA	Organización Auténtica
PSP	Popular Socialist Party
SAR	Society of Friends of the Republic

HYMN OF THE 26TH OF JULY

We're marching toward an ideal
Knowing we are bound to win;
For the sake of more than peace
   and prosperity
We will all fight for liberty.

Onward, Cubans!
May Cuba reward our heroism
For we are soldiers who are
Going to free the motherland.

Cleansing with fire
That will destroy this infernal plague
Of undesirable governments
And insatiable tyrants
Who have plunged Cuba into evil.

The blood that flowed in Cuba
We must never forget.
Hence we must remain united
In memory of those who died.

The Cuban people,
Drowned in grief and wounded,
Have decided
To pursue without respite a solution
That will serve as an example
To those who have no pity.
And we are determined to risk
Our life for this cause:
Long live the Revolution!

—Augustín Díaz Cartaya

History, Mythology, and Revolution

INSIDE THE CUBAN REVOLUTION revisits the story of one insurgent force in the 1950s, Fidel Castro's 26th of July Movement (M267), and its attempt to overthrow the regime of General Fulgencio Batista y Zaldívar. Though the standard periodization of the *lucha contra la tiranía*, the struggle against the tyranny, dates between 1952 and 1959, the book begins in the early months of 1957, when Castro's rebels were just finding their bearings in the Sierra Maestra mountain range, and the 26th of July Movement ranked as one of several opposition forces on the island. The story reaches its climax in April of 1958 and draws to a close in the middle of that year, six months before Batista's flight from the island, when Castro's organization had become the hegemonic force in the opposition. Based on documentary material from heretofore inaccessible government archives in Cuba, this book examines the internal battles within Fidel Castro's revolutionary organization over politics, tactics, strategy, and ideology. Most of the documents have never been published and debunk several battleworn myths about how and by whom the Batista regime was overthrown.[1]

One of the first pieces of conventional wisdom this book overturns relates to the Argentine doctor Ernesto "Che" Guevara de la Serna and his role in forging the historiography of the Cuban revolution. During the insurrection and until his death in Bolivia in 1967, Che played a central role not only in fighting the dictator but also in crafting the Cuban revolution's "founding fathers" myth: that a handful of bearded rebels with a rural peasant base singlehandedly took on and defeated a standing army, thereby overthrowing the dictator and bringing the revolutionaries to power. Che's role as historian emerged during the guerrilla war itself, when he kept a diary of the political and military battles of the twenty-five-month insurrection. After the revolutionary triumph, between 1959 and 1964, Guevara published polished versions of the diary entries in Cuban journals such as *Verde Olivo*. In 1963 he also published the complete (but still edited) war diaries, as well as a number of other articles comprising a body of revolutionary theory, known later as the *foco* theory, which reinforced the central mythology of the Cuban insurrection.[2]

Virtually all of the scholarly, historical attempts to tell the story of how Castro overthrew Batista start with Guevara's emphasis on the rebel army or guerrilla war as the principal cause of Batista's demise. Guevara delineates two competing camps within the 26th of July Movement: the *sierra,* the rebels in the Sierra Maestra, and the *llano,* the largely middle-class and professional Cubans running the urban underground in Cuba's towns and cities. The *sierra-llano* rivalry, or the ideological, strategic, organizational, and political polarization between the armed rebels in the mountains and the clandestine militia in the cities, remains the leitmotif for subsequent accounts of how the 26th of July Movement seized power in January 1959.[3]

During the insurrection, Guevara had strategic and ideological run-ins with several members of the urban underground leadership, whom he regarded as insufficiently revolutionary and misguided in their commitment to an urban-based insurgency. When I asked the revolutionary student organizer and current president of the Cuban National Assembly, Ricardo Alarcón, why Che seemed to loathe the movement's urban leaders, he sighed and said, "I don't like to criticize Che. But on that subject he really didn't know what he was talking about."[4] Nevertheless, Guevara's post-1959 writing about the Cuban insurrection contributed in large measure to widespread assumptions about the causes, evolution, and intensity of the *sierra-llano* conflict. It is significant, then, that the Cuban government, which has historically embraced the mythology that Che helped develop, has now released documents permitting a reinterpretation of this period in Cuban history.

THE SECOND myth this book attempts to overturn relates to the importance of the year 1959. Of course that year was a watershed moment in Cuban twentieth-century history. But almost all of the individual and institutional actors on the Cuban political stage in the late 1950s were consciously playing out a drama that in fact began during the Wars of Independence against Spain and the American intervention in 1898, and continued in the 1930s during the antidictatorial struggle to rid the country of President Gerardo Machado.[5] It was during the Machado period that a younger generation of Cubans, whose ancestors had fought in the wars against Spain, took on a leading role in the island's politics and in the effort to resurrect the ideals of unity, sovereignty, and independence best personified in the figure of José Martí. The University of

Havana spawned various opposition and clandestine political-military groups, such as the University Student Directorate (DEU), the elusively named "ABC" (which stands for nothing), and its left wing, the Student Left Wing. Another group, Joven Cuba, was led by the former minister of interior under the "government of 100 days." This transitional government emerged during the brief (1933–1934) presidency of a university professor, Ramón Grau San Martín, who had instituted a socially reformist, nationalist agenda. Grau San Martín had even abrogated the Platt amendment in 1933 before the United States officially repealed it the following year.

The 1930s also marked the period when the Communist Party, which grew to one of the largest Communist parties in Latin America, developed a significant political and organizational base among Cuban workers, particularly in the sugar industry, the lifeblood of Cuba's economy. During this period, the National Confederation of Cuban Workers (CNOC), a powerful trade union movement heavily influenced by the communists, exploded onto the Cuban political and economic scene. CNOC was capable, for example, of organizing some one hundred strikes between 1934 and 1935, when, with American encouragement, General Fulgencio Batista withdrew his support for the Grau San Martín government, causing its collapse.[6]

Finally, with respect to the United States, the 1930s provided an important lesson to a Cuban generation bent on forging an independent, democratic nation. The intercessions of Franklin Roosevelt's envoy to Cuba, Sumner Welles, to mediate the crisis between Machado and the Cuban opposition—a coalition that included students, intellectuals, a faction of the armed forces, labor, and initially the Communists—may have helped solve the immediate problem of removing a dictator from power.[7] But by relying on the Americans to solve their internal problems, Cuban political forces, including many but not all of the 1930s generation, gave the United States carte blanche to continue this role well into the future—as Welles's successor Jefferson Caffrey did together with Batista in removing the Grau-Giuteras regime. Indeed, Fulgencio Batista's cooperation with subsequent American governments, and the perils of alliances with the armed forces, haunted the next generation of Cuban revolutionaries, who came to believe that they would fail if they continued to rely on either the Cuban armed forces or the U.S. government to achieve their ideals of sovereignty, independence, democracy, and social justice. Indeed, repeated American military interventions between 1898 and 1924, followed by continued political interference in Cuban domestic affairs under the Good Neighbor policy of Franklin Delano Roosevelt, drove many

Cubans to seek to separate their country's political culture and economic life from the behemoth of the north. Yet FDR's New Deal also served as a beacon for many young Cubans, who believed that the distortions in the Cuban economy could be alleviated by a welfare state and a Keynesian economic model similar to that implemented by FDR.[8]

Between 1934 and 1940, starting with the first Grau presidency, Fulgencio Batista exercised de facto political control over seven nominally civilian governments, until agreeing to convene a constitutional assembly in 1939 and to hold democratic elections in 1940. Batista won these elections and, under the new and extraordinarily progressive 1940 constitution, presided over Cuba as a democratically elected president until 1944. The umbrella labor federation, by then named the Confederation of Cuban Workers (CTC), and the Communist Party participated actively in public debate and policy on labor rights, wages, and working conditions, while World War II boosted the development of domestic industries and small businesses on the island.[9] At the same time, Grau and his still substantial Partido Revolucionario Cubano–A (also known as the Auténtico Party), formed in 1937, successfully challenged Batista in 1944 elections, winning the presidency for Grau.

In the early years of his presidency of 1944–1948, Grau continued the moderate, reformist social agenda that a somewhat reinvented Batista had initiated under the auspices of the 1940 constitution. But as World War II ended and the Cold War heated up, Grau came under pressure from his base in the Auténtico Party to wrest control from the Communists over the increasingly powerful CTC. Grau and his minister of labor, Carlos Prío Socarrás, a former student leader and political prisoner from the 1930s, orchestrated an Auténtico-led purge of the Communists from the CTC leadership and from the federation's provincial councils. As historian Jorge Ibarra wrote,

> with the Auténtico party in power, the submissiveness and venality of the reformist labor leadership, headed by Eusebio Mujal, became manifest. Although the ascent of Auténtico unionists to positions of power in the CTC was the work of governmental and gang violence, and worker-employer relations from that time on were marked by corruption and capitulation to government policies, some reformist leaders managed to attain a certain prestige by satisfying demands of an economist character. The numerous mediations of the Auténtico governments in worker-employer conflicts were aimed at avoiding spontaneous or Communist-led strikes and protest movements by partially satisfying specific, limited worker demands, designed to strengthen the position of Mujal in the unions. The election of Auténtico labor leaders

in work centers became virtually a precondition necessary to ensure that the Ministry of Labor would show some favor to the workers in the conflicts with employers.[10]

There was a bitter irony in the way the Auténticos claimed the mantle of the thwarted revolutionaries of 1933, who had sought to forge a sovereign Cuban republic free of the trappings of both Spanish colonialism and American *"plattismo."* For in creating their new regime, the Auténticos had begun to slip into a pattern of corruption and political patronage that the party founders themselves had hoped to excise from the island just a decade earlier. In 1947, a splinter of the Auténtico Party broke off to form the Partido Revolucionario Cubano–O, or the Ortodoxo Party. Led by the nationalist, populist orator Eduardo Chibás, the Ortodoxos sought to recover and reclaim the mantle of clean government and realize the progressive vision of Cuba embodied in the 1940 constitution. In 1948 elections, the Auténtico candidate, Carlos Prío, won the presidency over Chibás, initiating a period considered among the most polarized, corrupt, violent, and undemocratic in Cuba's brief, post–Platt amendment, republican history.

A coup by General Batista against Prío on March 10, 1952, preempted presidential elections in which Batista was slated to run but unlikely to win against candidates from several opposition political parties, including Grau from the Auténtico Party and a second-tier candidate for the Ortodoxo Party, Roberto Agramonte, Sr. Agramonte had been chosen to run after the spiritual and political leader of the Ortodoxos, Eduardo Chibás, had committed suicide, perhaps accidentally, when he shot himself in a moment of high drama in 1951 during his weekly radio show in which he regularly excoriated the corruption of the Auténticos. Whether accidental or deliberate, the shot soon came to symbolize a wake-up call, or *aldabonazo*, for Cubans disillusioned with politics as usual. After the coup, both parties, by then bitter rivals, strained to build a political alliance, known in Cuban political parlance as a "pact," that would strengthen the opposition and weaken Batista's ability to stay in power. But a hard-core, Chibás-loyal wing of the Ortodoxo Party, of which Fidel Castro was a member, rejected all political alliances, coveting instead complete political independence as the path to Cuba's redemption. Militant anti-Batista groups such as the National Revolutionary Movement (MNR), led by a member of the Student Directorate of the 1930s, philosophy professor Rafael García Barcena, began to attract young professionals, university students, and professors. In 1953, the MNR attempted to stage an attack on a Cuban military base in a Havana suburb on Easter Sunday, but was preempted by Cuban police who arrested, tortured, and imprisoned García Barcena for two years.[11] Also at the universities, the Federation of University Students (FEU), led by the extraordinarily charismatic José Antonio Echeverría, developed a critique of Cuban politics and the *batistazo* with a strong social, political, and anti-imperialist bent. And Fidel Castro, who prior to the coup had prepared to run for Congress representing the Ortodoxo Party, soon abandoned the prospect for elections to bring about a peaceful, democratic transition and instead began recruiting men and women for clandestine preparations to assault an army barracks called Moncada. Of the 160 rebels, nearly half were captured, tortured, and murdered. Castro and twenty-six other surviving *moncadistas* and other supporters continued to collaborate in jail.[12] After his release from prison during an amnesty in 1955, Castro departed for Mexico to prepare an armed insurrection. During that time, the new revolutionary organization slowly blossomed, taking its name from the date of the Moncada attack: July 26, 1953. Many of García Barcena's followers, including Armando Hart, the young attorney who represented García Barcena and Faustino Pérez, as well as militant radicals from smaller clandestine organizations around the country such as Frank País, joined the 26th of July Movement after Castro's release from jail. Meanwhile, Carlos Prío, who managed to leave the country a wealthy man, funded an armed action group known as the Organización Auténtica (OA). Likewise, the FEU under Echeverría formed a militant offshoot, the Student Revolutionary Directorate (DRE). And though Batista had outlawed the Communist Party in 1952, Communists in local unions around the country, including sugar workers, continued to agitate and organize, even staging in 1955 (with Ortodoxo and independent trade union leaders and support from Echeverría's DRE) one of the largest strikes of sugar workers in Cuban history.

But in the middle of the decade it was by no means clear that armed insurrection was the only option for overthrowing the new Batista regime. Between 1955 and 1956, the moderate political opposition and civic groups formed the Society of Friends of the Republic (SAR), and attempted to negotiate as a bloc, and directly with General Batista, a solution to Cuba's political crisis. But the failure of those negotiations polarized Cuban politics further and for many, including the nascent insurgent groups, represented the nail in the coffin of a peaceful removal of Batista.[13] Indeed, Batista's refusal to participate in early elections threw the moderate opposition into crisis, reinforced the rationale for armed insurgency, and initiated a new era of competition to overturn the dictatorship within the moderate political opposition. The different approaches to ousting Batista were represented by, among others, the various factions and offshoots of the Ortodoxo and Auténtico parties, the radical, armed opposition, and armed insurgents fighting for tactical and strategic superiority in the drive not only to unseat the dictator but also to rid Cuba of corruption and longstanding *politiquería,* or dirty politics.[14] After Batista's New Year's Eve flight from Cuba on December 31, 1958, it was Fidel Castro's 26th of July Movement that had accumulated sufficient political and military capital to install the first revolutionary cabinet. But a number of the subsequent political conflicts in the 1960s, particularly between what came to be the three primary revolutionary forces, Castro's 26th of July Movement, the DRE, and the Communist Party, known as the Popular Socialist Party (PSP), had their roots in the conflict within and among those three groups during the anti-Batista insurgency, just as the Cuban political crisis of the 1950s had its roots in the events of a generation earlier.

THE THIRD piece of conventional wisdom this book overturns relates to the role of Fidel Castro during the insurgency. Because of his enduring command of Cuban events since 1959, many still assume that Castro also had his hands in all of the major and minor decisions of the 26th of July Movement during the insurrection and was responsible for all of its failures and successes. An important example is a critical event in the Cuban insurrection and the climactic event of this book: the general strike of April 1958. In part because of the lack of primary source documents from the 26th of July Movement, most scholarly and popular treatments of the Cuban general strike of April 1958 blame Fidel Castro for its conception, timing, and implementation. The most influential of these is the 1974 history of the Cuban insurrection by Ramón Bonachea, who was associated during the insurgency with the DRE and Marta San Martín. According to the authors, Fidel forced the strike upon the urban revolutionaries to do away with the *llano*'s challenge to his power within the movement, to frustrate the temptation by 26th of July's Civic Resistance leaders to forge an alliance with reformist military officers, and to force a direct military confrontation with the armed forces in the Sierra Maestra. The authors concluded, "It can be stated unequivocally that Fidel Castro was responsible for the conception of the strike and for its failure."[15]

Other scholars generally followed suit. For Tad Szulc, a Castro biographer, the strike became Fidel's mechanism for imposing revolutionary unity not only within the 26th of July Movement but upon all opposition forces.[16] Robert Quirk also argues that the National Directorate, or core leadership of the *llano*, opposed the strike but obeyed Fidel, who, by exaggerating the strike's chances for success, lured his city-based comrades into accepting his point of view.[17] Historian Thomas G. Paterson has written the best treatment of U.S.-Cuban relations during the insurgency. But on the subject of the insurrection itself, Paterson defers to earlier authors, arguing that Fidel imposed the strike over the objections of the *llano* and after its failure gained the political and strategic advantage.[18] Jon Lee Anderson understood correctly the movement's motives for the strike but misinterprets the *sierra-llano* relationship, suggesting that Castro regarded the urban underground as "perhaps the greatest threat to his power" before the strike.[19] Jorge Castañeda also attributes the planning and timing of the strike to Fidel, implying that in its aftermath Castro shirked responsibility for its failure, pinning blame instead on the *llano*.[20] Hugh Thomas properly locates the initiative for the general strike with the urban underground, noting in 1971 that Fidel Castro's own feelings about the strike "remain obscure."[21]

Among Cubans, too, even before Batista fled to the Dominican Republic on New Year's Eve of 1958, the unsuccessful uprising eight months earlier had become a watershed in the history of the Cuban insurrection, marking the demise of the *llano*'s hegemony within the 26th of July Movement. Writing in 1964 in *Verde Olivo*, the journal of the Cuban armed forces, Che Guevara summarized the effect of the strike's failure on the political and structural balance of power within the 26th of July Movement in a widely reproduced and cited article, "A Decisive Meeting."[22] In the twenty-five years after Guevara published the article, discussion or analysis of the strike remained taboo. Little has been published since except anecdotal first-person accounts of specific actions carried out by the underground prior to and during the strike. In 1988 and 1990 the history department of Havana's Communist Party released a two-volume collection of these articles accompanied by more analytic pieces written by Armando Hart Dávalos, who though jailed at the time of the strike was the movement's national coordinator in the *llano*, and by Faustino Pérez Hernández, the National Directorate's Havana representative and chief of the national strike committee.[23]

Likewise, the absence of Cuban documentation to date has hampered accounts of this period, creating narrative gaps between the April 1958 strike, the rebel army's defeat of a summertime offensive in the Sierra Maestra, and the political consequence of that military victory: the July 1958 Pact of Caracas, a unity agreement that marked the 26th of July

Movement's hegemony over revolutionary and opposition politics in Cuba.

This book begins to fill in those gaps with important new evidence. Contrary to standard accounts, which tend to depict the defeat of the movement's *llano* strategy as an immediate and unqualified victory for the *sierra*, for Fidel Castro, and for the M267 with respect to the other opposition groups, *Inside the Cuban Revolution* debunks the conventional wisdom that Fidel Castro deliberately sacrificed his allies in the *llano* prior to, during, and after the strike.[24]

In particular, the newly released documents provide a more nuanced picture of this controversial chapter in the Cuban insurgency, allowing a glimpse into the anatomy of the strike itself: the internal debates that preceded it, the operational plans that accompanied it, the multiple competing tactics that depleted the movement's resources to implement it; the impact of the strike's failure on the cohesion and balance of power within the 26th of July Movement and on its ties to Cuba's militant and moderate opposition; and how, despite their reluctance to do so, the revolutionaries rebuilt a political coalition to unify the opposition.

The Cuban documents demonstrate that until the last six to eight months of the two-year insurrection, the lion's share of decisions regarding tactics; strategy; resource allocation; political ties with other opposition groups, Cuban exiles, and clandestine adversaries; and relations with the United States (in Havana and Washington) were made by lesser known individuals from the urban underground—not Che Guevara, Fidel Castro, or his brother Raúl Castro. Had it not been for the work of the 26th of July Movement outside of the Sierra Maestra during the first seventeen months of the insurgency, from November 1956 until April 1958, the final period, when the antidictatorial struggle gained unstoppable military and political momentum, would simply not have been possible. To reach January 1, 1959, the day that marks the victory of the Cuban revolution, the 26th of July not only had to mount a two-year military campaign but also a political campaign against many of the forces that were also seeking an end to the Batista regime.

THIS STORY thus traces two dynamics between the early spring of 1957 and the middle of 1958. First, the new documents allow a close look at the internal battles that played out then within the 26th of July Movement. Since the vast majority of the new material on which this book is based comes from the individuals operating in the *llano*, this book resurrects, reconstructs, and assesses the real relationship between the *llano* and the *sierra*. The second dynamic is directly related to the first. As the 26th of July developed into a significant force of popular opposition during those first seventeen months, the underground leaders of the movement fought desperately to preserve tactical and political independence from the other opposition forces on the island—traditional opposition political parties, the Communist Party, and rival insurgent forces. At times the politics of the war played out on the island. At other moments, the theater of action shifted abroad to Miami, Washington, and Caracas, for example. To the extent that the 26th of July pursued an urban-based popular insurrection, the movement's leaders were forced to reconcile their desire for political independence with their tactical needs for cooperation and material support from groups and individuals outside of their own circles. As the M267's military strength solidified beginning in the summer of 1958, it became possible for the movement to relate to the broad anti-Batista opposition from a position of political strength. Indeed, the rebel army's military successes directly enhanced the movement's standing in the country, intensified the level of popular mobilization against the dictator by the second half of 1958, and allowed the M267 to leverage its new standing into political agreements with the opposition, on its terms: first in July of 1958 with the Pact of Caracas and later in January 1959 when the 26th of July alone put together the first revolutionary cabinet. The battle for Cuba's future "was a power struggle," the now deceased Comandante Manuel Piñeiro acknowledged to me, as much within the opposition as against the Batista dictatorship itself.[25]

While this book attempts to strip away some of the mythologies surrounding the internal dynamics of the 26th of July Movement, especially from the perspective of the urban underground, the full history of the Cuban revolution has yet to be written. This account does not represent an in-depth examination of all of the factors that contributed to the regime's collapse, such as the crisis within the Cuban armed forces, the fate of Cuba's moderate political opposition, the experience of the OA or the DRE, or even the military battles during the insurgency.

Chapters 1 through 3 of this story situate the 26th of July in the context of political debates taking place in Cuba during the spring and summer of 1957, examining how, under Frank País, the *llano*'s National Directorate sought to insert itself into those debates, expose the weakness of Cuba's nonviolent political opposition, and organize the movement—both nationally and province by province—to prepare for a general strike. Covering the period between August and December of 1957, Chapters 4 through 7 illustrate the effect on the *llano* and on the entire

26th of July Movement of the loss of one of the underground's most important organizers; negotiations between key members of the National Directorate and Joint Civic Institutions to form a provisional government; how the emergence in exile of a quasi-opposition government in Miami—the Cuban Liberation Junta—preempted the 26th of July's preparations for a post-Batista era; the effect of the Miami episode on the movement's relationship with other Cuban revolutionary forces in preparing for a general strike; and the process by which the *llano* and *sierra* decided to break publicly with the Cuban opposition.

In Chapters 8 through 12, the narrative follows the *llano*'s preparations for a general strike, tracing the evolution of the strike plans from a model that contemplated mobilizing Cuban workers at the center of a popular insurrection, to an approach that relied primarily on violence and sabotage to unseat the dictator. The climax of the story is the shift in the balance of power within the 26th of July from the *llano* to the *sierra*. In the denouement, Chapters 13 through 16, the rebels face and recover from the strike's catastrophic failure. As the rebel army beats back a summertime offensive by the Cuban military, Castro's representatives in Miami and Caracas begin negotiations for a new alliance—one whose formal agreement they delay until the revolutionaries recover sufficient military strength for the movement to accrue the political capital it needs to participate in an opposition coalition that promises to deliver weapons, money, and the public appearance of complete unity against the dictator. After the July 1958 Pact of Caracas, the story jumps ahead to November and December of 1958, summarizing the final months of the insurgency and concluding with a brief discussion of the first revolutionary cabinet, installed in January 1959.

1 "Tactics in Politics and Tactics in Revolution Are Not the Same"

FEBRUARY–MAY 1957

We aspire to remove, demolish, destroy the colonialist system that still reigns, to do away with bureaucracy, eliminate superfluous mechanisms, extracting our true values and, according to the particularities of our own idiosyncrasies, introducing the values of modern philosophical currents that currently prevail in the world. We aspire not to do this in a piecemeal fashion just to come out ahead but rather to conscientiously and responsibly plan the construction of the new nation with seriousness, intelligence, and dispassionate love of country that characterizes the 26th of July. This idea, these projections, should be widely disseminated and discussed by every part of the movement.

Frank País, to leaders of the 26th of July, May 17, 1957

ON MAY 14, 1957, JUDGE MANUEL URRUTIA Lleó of the district court of the province of Oriente issued a landmark ruling in a case brought by the state against 151 men charged with participating in various antigovernment activities. Among the defendants were twenty-two men captured in December 1956 after Fidel Castro's boat, the *Granma,* arrived in Oriente from Mexico, ready to take up arms in the Sierra Maestra against the Batista regime. Judge Urrutia's ruling dealt a major blow to the government by essentially legitimizing armed insurgency: it declared that "in view of the usurpation and illegal retention of power by Batista and his followers, the defendants had been acting within their constitutional rights."[1]

Among the revolutionaries acquitted and released from jail that day was an aspiring schoolteacher from Santiago de Cuba, Frank País. The twenty-three-year-old País had been active as early as 1953 in the clandestine resistance to General Fulgencio Batista y Zaldívar, who on March 10, 1952, had overthrown the democratically elected president, Carlos Prío Socarrás, in a pre-election coup. A member of the clandestine

Oriente Revolutionary Action (ARO) and later a leader of National Revolutionary Action, País merged his organization with the 26th of July Movement (M267) in 1955, becoming "chief of action and sabotage" in Oriente province. With his rare combination of meticulous organizational skills, keen sense of politics, and strategic vision, País's involvement in the Havana-based M267's plans was absolutely vital. País first met Fidel Castro in August 1956 while Castro was in Mexico, and from then until the end of the year he worked, at first against his better judgment, to plan and stage what was to be a major uprising in Santiago on November 30, 1956.[2] On that day, a popular insurrection in the provincial capital was to coincide with Castro's landing in the province, pinning down the army and police in order to give Castro and his men time to reach the hills. But only a handful of work stoppages and targeted acts of industrial sabotage were carried out, while most of Castro's *Granma* companions were either killed or arrested. Only Fidel and a handful of survivors made it safely to the nearby Sierra Maestra mountains.

Before his arrest in the ensuing police crackdown of the province, País and several 26th of July comrades visited Castro in February 1957 and brought along the veteran *New York Times* war correspondent Herbert Matthews. Matthews's front-page reports with photographs of Castro caused a major splash in Cuba because they contradicted earlier reports by the Cuban information ministry and UPI that Fidel Castro was dead. The new reports and pictures renewed the M267's notoriety and popularity on the island: they also gave the movement's key activists, who accompanied Matthews to the Sierra, the chance to sit down and hash out strategic and organizational plans with Castro and Che Guevara.[3] Before the talks, some activists wanted to convince Castro to abandon the Sierra Maestra, go into exile, raise money, and rally the international community to the cause of Cuban liberation. Instead, after two days of deliberations, the core of the M267 underground from Havana and Santiago agreed instead to Castro's plans to expand the underground's forces and the new guerrilla front. País, Faustino Pérez, Haydée Santamaría, Armando Hart, and the other underground activists left the Sierra meetings with a substantial undertaking before them: to build up Castro's guerrilla force, create new fronts, form an urban militia in each of Cuba's six provinces, build a national civic resistance of middle-class professionals, and organize the Cuban working class to take on the Batista regime in a "general revolutionary strike as the capstone of the struggle."[4]

País returned to Santiago from the Castro meeting energized and ready to tackle the considerable disarray that existed within the 26th of July Movement. Three weeks later, however, he was arrested and had to cool his heels in jail for over two months. Not until his release following Judge Urrutia's ruling was he able to rapidly set to work carrying out the monumental and multiple tasks that he was charged with as the movement's chief coordinator for the entire country. The main components of the insurgency—communications, organization, fund-raising, internal philosophical and ideological unity, "propaganda," organizing and arming an urban militia, sending men and material to Castro, and creating new guerrilla fronts—were each lacking both leadership and resources at this early stage of the insurrection.[5] The U.S. embassy concurred with País's assessment of the movement's disarray in the *llano*, writing that "embassy intelligence sources . . . add that while the forces with Castro are fairly well organized, and he is clearly the leader, the same cannot be said for his organization outside of the hills. While many people are either in the '26 of July' Movement or sympathetic to it, the organization is loose and confused and suffers from considerable inefficiency."[6]

At great personal risk and often with emotional angst, País laid down the organizational architecture and began to outline the 26th of July's strategy of overthrowing Batista with a nationwide general strike supported by armed struggle (a model that was to dominate the movement's operations for the following year). He began to build the urban underground into far more than the rearguard supporting the guerrilla struggle in the mountains. The scope of his initiative and decision-making authority, conferred by Fidel Castro himself, was vast. The guerrilla, or *sierra* forces, completely depended upon the *llano* for everything from medicines, weapons, ammunition, food, equipment, clothing, money, and domestic and international publicity. With more and more comrades falling into police custody, País carried the burden of satisfying virtually all of these requirements.

In one of several memoranda sent around the country to M267 activists, País also made it clear that the movement must avoid overtures from traditional opposition political parties and even from other insurgent groups. País explained the movement's place in Cuban history, its differences with the island's "pseudo-opposition," the problems in building unity, and the new ideology the revolution would seek to awaken. He determined why the Santiago uprising of November 30, 1956, failed: a lack of both preparation and ideological and organizational unity. "We are living a moment of great confusion," wrote País, "confusion the government welcomes and that shakes the pseudo opposition in its clumsiness, egotism, and unbridled ambition." País spared no pity for "the pseudo-opposition," which "in all its ambition, fights battles, criticizes itself, lacks unity, and is destroying itself, each one of its factions trying to occupy the position of leadership" in dealing with the government. As a result, one by one, opposition parties and politicians "converse and collaborate with the government, play its game, then look ridiculous accepting their so-called pacifist solutions, all while the government deceives and confuses" public opinion. The 26th of July, however, represented a departure from politics as usual, and País was intent on persuading the movement's cadre that they and all of Cuba must regard the movement as completely independent. As the opposition politicians "rub shoulders and smile with the regime's figureheads," he wrote M267 activists, "a gallant youth finds itself in the Sierra Maestra and a National Movement is laboring clandestinely every day, following its own orders." In the midst of such "demagogy, division, and lack of revolutionary ideas . . . we are forging and achieving a clean, intelligent and new program, with an honest, valiant, and revolutionary generation that captures in its ranks all of those who feel for and aspire to a true revolution."[7] País was keenly aware that the 26th of July was a heterogenous group of young men and women: Ortodoxo Party members, nationalists, social democrats, intellectuals, and socialists. Though many of the core cadre of the 26th of July remained deeply anticommunist, País sought to situate the 26th of July in a historical and ideological context that would appeal to the anti-imperialism of Cuba's Communist Party, the Popular Socialist Party (PSP), as well as to the nationalism of a population whose independence and sovereignty had been repeatedly thwarted since the turn of the century. The 26th of July, he wrote, represented "a new idea that captures the frustrations of Cubans from 1902 through today, and tries to take advantage of our historic experiences to unite them to our economic, political, and social needs of our country, and give them true solutions."[8]

País developed a new organizational plan for the movement that drew from the lessons of the short-lived November 1956 uprising and from his analysis of the ideological, political, and security environment in which the M267 operated. He centralized a "National Directorate" under the leadership of a core group that included himself and a longtime comrade from the underground, Léster Rodríguez. Meanwhile, Armando Hart, Faustino Pérez, Marcelo Fernández, Haydée Santamaría, Celia Sánchez, Vilma Espín, and Carlos Franqui would serve as "adjunct" members who, for the time being, were not responsible for the day-to-day management of the movement's plans. He divided the M267's tasks into six separate "sections": organization, labor outreach, civic resistance among the Cuban middle class, sabotage activities and an urban militia, propaganda to promote the movement's cause, and a treasury to raise funds. País moved the movement's headquarters from Havana to Santiago, where, compared to the capital, the M267 maintained cordial and cooperative relations with other opposition groups, such as the Organización Auténtica and the PSP.[9]

Moreover, País and the entire National Directorate had also committed to providing for the *sierra's* very survival as well as creating new guerrilla fronts, and recruiting, training, and arming members for a nationwide militia cell structure. Quickly, País sent a group of fifty reinforcements to the Sierra Maestra, among them René Ramos Latour and Jorge Sotús, both longtime co-conspirators from the Oriente underground. At the same time, he laid the groundwork for opening a second guerrilla front in the Sierra Cristal range of Oriente. He also asked comrades around the country to prepare to "quickly create several more fronts . . . to carry out intensive work in the regions that may be used for future fronts, studying them, making contacts, maintaining them, providing . . . all of the details to the National Directorate but discreetly, without awakening a stir, without promising anything, without talking more than is necessary."[10] Expanding the armed activities of the M267 increased the movement's vulnerability to penetration by government security or paramilitary forces. País thus warned that any leaks or betrayals would be punishable by death. Militia members in the "action and sabotage" cells were to keep "strict norms of discipline, silence and organization, punishing even with their lives those cases of mistakes or indiscretion. Anyone who is arrested and talks will be automatically sentenced and this sentence should be carried out in prison. Our sabotage machinery must be perfect; it cannot abide mistakes."[11]

País, who had operated only in Oriente and did not personally know many of those members from other parts of the country, nevertheless attempted to take charge and demand allegiance and obedience from his colleagues in Cuba's other five provinces. Just as Castro was geographically isolated from the urban movement, País was isolated in his Santiago safe houses and felt frustrated at the lack of response from activists around the country over whom the National Directorate hoped to establish control. Despite País's promotion to national coordinator, the movement's provincial coordinators in Las Villas, Matanzas, Pinar del Río, and Havana replied slowly, if at all, to his letters, memoranda, and orders. At this juncture, the movement's hold on anything that could be described as a national movement was so loose that in many cases, País did not know to whom to direct sabotage instructions or where to write to core members.[12] Yet, despite this abysmal lack of communication and the mere skeleton of a real organization, País ordered the five other provinces to prepare to unleash during June 1957 a flurry of attacks on bridges, highways, telephones, and electrical generators, to coordinate with "military actions" in his own province, such as the opening of the second front.[13]

The central strategy of the revolutionaries during this period was to organize a nationwide general strike, which was to be reinforced by military actions carried out by guerrillas in the Sierra Maestra. To succeed at such an undertaking, the movement would have to involve substantial numbers of Cuban workers in actively opposing the regime. While the failures of the November 30 uprising had encouraged País to promote a more comprehensive, horizontally organized national movement, that episode had its partial successes—particularly on the eastern end of Oriente province in the city of Guantánamo, as well as with the working class and PSP. In Guantánamo, under the direction of militia captain Julio Camacho Aguilera, who later became one of the movement's key liaisons with the Cuban military, the M267 shut down highway traffic and took over the Ermita sugar mill. In early 1957, the 26th of July worked with labor activists to stage "small attempts at general strikes," demonstrating to País that out of the Cuban working class it was possible to "create cadre and leadership, indoctrinate them, discipline them, and train them."[14]

Moving the M267 beyond what País nevertheless regarded as "superficial and superfluous" outreach to workers required overcoming several formidable obstacles deeply rooted in the historical role of organized labor and the PSP in earlier Cuban anti-dictatorial movements.[15] The movement's cadre also brought to their work political, ideological, and sectarian baggage that prevented most from seeing Cuban workers and organized labor as potential allies in the struggle against Batista. Anticommunism within the 26th of July cadre itself was common, both because of the Cold War climate of the 1950s and because the PSP, officially banned in 1952, had a reputation for having collaborated with Batista from the 1930s. Since 1947, Eusebio Mujal Barniol had controlled the Confederation of Cuban Workers (CTC). A former communist who joined the Communist Party in 1930, Mujal had orchestrated the purge of the PSP from the leadership of the Cuban trade union movement in 1947. Mujal injected the CTC's policies and statements with a potent dose of anticommunism and routinely oversaw the firing of workers who participated in antiregime activities or violated the CTC's standing policy prohibiting work slowdowns, stoppages, and strikes. In exchange for preserving a compliant working class, he secured salary increases and other benefits for the CTC's rank and file. His personal reputation for venality and corruption made him and his cohorts a target of numerous assassination attempts by the 26th of July "Action and Sabotage" groups. Yet, despite the corruption and conservatism of the CTC leadership, throughout the decade dissident factions and affiliates—many of them communists, Ortodoxos, or independents—rejected collaboration with the regime and actively supported and worked with the 26th of July and other opposition groups.[16]

Cooperation between the 26th of July and the PSP, however, was key to a successful national strike given the party's longstanding ties with workers, particularly those in sugarcane production and cultivation. Among sugar, tobacco, and transportation, and to a lesser extent the electrical and banking sectors (those trades where organized labor had not been thoroughly depoliticized during the Mujal era), the PSP exercised some influence on organized labor, though other than in Oriente it had lent only nominal, conditional support to the 26th of July. In the areas surrounding the major towns of Oriente—Bayamo, Manzanillo, and Guantánamo—where both sugar and tobacco were cultivated and processed, the party remained active, making the province, in País's view, a potentially fertile ground for collaboration between the PSP and the movement.[17]

País did not have such high hopes for the movement's potential collaboration with its rival insurgent forces, the Student Revolutionary Directorate and the Organización Auténtica (OA). On March 13, 1957, forces from both organizations staged a frontal assault on Batista's presidential palace. The premise of their plan was that a successful assassination of the dictator in his own office would, with one single blow, bring an end to his entire regime. Though the Directorate's "chief of military operations," Faure Chomón, and the M267's Faustino Pérez had discussed the possibility of the movement joining the assault, bringing Herbert Matthews to the Sierra took precedence for the 26th of July. Acting as Matthews's guide, Pérez stayed in Oriente until after the palace attack with no intention of returning to participate. In fact, though many of the 26th of July's members were close friends and collaborators of José Antonio Echeverría and other DRE members, and the two organizations had hashed out a joint statement of objectives during Castro's tenure in Mexico, the rivalry between the two organizations was unmistakable, as the M267 developed plans to form its own separate provisional government based in Santiago if the assassination attempt succeeded.[18] But the assault on the palace failed miserably, at great cost to the assailants and their organizations. More than forty men were killed in the attack, including Echeverría, the charismatic Directorate leader and president of the Federation of University Students, a multiclass student organization with roots in the anti-Machado uprisings of the 1930s.[19] The U.S. embassy reported that "the government's reaction was swift and violent," with "as many as 400 arrests," while others "died under mysterious circumstances."[20] Indeed, the government crackdown did not discriminate between revolutionary organizations. By the end of March 1957, Frank País, Faustino Pérez, Carlos Franqui, and Armando Hart also found themselves in jail.[21]

Despite the debilitating arrests of nearly half the National Directorate's members and the crushing loss of Echeverría, the 26th of July was quick to benefit from the attack's failure. On the afternoon of the palace attack, three members of Havana's underground commandeered a truck full of weapons that the DRE had left on a side street near Batista's palace. After storing the weapons in the home of the man who later became the founder of Cuba's intelligence services, the underground operatives shipped them in several cars to a safe house in Santiago. Though the Directorate demanded that the M267 return the weapons, Frank País was able to use the arms for his plans to open a new guerrilla front in Oriente.[22]

The OA was another armed insurgent force loyal to and funded by Carlos Prío Socarrás, Cuba's president from 1948 until the coup in March 1952. After the palace attack, virtually all of the surviving members fled the country, many settling temporarily in South Florida or in the Dominican Republic, where they trained for eventual guerrilla operations back in Cuba. Just as the DRE had ample reason to resent the 26th of July first for not participating in the attack and then for stealing their weapons, the 26th of July harbored equal if not more rancor toward the OA for similar reasons. On the eve of the November 1956 uprising in Santiago, País asked the OA to contribute some weapons they had been stockpiling and to stage some support actions in Havana to coincide with the *Granma* landing. But when push came to shove, the OA did neither and the 26th of July was left without the assistance it expected.[23]

País did not hesitate to voice his dismay at this slight. After his release from jail in May, he found a letter waiting for him from Alberto Bayo, the Spanish Civil War veteran who had trained Castro's own expeditionary forces in Mexico in 1955. Bayo was then under contract with Prío to train OA forces for their imminent return to Cuba. Knowing that the movement was vulnerable to accusations of a "lack of national cooperation," Bayo asked for the 26th of July to support the OA landing. The cheekiness of the request incensed País, who accused the OA of "selfishness" and "undignified behavior" in refusing to give weapons to the M267 during the November 1956 uprising. "I suppose," País wrote Bayo, "that those of you over there don't know the cowardly and irresolute [character] of your cadre here. I sincerely do not understand their game nor what they are pursuing, because tactics in politics and tactics in revolution are not the same." Whether the OA had actually "turned over arms to the government in exchange for money" or lost them "by mistake," País warned Bayo to beware of "the thousands of intrigues and jealousies consuming the exiles' time and energy." But he stopped short of rejecting the OA request for assistance.[24]

País assured Bayo that the movement had "never been reluctant to accept an agreement" as long as it is "effective and yields practical results."[25] He recognized the imminent arrival of an OA force—known as the *Corinthia* expedition—as an opportunity for the M267. He planned to support them in opening a new front in Oriente's northern stretch of mountains, the Sierra Cristal, in order to advance the movement's own plans for a second guerrilla front.[26] Carlos Prío sent an envoy to Oriente to deliver a personal gift of ten weapons and one thousand dollars for Fidel Castro with the message that the *Corinthia* expedition would not depart without Castro's green light. But País was extremely skeptical of the sudden show of interest in joint action and had no intention of allowing a rival organization to form an autonomous guerrilla group in the same mountain range where he planned to deploy the movement's second front. Indeed, without word from Fidel, País, or Prío's envoy, the *Corinthia* set sail on May 19, 1957.[27]

Given that Prío stood to provide financial assistance to the 26th of July Movement, País understood it would be highly expedient to demonstrate some sign of support for the rival expedition. If the OA agreed to establish a consolidated front under M267 command, he planned to supply them with food and clothing. If they refused to subordinate themselves to the movement, he planned to "leave them alone so that they can try out a bit of life in the Sierra without supplies or support . . . as they did to us on November 30." Prío's forces, however, did not survive to face the choice. After landing east of Mayarí on the northern coast of Oriente, local peasants informed the army, which surrounded the expeditionaries and assassinated all but a few on sight. The M267 underground later hid some who had managed to escape.[28] With the Directorate's palace assault and the OA's expedition both ending in bloody failure, by the end of May 1957 the 26th of July appeared to be the only viable insurgent force on the island.

During the spring of 1957, Frank País operated with the support of both emerging tendencies within the 26th of July Movement, *sierra* and *llano*. Barely two weeks out of jail, he established a framework for an island-wide underground movement. He reinforced the Sierra rebel forces; trained and recruited men and amassed weapons for a second front; stopped a second M267 expedition from coming to the Sierra from Mexico; initiated talks with dissident members of the Cuban armed forces; and sent out feelers to leading Cuban political figures who sympathized with the 26th of July. At the same time, increased sabotage of utilities, sugar mills, and other economic and political targets in the *llano* heightened the movement's public profile without significantly weakening the Cuban economy.[29]

Despite the physical isolation of both Castro and País in the Sierra and in the Oriente underground, the 26th of July hardly operated in a political vacuum. After enduring the DRE-OA assault on the presidential palace, a month-long state of emergency, and some pressure from opposition political parties, Fulgencio Batista allowed the suspension of constitutional guarantees to lapse, ended some government censorship of Cuba's many weekly and daily periodicals except for Oriente province, and announced that he would hold presidential elections in June 1958.[30] Batista's recent electoral record inspired little confidence. Shortly after the 1952 coup, he announced presidential elections for November 1954. When the Auténtico opposition candidate, Ramón Grau San Martín, withdrew his candidacy at the last minute, Batista nevertheless proceeded with the elections, won by default, and took office, leaving the political opposition profoundly skeptical about his commitment to a democratic transition.

Though the government continued to prohibit press reports and analysis that could be construed to promote revolution or insurgency, a public debate unfolded. The discussions, which involved both major and minor actors on the political stage, aired various alternatives for redressing the political crisis that had enveloped the country for most of the decade. Pundits and politicians associated with the major opposition political parties—the Ortodoxo Party and the Auténtico Party and their various factions—as well as several smaller opposition parties and groups, presented five alternatives for a transition to the Cuban public: elections orchestrated by Batista; elections following Batista's departure from power; a coup d'état and installation of a military junta; a coup d'état and installation of a mixed civilian-military junta; or armed insurrection and revolution.[31]

The 1952 coup that overthrew Auténtico president Carlos Prío Socarrás and preempted elections scheduled for November of that year catapulted both the Ortodoxos and the Auténticos into the opposition, deepening a political and moral crisis that had begun to unfold throughout the late 1940s and early 1950s. In 1948, Eduardo Chibás had founded the Ortodoxo Party as a spinoff of the ruling Auténtico Party, adopting the image of a broom and the slogan "honor against money" to express the Ortodoxo commitment to clean government and its repulsion with sky-rocketing corruption in Cuban politics. Chibás's perhaps inadvertent sui-cide in 1951 during one of his live weekly radio broadcasts (he shot him-self on the air for dramatic effect), as well as the coup, caused members of the party's "youth" section, like Fidel Castro, to defect from the party and traditional politics, opting instead for revolutionary insurrection.[32] By 1957, the leaderless Ortodoxos had split into three separate factions.

The largest wing, the Ortodoxos-históricos (historic), was loosely orga-nized around three individuals: Eduardo's Chibás's brother Raúl Chibás, director of a military academy; Roberto Agramonte, Sr., a sociology pro-fessor and the party's candidate for the unrequited 1952 presidential elections; and Enrique Barroso, president of the party's youth group. The históricos believed that participating in elections orchestrated by the Batista government would inevitably produce a fraudulent outcome; in-stead they advocated organized "civic resistance." A second faction, the Ortodoxos-abstencionistos (unregistered), led by an attorney and politi-cal science professor who had presided over the constitutional assembly of 1940, Carlos Marqúez Sterling, had also by 1957 steered away from supporting elections under Batista, advocating civic resistance as well. Marqúez Sterling had served as an aide to a veteran of the War of Inde-pendence, Don Cosme de la Torriente, who led the Society of Friends of the Republic, or SAR, "the closest the mainstream opposition ever got to a united civic front against the Batista dictatorship."[33] During 1955 to 1956, the SAR and Don Cosme unsuccessfully attempted to negotiate Batista's departure through an accelerated election schedule. At the time, however, Marqúez Sterling had incurred the ire of the históricos faction of the Ortodoxos by supporting the notion that political pacts even with their mortal enemies, the Aútenticos, or elections might strengthen the anti-Batista opposition.[34] And a third faction, the Ortodoxos-inscritos (registered), under Emilio "Millo" Ochoa, was prepared to participate in elections held with Batista in power, provided Batista first restored the 1940 Constitution. Throughout 1957, the three factions grew progres-sively weaker as waves of police brutality, repression, and assassination drove their leaders in and out of exile.[35] Moreover, the Ortodoxos had been further divided by splinter groups such as the Movement of the Na-tion, founded by the Harvard-trained journalist Jorge Mañach, and other opposition movements such as Amalio Fiallo's Radical Liberation Move-ment.[36]

The Auténtico Party had also split into two factions, each headed by former presidents. The Auténticos-inscritos remained loyal to the aged former president Grau San Martín, who governed Cuba from 1944–1948 and had indicated his desire to run for the presidency in the June 1958 elections. Carlos Prío Socarrás and his former prime minister, Manuel Antonio "Tony" de Varona, led the Auténticos-abstencionistos from their exile in Miami Beach, Florida. Prío sought a return to power by virtually any means possible. He funded the OA and flirted with the possibility of enticing senior officers in the Cuban armed forces to stage a coup d'état against Batista. He also indicated a willingness to participate as a candidate in elections under certain circumstances. Both parties included individuals of some prestige in Cuban society for whom resolving Cuba's political crisis became an opportunity to institute economic and social policies in Cuba that would help modernize the economy. These reforms included decreasing the island's dependence on sugar revenue, reducing gambling and other mob activities, and establishing greater political and economic independence from the United States. Many of them became increasingly open to the option of armed insurgency as Batista's intransigence grew and as opposition party leadership proved unable to challenge his reign effectively.[37]

By the second half of the 1950s, Miami was providing a safe haven to the insurgent and moderate anti-Batista opposition groups, including the 26th of July, the OA, the Student Revolutionary Directorate, the AAA of Aureliano Sánchez Arango (an education minister under Prío), and various self-exiled politicians and military officers. From his Miami Beach apartment, Carlos Prío tried to build support for his return to the presidency with a coalition of the military, the insurgents, the opposition parties, and the progovernment political parties. After the OA had suffered two blistering defeats—one in the March 1957 palace attack and the second in May when Colonel Fermín Cowley assassinated most of the OA's combatants on the *Corinthia* expedition—Prío published an open letter to the most important news source for the Miami exile community, *Diario las Americas,* calling for a military junta to restore the 1940 constitution and oversee elections.[38] While publicly and certainly privately courting both pro-Batista and reformist officers, Prío made regular appearances at staunchly anti-Batista opposition gatherings. For example, immediately following his public offer to return to Cuba through the work of the military and elections, he addressed a unity rally in Miami convened by the radical opposition that had flatly rejected elections—the OA, the AAA, the Civic Front of Martí Women, the Revolutionary Directorate, and the 26th of July. Making no mention of coups or elections, he gave the keynote address as the de facto leader of the Cuban opposition and exhorted all Cubans to put aside their factions and rivalry in order to free Cuba.[39]

Indeed, back in Havana at the El Principe prison, sheltered from the day-to-day compartmentalization of clandestine warfare, political prisoners from the M267, the DRE, OA, and Communist Party forged ties despite the sectarian rivalry that prevailed outside the prison gates. There Alberto Mora, Jr., a Directorate member whose father had died in the palace attack, and Faustino Pérez, the M267 Havana coordinator, had approached each other and consulted with their comrades about the possibility of forming a unity pact between the DRE, the M267, and the OA.[40] Pérez supported the "idea of an integration, or at least coordination of forces" as "useful for now and for later" and alerted his M267 colleagues that the DRE had already met with Prío "to propose the constitution of a junta with representatives from the Directorio, the 26 and Prío's Auténticos," to "move toward unity with the Directorio and with Prío, [and to] coordinate action if possible."[41] Pérez knew that at this stage of the anti-Batista effort, Carlos Prío and the Cuban political opposition had a stake in Fidel Castro, who represented "the materialization of a state of opinion" against Batista. Though Castro's presence in the Sierra Maestra was both destabilizing and embarrassing to the dictator, Prío did not want the M267 to emerge as a force that stood any chance of governing the country.[42] And given his flawed record at democratic governance, without the participation of the 26th of July, which by June of 1957 had emerged as the only insurgency to stake out and hold a position on Cuban territory, Prío had limited credibility to lead a unified, exile-based revolutionary opposition force on his own.[43] For its part, the M267 was too weak, badly armed, and underfunded to contemplate a break from Prío and his money and material assistance. Thus, for the time being, Prío and the 26th of July kept their doors open to one another.

The PSP also joined the debate over Cuba's future—in fliers, underground press statements, and through sympathetic opinion pieces. The PSP's secretary general Blas Roca and president Juan Marinello were virtually the only voices in Cuban politics to articulate an anti-imperialist view of the island's political crisis at the time. In their analysis, Batista remained in power because of the assistance of his "imperialist masters." In order to remove Batista from power and sever Cuba from the grasp of American hegemony, the Communists proposed forming a united front of the masses and the opposition political parties. The 26th of July's strategy to target industry, agriculture, and infrastructure for sabotage scandalized the PSP, which believed that such tactics would terrorize—not energize—the very workers whom the party hoped would rise up against the dictator.[44] The PSP energetically opposed the Directorate's "putsch," or palace attack, as well as the 26th of July's "*cuartelazo* and terrorism," a reference to the 1953 Moncada assault and subsequent militia sabotage.[45]

Facing demands to restore the constitution and hold elections, Batista and the progovernment coalition of political parties represented in the Cuban congress convened a series of political rallies, voter registration drives, and early campaigning to prepare for elections. A congressional committee gave opposition parties a role in negotiating the conditions under which they would participate in these elections. On any given day throughout June and early July of 1957, as many as seven opposition parties joined and withdrew from committee debate. A brief interlude of unity within the electoral opposition followed, only to fall apart over procedural matters, failure to agree on one unity candidate, and the government's refusal to meet some of their demands. According to the U.S. embassy, the government "was determined to hold elections whether or not the opposition participated," which amounted to a "complete about-face from" its earlier position that elections were intended to permit a genuinely democratic transition.[46]

After three months of relatively open debate, the political opposition lacked a presidential candidate, and the government appeared to be dead set on holding elections with or without the opposition. This stalemate strengthened the 26th of July as it sought to expand its appeal to the Cuban public. To the extent that the Cuban people viewed elections as neither legitimate nor plausible, the 26th of July, the only active armed force on the island at the time, gained in national appeal and stature. Also, the key to public opinion at the time was the Conjunto de Instituciones Cívicas, or the Joint Civic Institutions—nearly two hundred civic and professional organizations representing approximately 300,000 Cubans, including doctors, lawyers, accountants, engineers, teachers, accountants, and fraternal and religious organizations such as Catholic, Protestant, and Baptist groups; Masons, Lions, and Rotarians; Knights of Columbus; Catholic Youth; and the Catholic Teachers League. With municipal, provincial, and national chapters, the Civic Institutions were led nationally by the president of the Cuban Medical Association, Raúl de Velasco, and included other prominent professionals such as José Miró Cardona, president of the Havana Bar Association. As the key constituency to which both political parties and the revolutionaries appealed, the Civic Institutions, civil society in today's political vernacular, occupied the middle ground between the state and the population, and were fast becoming a critical voice against violence, the civil war, and the dictatorship, particularly as the economy began to take a downward turn.[47]

In Oriente, where opposition to Batista was generally more overt and widespread than in the rest of the country, the Civic Institutions openly criticized the army's forced evacuation of rural squatters living near the rebels. They also considered issuing a public demand for Batista to resign.[48] For a group of generally apolitical professionals fearful of jeopardizing their personal safety, such a step risked exposure to extreme police brutality. Veteran *New York Times* reporter Herbert Matthews wrote in his notebooks of one episode that illustrates the danger involved in opposing the regime in the spring of 1957. During one of his regular visits to the island, Matthews learned of

> a respected Cuban citizen who had taken no part in revolutionary activities in Havana . . . informed upon to the police by a *chivato* (snitch). They came for him one night, bound his hands, put a hood on his head and threw him in the bottom of a car . . . When the hood was taken off he was in a bare cell with two men who worked on him for twenty-four hours almost without let up. Then he was let alone as he had nothing to tell and they could get nothing out of him. The family was influential and able to get lawyers busy. This was just after constitutional guarantees had been restored so they got a writ of habeas corpus. The police, learning this, turned the man loose . . . The doctor who examined him afterwards found, among other things, that his back was completely raw from blows of the *picho de buey* [whip], his buttocks were blue and swollen from cat-o'-nine tails with lead at the end of each thong. One ear had almost been torn off simply from repeated blows of the fist. The doctor said that if he had not been a big strong man of 33 he could not have survived the treatment. His family had friends in the Guatemalan embassy, and it was arranged to give him asylum there.[49]

Though the Batista government "ruthlessly brushed aside" one of the first public statements by the Civic Institutions against the civil war, the group's statements reflected "the anxiety" permeating Cuba's professional classes at the time. And while the Civic Institutions were as yet unprepared to support an alternative to elections, the 26th of July welcomed their progressive alienation from the prevailing order in Cuba and endeavored to gain their support in overturning the Batista regime.[50]

The government kicked off the election season by staging two summertime political rallies in Oriente province designed to demonstrate its confidence that the electoral process could proceed apace. The regime dismissed or even ignored the presence of a guerrilla campaign in a nearby mountain range and active rebel sabotage in the province's main cities.[51] Batista's cabinet; municipal and provincial officials; hundreds of members of a quasi-paramilitary force led by Rolando Masferrer, the notoriously corrupt and violent congressman and paramilitary leader; as well as the national and foreign press corps flew to Oriente to attend the rallies. While the government press reported that some one hundred thousand Oriente citizens attended the first rally, held in Santiago, one observer described a virtual boycott, reporting that "no more than four thousand" were there. Those participating included mainly government officials with their supporters, Masferrer's paramilitary Los Tigres, easily identified by their white baseball caps, and police dressed in full battle gear with thousands of troops and tanks.[52]

The 26th of July tried to neutralize the government's show of force to demonstrate that Batista could no longer conduct business as usual in the province. First, sabotage militia planted a time bomb under the stage in Santiago where government spokesmen were to deliver their speeches. But the bomb did not go off. With País's key operative sick in bed, all the movement could muster was to interrupt Masferrer's speech briefly by broadcasting its own message to the crowd.[53] Second, the movement's effort to launch dramatically during the rallies a second guerrilla front in the province was derailed the day of the first rally. At that point, local peasants leaked to local army officers the location of over forty M267 men, forcing the nascent second front to disband before it could even establish itself.[54] Worst of all for Frank País, Oriente's most important underground leader at the time, Masferrer's Tigres assassinated his younger brother Josué and two other comrades.[55] At the second rally, held on July 15 in Chivirico, some forty miles from the Sierra Maestra, the Batista government adopted what one observer described as "vulgar blackmail of the people and the opposition": if the opposition did not participate in the elections, Batista would cancel the elections and install a junta, giving the military power indefinitely.[56]

Throughout all of this activity, however, the key question was which alternative the Civic Institutions would support: elections, a coup, or insurrection? With Batista's promise to remain in power during the election process, the continued repression (especially in Oriente), and the opposition's failure to unify around one anti-Batista candidate, the electoral route began to lose ground as a credible way out of Cuba's political crisis. The abstentionist opposition parties offered no viable alternative because they were justifiably reluctant to engage in a political process—elections—that stood to legitimize Batista himself. Likewise, their adversaries in the electoral opposition could not agree on a ticket to challenge Batista's candidates. Oriente was practically in open rebellion, with Castro's rebels becoming more popular by the day, and the underground's sabotage was increasingly shaking key industries. With such chaos, a military junta loomed as a distinct possibility in Cuba. If the armed forces came to view the electoral route or growing civic activism as destabilizing, they would not hesitate to step in, particularly if, wrote one columnist, "the insurrection had a chance to triumph or if Batista reached the end of his term without elections."[57]

While the "extremely individualistic" opposition maintained an undeniable capacity to agitate, it had not removed Batista from the seat of power. Still, the U.S. embassy observed, elections remained Cuba's most promising option: "All of the government parties and six of the opposition are electoralist . . . only two opposition parties are abstentionist, and the *insurreccionalistas* in fact have been reduced to only one: the 26th of July."[58] The way in which the 26th of July Movement took advantage of the political moment and the reprieve in press censorship soon drowned out the other voices on Cuba's political scene.

2 | The Sierra Manifesto

JUNE–JULY 1957

I have no greater interest than to live in a country where popular will and the law are respected; where leaders who dissent are not tortured or persecuted . . . Some Cubans still blanket themselves in the illusion that they ought to embrace the flag of peace in dealing with the regime. I sustain the conviction that peaceful talks with the dictatorship are not possible while our rights are denied.

Raúl Chibás, July 14, 1957

IT HAD BECOME COMMON PRACTICE FOR leaders of the 26th of July Movement such as Armando Hart, Haydée Santamaría, Vilma Espín, and Luis Buch to meet with American officials based at the Santiago consulate. Among these officials were William Patterson, the vice consul, and another officer, Oscar Guerra, both of whom were more than likely CIA intelligence officers.[1] Indeed, the rebels had something of a cheering section back at the analytical section of the CIA, where "my staff and I were all *fidelistas*," the lead desk officer for Cuba later noted.[2] After his release from prison, Frank País continued the talks, engaging in lengthy discussions with Patterson in particular. These conversations left País eager to take steps to soften Fidel Castro's public image. The American officials had convinced him that, as he wrote to Castro, "the real fear of the financial sectors . . . is that when Batista falls we won't have sufficient power to constitute our own, stable government, and instead we will have to call upon all of those parties, movements and submovements that every day divide and separate more." País wanted to head off any anxiety or "fear that Cuba would become another Haiti," a country only thirty miles along the Windward Channel from Oriente province that had endured a series of coups and countercoups throughout the 1950s. The endorsement of prominent figures from Cuba's opposition political parties and the Civic Institutions would, País felt, send a signal of moderation and stability to Cuba's political and economic elite, to the United States, and to the movement's own membership.[3]

Without Castro's knowledge, País took advantage of the political debate in Cuba and of the break in press censorship by launching a secret initiative "to recruit a series of highly representative and valuable men from national public life and link them closely" with the 26th of July.[4] País sent to Havana Haydée Santamaría, one of the few National Directorate members who was not then in jail, and Javier Pazos to sound out various well-regarded individuals about their interest in the movement's proposal. Santamaría, known as María or Yéyé in the underground and by her close friends, had worked closely with Fidel Castro since 1953. Her brother Abel and boyfriend, Boris Luis Santa Coloma, had helped Castro stage the attack on the Moncada barracks in Oriente. After the raid, Batista's police spared Santamaría's life but tortured her brother and boyfriend to death. In developing M267's ties with various political figures in Cuba, she began to demonstrate her considerable diplomatic and strategic abilities, talents that were to serve the movement well during the insurrection. Javier Pazos was the son of Felipe Pazos, president of the National Bank of Cuba under Carlos Prío. In the 1940s, Javier went to high school in Washington at the Sidwell Friends Quaker school while his father worked at the Inter-America Development Bank. After the 1952 coup, "Javierito" joined the 26th of July to serve ultimately as a courier, translator, and gunrunner.[5]

Santamaría and Pazos started their domestic diplomatic tour by meeting with Raúl Chibás, Felipe Pazos, Enrique Barroso, Roberto Agramonte, Jr., and Justo Carrillo to discuss "the possibility of forming part of a revolutionary government."[6] Raúl Chibás, a native of Santiago who held a doctorate in the humanities and had studied at Columbia University, was the brother of Ortodoxo Party founder Eduardo Chibás and director of a military academy in Havana; Enrique Barroso was president of the youth sector of the Ortodoxo Party; and Roberto Agramonte, Jr., an engineer at Cuba's largest concrete firm, was the son of Roberto Agramonte, the exiled sociology professor, former ambassador, and Ortodoxo presidential candidate who had advocated civic resistance to the dictatorship. Justo Carrillo, a founder of the anti-Machado student movement of the 1930s, led the Montecristi Group (Agrupación Montecristi), which Herbert Matthews described as a "group of highly qualified intellectuals with tremendous support from big business, banks and the professions." The group was planning a provisional government and regarded Carrillo as a possible next president.[7]

Of the five men, only Carrillo rejected Haydée Santamaría's offer to join a revolutionary government, preferring instead to keep Fidel in the Sierra Maestra more as a symbol of national defiance than as a serious contender for power. In a long letter to Fidel explaining his decision, he posed a number of questions about various transition scenarios: whether to have a military junta or a mixed civilian-military junta; who should be in the junta; the duration and function of a transitional government; how a transitional government would engage the Cuban population, via a constitutional assembly or elections; and the function of the military prior to installation of a transitional government. Carrillo warned that momentum for overthrowing Batista was building from within the dictator's own ranks, an alternative that could rapidly cast to the margins of the Cuban drama the political and psychological power of the Sierra struggle, particularly if the Civic Institutions regarded a military junta as a legitimate means to end violence, oversee a transition, and credibly restore a measure of democracy and economic stability.[8]

País succeeded in bringing respected societal leaders on board with the M267's insurrectionist strategy when Pazos, Agramonte, Chibás, and Barroso agreed to make the trek to meet with Fidel Castro. Rumors of an alliance between Fidel Castro and "leading intellectual oppositionists" such as Pazos and Chibás, reported the U.S. embassy, "if true, would be quite significant, as both men have large followings."[9] Indeed, amid competing rumors that a military coup was pending and fearing that the Cuban public would accept Batista's call for elections even without a true opposition candidate, the M267 underground hastily shuttled Chibás, Barroso, Agramonte, and later Pazos from Havana, to Santiago, to the coastal city of Manzanillo. The gateway to the Sierra Maestra for men, weapons, supplies, and correspondence from the *llano*, Manzanillo is some one hundred miles west of Santiago on Guacanayabo Bay. From there, they would make the trek up to Fidel's headquarters in the Sierra Maestra. País took great precaution with security on this trip: he kept even the closest of comrades on a need-to-know basis. Thus when the group arrived in Manzanillo in early July 1957, Celia Sánchez, an important collaborator and daughter of a well-to-do physician, was caught completely by surprise.

Though it was an open secret that the well-known group was heading for the Sierra Maestra, Celia successfully hid them for several days while outfitting them for their trek and waiting for Fidel's authorization to send them to him. Though she complained to Fidel of how difficult it was to accommodate, equip, and hide them, she reassured Fidel that the initiative would be positive for the movement. "You have no idea the effect all over of the news that they are arriving in the Sierra," she wrote him. Felipe Pazos's arrival, she wrote, could be "another coup . . . In every sense it is useful that these people are up there and for you personally most of all, pestered as you are by work; it is impossible to stay on top of everything with the growing number of men. Now with them you can distribute responsibilities."[10]

Chibás, Agramonte, and Barroso reached the Sierra on July 5, followed by Pazos on July 10.[11] Even before Pazos arrived, the movement sought publicity for the visitors' presence in the Sierra, sending via Celia several rolls of film of Castro and the first three guests to the editors of *Bohemia*, Cuba's leading weekly magazine.[12] The next week's issue of *Bohemia* ran a two-page photo spread of Fidel with the three Ortodoxo Party figures, each dressed in drab green uniforms and seen deep in conversation with the rebel leader, who smoked his then ubiquitous cigar and gazed intently through black, thick-rimmed glasses. The magazine hailed Chibás as Cuba's "personality of the week" and declared his meeting with Castro a "blow to those who have been assuring us that the opposition is only a focus for rotten ambitions and small-minded egotism."[13] Though as yet uninformed of exactly what Frank País had in mind in terms of creating a revolutionary government formed in the Sierra Maestra, Fidel concurred with the importance of publicizing an open alliance with the Ortodoxos-históricos, writing Celia that it "would be extremely advantageous to form a revolutionary government presided over by Raúl Chibás."[14]

The U.S. embassy, however, reported different explanations for the trip to the Sierra. Some observers believed that they had gone up to the mountains to work out "a plan of action" were Castro to succeed militarily. Other embassy contacts, described as supporters of the 26th of July, reported that in light of rumors that Castro planned to nationalize Cuban industries, Pazos's motivation in particular was to "steer Castro's political policies and to safeguard the considerable investment they have in Castro and his operations."[15] Chibás and Fidel may well have discussed forming a revolutionary government, but Pazos's arrival as well as Justo Carrillo's input had clearly altered the direction of conversations, and of Castro's sense of how best to capitalize on the political moment.

THE "MANIFESTO to the Cuban People," the document that Castro, Pazos, and Chibás finally settled on, came to be known as the "Sierra Manifesto." Its contents filtered gradually into the public domain, with a portion first summarized and published in the local Santiago press and then broadcast on Havana radio; the document was published in its entirety by *Bohemia* on July 28, 1957. Castro had not intended the manifesto to leak out in dribbles from Santiago to Havana, but rather to be released in full by *Bohemia* magazine. He sent copies to Celia to send to

Havana and to País in case the Havana route failed. But, wrote Celia, "one of Alejandro's [Fidel's] *guajiros*" (peasants) who carried the manifesto to Havana stopped in Santiago to deliver a love letter to a girlfriend of one of the rebels and leaked news of what Fidel and the Ortodoxo figures had in store.[16]

Fidel may well have been the document's primary author, but the timing of its release, the ideas it expressed, and the message of moderation it sent were not "the product of his imagination and manipulative talent." Nor, as has been widely assumed, was the alliance with Pazos and Chibás—or the document announcing it—an attempt to punish Frank País for exercising autonomy and independent decision-making in his organization of the movement.[17] Rather, it is now clear that the Sierra Manifesto was the fruit of input from both *sierra* and *llano* and from others outside the movement. Far from a repudiation of the underground's coalition-building strategy, the Sierra Manifesto represented the culmination of plans that País had initiated since his release from prison two months earlier.[18]

In fact, País's attempt to cleanse Fidel and the movement's public image by orchestrating the visit to the Sierra Maestra by Chibás, Pazos, Barroso, and Agramonte came as a complete surprise to Castro, just as it had to Celia Sánchez. Neither apologetic nor defensive with Fidel in explaining his hushed approach, País acknowledged that Castro "had not been informed of the notice of the [group's] arrival" in the Sierra, and especially understood the "surprise you must have had when you learned" of their desire to discuss Haydée Santamaría's "proposal" to form a "civic-revolutionary government" with the 26th of July Movement.[19] In a letter reaching Fidel with Chibás in the Sierra Maestra and Pazos on his way, País explained that he had taken the initiative because "I think it is necessary for you to have a general staff with certain outstanding personalities, to give it prestige and an even greater aura of danger for all the sectors of the nation who look upon you—romantically, perhaps?—with certain reservations. But when they see you surrounded by people of this kind, they will think you are trying to establish programs and concrete government projects, and at the same time, a civilian-revolutionary government that will provide our movement with still more prestige and enhance its militancy."[20]

Though the conventional wisdom has been that Fidel Castro alone sought an alliance with Cuba's political opposition to reassert his power within the movement and to stop País from developing his own power base in the *llano*, a previously unpublished portion of a letter dated two days later, a crucial political and organizational strategy document, in fact illustrates País's role in the substance, timing, and function of the alliance.

> The last point about which I wanted to speak with you is the formation of a Civic Revolutionary Government. It seems to me that the situation for one is not at all bad, I would even say favorable. You must have heard that it has been widely commented upon, especially the involvement of Raúl Chibás in such an eventuality, and I, who hear the people's reactions, see that they are favorable, even though they don't understand well what it would actually be nor what implications it would bring. It seems to me that when Javierito's father arrives you should sit down and study these possibilities and begin making the necessary plans for such an end, as well as begin dividing up the work in order to publicize it. You could go about this in two ways, one that we would manage, explaining what a revolutionary government would consist of and which we would carry out, and the other through publicity in foreign and national magazines and newspapers. This publicity should be carried out in steps, beginning with photos and interviews of the three or four together, followed by declarations, etc. and culminating in the formation of a civil government one or two months before the final stage, coinciding with the publication of the program, or naturally, if you think this would be viable or more effective, earlier.
>
> In making this recommendation to you, I have done it thinking about the subtleties and complications that might go along with some aspects of a revolutionary government, such as tax contributions, etc., about which I have already heard some commentaries, like "imagine, we'd have to pay two contributions." Javier's father, far better than I, can plan for this, as he is an authority.[21]

In the same letter, País recommended that the movement time the announcement of a such a revolutionary government to coincide with the final stage of general strike, which he explained would culminate within months.

AS PAÍS had hoped, the manifesto responded to the questions of the day. Were elections possible under Batista? What was the proper role of the armed forces in a transition? What was the role of the United States? What sector of Cuban society would produce the new kind of leadership that Cuba needed? What were the revolution's substantive goals? By putting civil society at center stage in Cuba's transition, the manifesto sought to push the Civic Institutions beyond its pacifist position of calling upon both the regime and the revolutionaries to stop the violence.

Granting the power of naming a provisional government to the otherwise apolitical Civic Institutions, the manifesto endeavored both to politicize civil society, depoliticize traditional politics, and purge *politiquería*, or dirty politics, from the island while leaving the door open for the new revolutionary generation to gain access to power through insurgency.[22]

The document blamed the country's political impasse on the impotence and lack of vision of its public officials. At its core, the manifesto was a skillful attempt to wrest the political initiative from the Batista government and expose the disunity and weakness of Cuba's opposition political parties, which Batista had so ably promoted and exploited. If, warned the manifesto, "the dictatorship managed to defeat the rebel bulwark of the Sierra Maestra and crush the underground movement," the population's "general grief and skepticism" would make any chance of honest elections remote. This is because the electoral process has ignored the "two forces that have made their appearance in Cuban public life: the new revolutionary generation and the civic institutions," which alone were "much more powerful" than the political "clique[s]" then vying for power. Lacking a place for those two forces in the country, the electoral solution "could only prosper on the basis of the extermination of the rebels." Instead, patriotism demanded unity of all antidictatorial forces—whether political, revolutionary, or those emerging from the civic institutions—which shared the goal of eradicating a regime "based on force, the violation of individual rights, the infamous crimes," and which had "the desire to seek the peace . . . by the only road possible, the democratic and constitutional path of our country."[23]

According to the manifesto, the 26th of July Movement, "more than anyone else," wanted free elections and constitutional government. Its supporters had died in the mountains, streets, and prisons for this very reason. But elections under "antidemocratic and partial" tyranny with "the closing of radio stations" and "mysterious deaths" could not be "truly free, democratic and impartial." Proof of the regime's dubious faith in elections was its reliance upon repression: "With more blood, they want to put an end to the rebellion; with more terror, they want to end terrorism; with more oppression, they want to put an end to the desire for freedom." The only chance for elections to safeguard democracy in Cuba was for "all opposition parties, all civic institutions, and all revolutionary sectors" to create a "civic-revolutionary front with a common strategy of struggle," and for the Civic Institutions to designate an individual to preside over a "provisional, neutral government." With the provisional government in waiting, the Civic Revolutionary Front would call upon Batista to resign and transfer power to the provisional president.[24]

The program of such a new government closely reflected the long-standing platform of the Ortodoxo Party, which called for the release of all political prisoners, free speech, free press, and a crackdown on corruption; the creation of a career civil service system; democratization of the trade union movement; campaigns to improve literacy and civic education; agrarian reform; and currency stabilization and import substitution industrialization. As for the standing army, the "civic revolutionary front" would "separate the army from politics . . . to guarantee the apolitical nature of the armed forces." Neither a military junta, foreign mediation, nor any scenario involving the traditional sources of state power in Cuba could guarantee a democratic transition in Cuba, according to the manifesto, which called upon the United States not to intervene in or mediate the conflict but only to suspend weapons shipments to Batista. The manifesto called upon Cuban emigrés in the United States and elsewhere to petition the United Nations and other international fora to denounce human rights violations under Batista. After one year, the provisional government would oversee national and local elections under the 1940 constitution and the 1943 electoral code, and "power will be given immediately to the elected candidates."

The manifesto strategically called for the Civic Institutions, not the political parties, to designate the provisional president, arguing that public opinion rooted in Cuban civil society would shelter the new president from the usual trappings of commitments and obligations that a nomination from Cuba's opposition parties would necessarily entail. To make their entry into Cuban politics more appealing, the manifesto did not ask the parties or Civic Institutions to "embrace the insurrection thesis" and join Castro in the Sierra but only to abandon the electoral process and demand Batista's resignation, as the Ortodoxos históricos and abstencionistas had argued. Castro's representatives, the manifesto proposed, were prepared to discuss their proposals in Mexico, Havana, "or wherever." All the political, revolutionary, and civic sectors needed to do was "organize the front that we propose and the downfall of the regime will follow." If the call to unity fell on deaf ears, the rebels would fight on in the mountains, already "an indestructible bulwark of freedom," because no one could prevent "the victory of the people."[25] By stopping short of calling for the formation of a revolutionary government in the Sierra Maestra, the manifesto envisioned a more gradual transition than Frank País had first imagined. Nevertheless, in its broad outline and political significance, the manifesto reflected País's view of the political opportunity facing the 26th of July, and it corresponded to País's time frame: he was planning to execute a national strike to unseat Batista by the end of 1957.

With the manifesto in the public domain after the group's visit to the Sierra, Castro sent País a forty-two-page handwritten letter addressing "all your communications I have received during the last two or three weeks . . . especially your typewritten report about the work plan for the months ahead and your reports on the labor sector" (a reference to the July 7, 1957, strategy document Castro received while hosting his visitors). Fidel explained to País his decision to call for a revolutionary front as opposed to a revolutionary government as primarily an attempt to undermine the credibility of elections and those advocating them.

> It is not that I have illusions about the political parties, but it will show them in the eyes of the country to be the allies of the Dictator, whose resignation we are asking for, while they accept the absurdity that this same dictator can be the guarantee of fairness and democracy; and in the eyes of the Civic Institutions, by rejecting the only formula that is theoretically unobjectionable and situates said institutions as a determinant factor in this struggle. Moreover, in the Manifesto we respond to many questions of the moment. I only lament not being able to accompany words with deeds at the same time.[26]

Castro had several objectives. He wanted to undercut those factions of the Ortodoxo, Auténtico, and other opposition parties that regarded elections under Batista as offering a credible prospect for a peaceful transition. Likewise, by giving the essentially apolitical Civic Institutions a starring role in forming a provisional government and overseeing the country's transition, the Sierra Manifesto attempted to draw the Civic Institutions away from the *"tesis electoral"* toward supporting the *"tesis insurreccional."*

INDEED, EVEN before the manifesto's release, the U.S. embassy reported that this strategy had begun to diminish the credibility of political parties, noting that "the abandonment of the party" by Raúl Chibás, "the strongest unifying force of the Ortodoxo Party" after his brother's death, "appears to doom it as a unified and nationally effective force."[27] Just as Castro had predicted to País, the manifesto pushed the hopelessly fickle and divided opposition, led by the likes of Tony Varona, José Andreú, Ramón Grau, and Emilio Ochoa, to issue their own manifesto calling for a United Opposition Front that would name Cuba's ranking supreme court justice as the head of a provisional government and request elections within ninety days. If that proposal failed, the new front would "unite behind a prominent nonpolitical figure and defeat the government in the elections scheduled for June 1958." The new initiatives were described by the U.S. embassy as "the most unity the opposition has shown for many months, but the Americans regarded "the attempt to force the Government to resign [as] unrealistic, unless the proponents of the United Front plan" expected key figures in the armed forces to defect. Though the embassy lauded the "serious attempt to develop a unified attack" against the government via "the electoral rather than the insurrectionary process," the reporting officer judged its chances of success as "problematic at best." Grau and Ochoa commanded "sizable followings," Prío was "somewhat discredited with the Cuban people," and Andreú represented "little more than himself and his wife."[28] Thus, the Sierra Manifesto exposed the opposition's willingness to support the Batista regime's plan for elections, despite significant evidence—the 1952 coup and the 1954 elections—that Batista had no intention of allowing a genuinely democratic election to take place.

The Sierra Manifesto appeared to indicate that the 26th of July was willing to participate in a united front composed of many opposition groups. Indeed, the timing, symbolism, and substance of the document jump-started the opposition not in Havana or Mexico, but in Miami, where the Auténticos, Ortodoxos, Civic Institutions, and revolutionary groups would soon respond to the 26th of July's invitation to unite against the dictator.

3 | "We Had to Act a Bit Dictatorially"

JUNE–JULY 1957

We have to begin preparing the working masses for the struggle ahead. This is without needing to reach extremes that might result negatively at this moment. Understand as negative any action that is violent and underutilizes our ties with the working class, in their efforts to indoctrinate and organize for the General Strike. Nevertheless, the workers need now to carry out an action felt nationwide . . . In addition to producing enormous psychological effects in terms of the capacity of the 26th of July and Civic Resistance to mobilize the working masses around a specific slogan . . . it would also have the effect of impressing groups that remain skeptical of our organizing capacity to generate a labor movement into a total strike.

Frank País to Labor and Civic Resistance leaders, July 1957

THOUGH THE 26TH OF JULY MAY VERY well have emerged as the strongest insurgent force at the time and even with the political opposition further divided by the Sierra Manifesto, Frank País was painfully aware that his organization still lacked clear channels of communications, structural and philosophical cohesion, cadre discipline, sufficient security against police surveillance and penetration, and enough money and arms to overthrow the dictator in a matter of months. The movement represented "an instrument totally removed from the political past," País believed. With the popularity and timing of the statement by Castro, Pazos, and Chibás, he felt that the M267 must rapidly develop into a truly national organization in order to match the rising tide of "popular intuition" and the response that Castro's recent message had inspired.[1] Fidel and the 26th of July were fast becoming larger-than-life symbols of a national sentiment for change. But the movement was becoming too big for its organizational britches and faced a growing disparity between its own real capacity and popular demand for an all-encompassing organization that could focus and direct the antidictatorial struggle among all classes.

Communication among even the closest of collaborators within the National Directorate was sparse both before and after issuing the Sierra Manifesto. Nearly three weeks after he had sent Haydée Santamaría to Havana to send out feelers to Pazos, Chibás, and others, País had yet to receive updates on the talks.[2] Nor had País heard from Armando Hart or Faustino Pérez, who were able to send and receive mail from jail. The Havana militia and finance coordinators ignored País's requests for information, meetings, and money. País did not even have an address for local organizers in Pinar del Río.[3] Throughout the month of June, País implored the movement's activists around the country to send money and weapons to Santiago for the Second Front, the Sierra Maestra, and the national movement. Even when he did receive contributions from the provinces, the process was infuriating and demoralizing. For example, in June when the Matanzas coordinator got his hands on a load of dynamite, he dispatched a courier to Santiago empty-handed to ask País to pay for the dynamite first, instead of simply sending it as instructed.[4] In Camagüey, local activists spread "false and tendentious reports" challenging País's authority and forced him to spend precious time defending an otherwise straightforward personnel change.[5]

Despite having trained activists to raise money, recruit members, and carry out sabotage in the towns of Las Tunas, Palma Soriano, Contramaestre, Mayarí, and Nicaro, by the end of June a frustrated País was complaining that not one of the newly minted M267 leaders had "delivered anything to [his own] headquarters [of Oriente] despite the previous circular's advisory of the conditions facing the struggle in the Sierra and by the movement nationwide."[6]

Indeed, the worst offenders were based in Manzanillo, a vital city of Oriente second to Santiago. There Celia Sánchez functioned as the movement's general coordinator and liaison with the Sierra Maestra. País had also appointed two others, one for "action and sabotage" and the other for filtering men to the Sierra Maestra. As member of the National Directorate and intimate of Fidel Castro, Celia (also known as Norma) had jurisdiction over the other two, and País over all of them. But Celia had failed to report on whether she had appointed the movement's *responsables* for organization, treasury, action, labor, resistance and propaganda; whether she was successfully sending people to the Sierra; or, for example, whether weapons and equipment that País had sent to Fidel via Manzanillo had reached their destination. The other Manzanillo activists, for their part, had defied instructions from País regarding the selection of men for the Sierra. Horrified at their poor performance, he wrote to them that

the things that are happening in your territory are, let us say, extremely unpleasant. It is hard to believe that your district, which should be head and
shoulders over the rest, in organization, unity and spirit, is not. Each of you
is working on his own, unaware of, or trying to ignore, the work of the others
without respecting hierarchies and mutually interfering in one another's
work, resulting in a poverty of efforts and leaving a bad impression among
those familiar with these problems. I must insist on respect, discipline, and
authority but since we have tried to get you to repair these problems yourselves and you have not, we will have to send a delegate from the National
Directorate with complete responsibility and authority over all of you, and if
you don't comply yourselves, this National Directorate will make sure that
you do.[7]

It was not humanly possible for País to exercise complete control over
the flow of men to Sierra. Though he actively recruited men from around
the country expressly to join the guerrillas in the Sierra Maestra, the rebel
army also provided a safe haven for underground fighters who, because
of their activities, could no longer operate safely in the cities. País had
prohibited most of these "burned" underground fighters from fleeing to
exile, and felt, given his objective of creating a national organization,
that it was politically necessary to permit activists from all over the country—not just Oriente—to join the rebels.[8] These factors increased the
pressure on Manzanillo, but País had yet to assert his authority over
groups there and in other regions that believed that sending new recruits
to Fidel was a priority for the movement and did so routinely without
clearing it through proper channels.

País's objections to these breaches in discipline was primarily a response to the tremendous security problem the movement faced as it
and the rebel army expanded. Already, Rolando Masferrer's paramili-
taries had attempted to infiltrate the organization as had Batista's intelligence operatives. The movement's action and sabotage cells were particularly vulnerable to penetration by government agents and the
"gangster element" in Cuban society. This latter crop of individuals—
many of whom were also government informants—were capable of
carrying out effective sabotage—but they also were prone to stealing
the movement's money and selling its weapons to the highest bidder.[9]
País thus begged his Manzanillo colleagues to respect a "national organization in charge . . . that has commitments with all of the provinces
and that selects and chooses nationwide which individuals should go
and fight." He further chastised, "The fact that you are in a preeminent position does not give you the right to anarchy; you must learn
to play the double role of municipality and national link to the *sierra*,

the first dependent upon you, and the second upon this National Directorate."[10]

The wave of sabotage acts claimed by the 26th of July throughout Oriente and in Havana, Las Villas, and Camagüey that summer gave the impression that the movement was large and tightly knit, with sabotage cells in every province and many counties across the country.[11] But most of the sabotage undertaken was spontaneous rather than being ordered from the top down or even coordinated at the provincial or local levels. Sabotage became a relatively easy way for many individuals to repudiate the regime, whether by cutting a telephone wire or throwing a stick of dynamite into the home of a government official. For example, fourteen-year-old Daniel Rodríguez became chief of two separate cells of "Action and Sabotage" in Havana. One was in the white working-class neighborhood of Lawton and the other in the black working-class waterfront neighborhood of Guanabacoa, where his father ran a metal shop. Rodríguez was the son of Spanish communists who fled to Cuba from Franco's Spain. This background suited him well in Lawton, but to gain acceptance in Guanabacoa, he was inducted as a *nañigo,* or priest, into the Santería religion. Rodríguez's involvement with the 26th of July, like that of many in both neighborhoods where he operated, evolved over time. Initially he and his buddies took aim at symbols of the dictatorship without any direction from anyone identified with the M267, and it was random acts of violence of this sort that the movement sought not only to take credit for but also to incorporate into its own underground strategy.[12]

País had a truly remarkable ability to manage simultaneously many competing demands of the movement. The failure of the second front weeks earlier had forced him to think more strategically about a general strike in towns and cities throughout the country as a viable, tactical complement to guerrilla warfare in the mountains. With most of his closest colleagues either in jail or exile, he drafted the organizational model he hoped would allow the movement to better coordinate the rapidly growing popular antidictatorial movement by managing a general strike throughout the country while maintaining the rebels in the Sierra. Outlining for Fidel the progress he made since his release, he explained his plans to revamp the movement's underground organization in a long, typewritten letter—the same letter in which he explained his rationale for proposing a civic revolutionary government.[13] Arriving by courier during the Chibás-Pazos Sierra visit, the letter set forth the blueprint for the grassroots organizing of a general strike as well as a new geographic and substantive division of labor for the National Directorate—both of which guided the underground for the year to come.

Without access to the full set of País's correspondence, several authors have interpreted the initiative as an "inexcusably high-handed" attempt by País to impose his and the National Directorate's authority and control over the *sierra* or as a ploy by País and Armando Hart (then in jail) to exercise a "major curtailment of Fidel's powers."[14] It is assumed that Fidel retaliated against País for reorganizing—and apparently expanding—the powers of the National Directorate by personally sending for Pazos and Chibás and forming the Civic Revolutionary Front announced in the Sierra Manifesto.[15] We now know that the plans for building the underground set forth in the letter are actually the crystallization of the *llano's* work in the two-month period since País's release from jail. Like his political initiative to bring the politicians to the Sierra Maestra, the reorganization of the movement reflected both País's autonomy from the *sierra* and Fidel, and Fidel's confidence in and dependence upon País. País deliberately sent the letter to Fidel during the Pazos-Chibás visit because he wanted Castro to incorporate the movement's plans and his own views into whatever agreement would result from negotiations then under way in the Sierra Maestra. From his perspective, the timing for the underground's national strike strategy depended upon the outcome of the movement's political overture, and vice versa.[16] País wrote Fidel that "the country's situation, your pressure, and the regime's tenacity have granted us enormous recognition that places us at the axis of every possible solution," requiring that, with the others jailed or in exile, País steer the movement forward essentially on his own.[17]

Despite the numerous internal problems that had made País "act a bit dictatorially, dictating orders and being a little strict," País wrote that his heavy-handed manner was beginning to pay off with labor, civic resistance, and the militia. He believed he had successfully converted Oriente province into the testing ground for a nationwide attempt to resurrect the general strike that had failed the previous year. To that effect, he wrote to Fidel that the complementary activism of labor, the militia, and civic resistance demonstrated that "a successful general strike is possible [and] that it is necessary." Local labor cells had already carried out mini-shutdowns, and walkouts were operating under a real structure. The province possessed a "Provincial Labor Directorate with its own Municipal Directorates functioning at full force and with a good deal of financial and propagandistic independence," he wrote. País planned to extend this model throughout the country by creating a National Labor Directorate to plan the national strike and its precise timing. Indeed, an "executive agent," or steering committee, had convened labor groups in Camagüey and Santa Clara and had already begun work in Havana, Pinar del Río, and Matanzas. Therefore, according to País's timeline for the strike, "all of our labor organizations should be created and unified" within one month, or by August 1957.[18] The National Labor Directorate would then name a coordinator, who would also become a member of the 26th of July's National Directorate. By October, he expected workers to have defined a program complete with slogans and propaganda to coalesce behind "the final plan."[19] Likewise, País projected that building municipal, provincial, and national sections of "professionals, merchants, and industrialists" in the Civic Resistance Movement would be complete by September 1957. Also, following the labor organizing model, the national coordinator for Civic Resistance would also become a member of the *llano*'s National Directorate.

Once the labor and civic resistance groups were fully operational, each "front" would then appoint a representative to the newly created National Strike Committee. País assured Castro that while the 26th of July would maintain control over the civic resistance and labor directorates, he intended the National Strike Committee to appear independent from the 26th of July, in order to attract those "civic, political, religious, business and worker organizations, sectors and figures" who "don't wish or cannot have sectarian links to a Movement like ours, but who agree with carrying out a national shut-down in order to overthrow the regime." País designed the National Strike Committee to be diverse, heterogeneous, and nonsectarian because he was confident that the movement's "strength lay in our active belligerency and in our labor and resistance cadre who have an extremely powerful force and who in the reality of any circumstance that might arise would always follow the guidelines of the planned upon revolutionary direction."[20] Under País's direction, the notion of opposition unity meant cultivating the appearance of diversity while maintaining the ability for the 26th of July to exert total control first behind the scenes, and when stronger, openly.

While not every member of each labor group was required to be a militant of the 26th of July, País assigned members of the movement's Action and Sabotage groups to each labor cell. Although País appeared to understand the risks of excessively militarizing the strike effort, the model he designed to involve the Cuban working class in the insurrection suffered from a contradiction: rather than rely on walk-outs and strikes as the primary expression of workers' repudiation of the Batista regime, or addressing worker-specific grievances explicitly, such as the prohibition on strikes or the CTC's corruption, labor activism was to depend primarily on workplace sabotage and violence. As País conceived it, the glue that would secure a coordinated effort between labor and civic resistance was neither the National Directorate itself, nor the force of País's organizational and leadership skills, nor the political alienation and economic stagnation of Cuban workers, nor even the Batista regime's violent repression. Preferably, a "disciplined, aggressive, and audacious militia," which had accounted for the underground's greatest successes to date, would propel and sustain the strike long enough to overthrow the dictator. País wrote Castro that

> when the order is given to maintain the state of insurgency, to give them experience and slowly increase . . . tension in the country until we reach the boiling point, that will be the moment when all of the [Civic] Institutions and all of the groups belonging to our Strike Committee will launch in unison the urgent demand that Batista leave! To resolve the situation and before the Regime has time to draft its response, all of Cuba will ask Batista to leave and before the uncertainty of such a strong, audacious, and national declaration, all of Cuba will launch the General Strike with a wave of worker, white-collar, and revolutionary sabotage never seen before.[21]

País believed that industrial, agricultural, and workplace sabotage, carried out by a streamlined militia working from within the strike committee's local cells, would create collective self-confidence and provide a psychological boost to labor and civic resistance activists. To strengthen and expand the movement's armed efforts further, País wrote Castro that he planned to purchase and introduce "arms into the zones that show the best discipline and organization . . . expanding and reinforcing the Sierra front and opening new fronts."[22] According to País's blueprint, Cuba would be convulsed in a general strike by November or December 1957.

País felt that the new model for overseeing the *llano*'s affairs would better distribute pressures and responsibilities, both geographically and substantively. An executive council within the National Directorate would include the six national division coordinators: propaganda, treasury, labor, civic resistance, militia, and a general coordinator. Simultaneously, a provincial coordinator from each of Cuba's six provinces (Oriente, Camagüey, Las Villas, Matanzas, Havana, and Pinar del Río) would also become a member of the National Directorate. País assigned a thirteenth slot to Celia Sánchez, whom he proposed as the *sierra*'s delegate to the National Directorate. Because of her geographic proximity to the mountains and her close, almost godmotherly ties with Fidel, Celia focused her attention on equipping Fidel and his men, whether by sewing and sending uniforms; relaying watches, boots, blankets, food, and medicine; or raising money from her substantial circle of well-off friends and acquaintances. While País turned his attention to coordinating the various tasks of the National Directorate around the country, Sánchez could give voice to the eternal and insistent demands of guerrilla warfare.[23]

The general strike strategy that País outlined complemented Fidel's guerrilla war in the Sierra. Indeed, his plan to restructure the National Directorate suggests a vision of the two revolutionary strategies, urban insurrection and guerrilla warfare, as mutually reinforcing but tactically separate in terms of day-to-day operations. The function of the National Directorate was not to run the entire war effort. Instead, País designed it to help him manage the underground's affairs and to impose a 26th of July superstructure onto the rapidly growing popular movement against the dictator. The urban underground had little say in Castro's conduct of the war in the Sierra Maestra, and País did not ask Fidel for the *llano* to have any say in the Sierra's tactical decisions. But País accorded the *sierra* a seat at the *llano*'s decision-making table in recognition of Castro's leadership and as the movement's only nationally known figure—and because supplying the *sierra* rebels remained an important part of the movement's focus.

Until now, there has been little conclusive evidence of how Fidel responded to País's plans to expand the militia, to restructure the National Directorate, or to funnel the lion's share of the movement's resources into a general strike to force Batista's resignation. Another part of Fidel's response to País's strategy in his forty-two-page letter of July 21, 1957, addressed the "opinion you asked for regarding the plans to be developed over the next months." Fidel wrote,

> I sincerely believe that you have performed a formidable task in this regard. Armando well knows how many times I insisted, after leaving prison, that it was the correct strategy, as opposed to the thesis of a military coup or a putsch in the capital. I see this so clearly today that if given a choice between a victory of days from November 30 and our landing, or victory one year later, without hesitation I would prefer the victory that is brewing through this fantastic awakening of the Cuban nation. What's more, I believe that the fall of the regime within one week would be much less fruitful than its fall within four months. Here, as a joke, I often assert to the comrades that we don't want a seven-month revolution.[24]

For Fidel, the country's festering under Batista's repression, while the *sierra* built up its forces and directly engaged the military—as País unfurled his four-month general strike plan in the cities—would only broaden and deepen the popular appeal of the revolution. Castro, confident in his ability to demoralize Batista's military and that the Sierra was home to the heart of the revolution, signed off on País's plan with aplomb. Castro encouraged País to move forward with his strike plans, but at the same time let the *llano* leader know that in his view guerrilla warfare in the Sierra remained, in Fidel's words, the "axis" of Cuba's political solution.

With his approval of the strike plan and implicitly of the new National Directorate, Fidel implored País to step up the supply of weapons and equipment to the Sierra, reproaching himself for "the generosity with which I suggested you use some of the arms headed for us for the S. F. [second front]; at the time, I was heavily influenced by the fact that then we had men carrying two weapons on their backs; today we have unarmed men who are like empty holes in our ranks."[25] País reassured Castro that in exchange for Fidel's support of the underground's plans, he would step up supply efforts to the Sierra.[26] On the fourth anniversary of Castro's Moncada attack, País explained, "I am very happy that at last you have touched upon the themes I asked of you. I will take note of everything and will try to do them as quickly as possible. From this month on I take responsibility for supporting you," beginning by sending more weapons and bullets and at least thirty men whom Castro had requested.[27] Thus, the *sierra* and *llano* agreed to pursue two potentially complementary tactics as part of a strategy to bring down the regime: guerrilla war in the mountains and a general strike in the cities. But neither Fidel, País, nor the 26th of July Movement had time to take advantage of this newfound harmony.

According to the American consulate in Santiago, the city's new chief of police, Lieutenant Colonel José Salas Cañizares, was sent to the Oriente capital to "apply extreme measures to terrorize the generally anti-Batista Santiago population."[28] Throughout the summer of 1957 País lived in ever greater personal danger, frequently changing safe houses more than once a day and narrowly escaping capture by forces under Salas Cañizares's command. At the end of July, Raúl Pujol, the owner of a local hardware store and a civic resistance activist, had volunteered his house to shelter País. Acting on an informant's tip one sweltering afternoon, the local police set up a blockade on either end of Pujol's street when both Pujol and País were in the house. Inexplicably, País and Pujol left the house and walked down the street together. At the end of the street, the informant, or *chivato* (who was a former classmate), identified País for the police, who forced País and Pujol into a waiting car, drove them to an alley two-and-a-half blocks away, and pulled them out to be shot in the back of the neck by Salas Cañizares at point-blank range.[29] Frank País was twenty-three years old.

4 | Defining Opposition Unity on the Ground

AUGUST–OCTOBER 1957

> The strike has arrived . . . How the province has responded! We've had 24 hours of complete paralysis: industries, businesses, offices, banks, private and rental cars, cafes, and private clubs closed, closed, closed. No one is going out in the street, only soldiers, police, and SIM [military intelligence services] are able to get around with so many *grampas* that have come down on them. I told Civic Resistance to convene a local demonstration; we had another tonight. Today they've fired shots, broken down windows and doors. They are real lions.
>
> Celia Sánchez to Haydée Santamaría,
> July 31–August 2, 1957

THE DAY AFTER PAÍS WAS ASSASSINATED, most Santiago businesses closed their doors in mourning. Some sixty thousand Santiagueros, from local Communist Party members to the leadership of the Santiago Civic Institutions, attended País's funeral.[1] Even the M267 underground emerged to grieve publicly, openly donning their black and red arm bands. Workers of all stripes went on strike "by voluntary action" for several days afterward, requiring "very strong measures by Government forces . . . [to] restore a semblance of normalcy," the American consulate reported.[2] The work stoppages were voluntary but not exactly spontaneous. Indeed, just one day before he was murdered, País had successfully orchestrated a provincewide fifteen-minute workplace shutdown organized by Civic Resistance and labor cells, as a finale to several similar actions that had occurred throughout July.[3] The government responded to the "serious situation in Oriente Province and the threat of a general strike" with a forty-five-day suspension of constitutional guarantees, including "freedom from search and arrest without cause and legal process, habeas corpus, prompt trial, movement, communication, speech, press, and assembly." The U.S. embassy regarded this measure as "an indication of combined arrogance and fear by the regime."[4] By the first of August, the regime had renewed censorship of the print, radio, and television media, with each measure rapidly rubber-stamped by the Cuban congress—the very same institution that was also debating ways to implement a democratic transition on the island.

Inspired by the scale, passion, and duration of Oriente's reaction to the País assassination, the 26th of July Movement decided to take advantage of the new agitated climate and accelerate País's plans to prepare immediately for a nationwide general strike. Celia Sánchez wrote to Haydée Santamaría in Havana that "Frank's absence has left me in such profound pain . . . but I know we are all feeling overwhelming grief." Indeed, within a week his assassination had forced País's closest colleagues in the *llano*—Celia, René Ramos Latour, Vilma Espín, Enrique Oltuski, Marcelo Fernández, Armando Hart, and Faustino Pérez—both to grieve personally and respond rapidly to a tragic but nevertheless welcome political opening for the movement. Sánchez did not "know how Santiago would cope without Frank and with Bienvenido's [Léster Rodriguez's] absence." She attempted to fill País's enormous shoes in the underground, while René Ramos Latour, or "Daniel," whom the Havana-based members of the National Directorate did not know personally, worked with Celia to cover País's responsibilities for the *sierra*. Latour formally assumed País's duties, in particular the task of expanding the underground's urban militia.[5]

Latour was convinced that the mass mobilization and protests over the assassination demonstrated that "the people of Santiago are ours, and they mean to show that they no longer cared about being found out by their oppressors." The protests were a sign that País's death had "broken down all barriers. There were no conservatives or radicals, rich or poor, blacks or white." Latour believed that the Santiago response could be replicated around the country, because "if it doesn't spread to other cities, it will be extinguished."[6] Latour readily acknowledged that the movement lacked the human and material resources to respond to an escalation of state violence but proposed that the M267 overwhelm the regime with a protracted nationwide shutdown that included Cubans of all classes and races. In Havana, Armando Hart escaped from jail and Faustino Pérez was released; both rejoined Enrique Oltuski and Haydée Santamaría, their colleagues in the National Directorate (DN). The freed men were surprised by the sudden surge in popular mobilization. Though they recognized that their organization in Havana was not ready to pull off anything like the spontaneous response of Oriente, they wrote Latour that they would make "every effort possible to convert the martyrdom of Salvador [País] into the most useful death in the struggle against the tyranny."[7] Like Latour, the Havana underground feared that the regime would respond with "brutal repression against business and workers that undoubtedly would suffocate the strike unless our own action apparatus responds with even greater repression." They also agreed with Latour that the movement's best response would be to match the regime's violence with their own. "It is sad," wrote Hart and Pérez, "but the time has come to apply maximum violence against the agents who open their businesses. When groups of them fall, it will provoke panic among their own kind. This very panic is that which the regime hopes to use against the people. Whoever applies it with greater efficacy will achieve victory."[8] The politically risky militarization of the underground through assassination attempts and sabotage was to intensify over the next year.

Whatever desire the National Directorate may have had to match the state's violence, the Havana underground "lacked, the same as always, sufficient organization to coordinate and sufficient efficacy in our Action cadre." The movement's civic resistance, propaganda, and labor sectors had managed only to publicize some revolutionary strike slogans. While the Havana underground hoped for some "labor actions" to "culminate in the days ahead in a strike," the "truthful situation," they wrote Latour, was that the Oriente underground should not hold high expectations for a massive shutdown of Havana because "the necessary worker coordination does not exist." If, on the other hand, the other provinces could hold and continue a strike, perhaps Havana would "carry out certain already conceived plans that might yield positive results."[9]

One cause for the Havana underground's skepticism was the reluctance of the local Civic Institutions to support publicly a general strike in the capital. At the time, Enrique Oltuski, the son of Polish-Jewish immigrants and a U.S.-trained architect, acted as the movement's liaison with the Civic Institutions. An executive at Shell Oil, Oltuski was a member of the Havana Rotary Club and unlike many of the movement's top cadre lived a double existence, with an aboveboard professional, social, and personal life as well as a clandestine, revolutionary one. Oltuski met frequently with the Civic Institutions' president, Raúl de Velasco, who was also the president of the Cuban Medical Association. Hoping that Batista's collapse was imminent, Oltuski held several conversations with de Velasco, attempting to persuade him that the time had come for the Civic Institutions to move beyond their prior calls for an end to violence and instead to demand Batista's resignation in the spirit of the Sierra Manifesto. But the Civic Institutions were "cowardly in the end. Its members agreed to call for Batista's resignation but only if the strike was successful," leaving the lion's share of heavy lifting squarely on the 26th of July's limited capacities.[10] If the 26th of July could force Batista's collapse through a general strike, then the Civic Institutions would endorse the new status quo.

With the movement's tactical and organizational preparedness under-developed at best and the Civic Institutions reluctant to call publicly for Batista's resignation, Armando Hart and Faustino Pérez also considered a more expedient scenario for driving out the dictator: developing an alli-ance with dissident navy and army officers who were contemplating a coup. The upheaval in Oriente had caused Havana to vibrate with "mili-tary conspiracies everywhere" and they were talking with a dissident navy officer who agreed that the popular reaction to the País assassi-nation had caused "the two months . . . [needed] for the definitive ac-tion to have elapsed in one week," and prompted the officer and his co-conspirators to accelerate plans for a mutiny at every naval post on the island.[11]

As a result of their talks, Hart and Pérez wrote Latour that they were se-riously contemplating "forming a mixed Junta between the army, navy, and 26th of July." Glossing over the obvious contradiction between the Sierra Manifesto's rejection of coups and military juntas, Hart and Pérez assured Latour that "it appears the thesis of the Sierra Manifesto will be accepted in terms of the nature and form of government that will replace the current one," if not the actual process for overthrowing the dicta-tor.[12] Still, they understood that with so many individuals and political forces jostling for position, there was no guarantee that the 26th of July would have a seat on such a junta. Thus they tried to coordinate with Oriente in planning for three possible outcomes after the mutiny: a new government that would include the M267; a new government that the 26th of July would not be able to formally support; or a government that the movement would reject entirely. They knew that the first scenario was the least likely but advised Oriente and the other National Director-ate members to "take advantage of Batista's fall to take over as much command as possible." The gamble was logical enough: to the extent that the movement could establish control in a chaotic situation, its po-sition in a new government would be strengthened. "Of course," they wrote, "since we would be dealing with a government supported by the Movement everything would be conditioned by what we tell you. But re-member that a fait accompli is the best revolutionary guarantee. The only one." Under the second scenario, Hart and Pérez instructed Latour to form a separate revolutionary government with the Santiago Civic In-stitutions and "any other force it seems necessary to include," explaining publicly that the M267 was forming the new government "to guarantee the spirit of the Sierra Manifesto, and we are now preparing the reception of Fidel Castro, leader of the Revolution, who together with the governing junta and the people will put forward the Revolution's thinking regarding recent events." Under the third and most likely scenario, "a *batistiano* government without Batista," which was "apparently in the making," the Oriente cadre would have to quickly and categorically denounce the Havana regime and form a revolutionary government in Santiago.[13]

GIVEN THE possibility of being preempted by a military coup, but not wishing to watch passively as the mobilizations in Oriente continued, the Havana-based members of the movement found themselves at a moment of both risk and possibility. The strike went forward, but fell light years short of paralyzing the country—it had little effect in Havana, the other provinces, and even, in the end, in rebellious Oriente, the movement's "best guarantee." One of the major impediments to a successful strike derived, as predicted, from the M267's limited ties with organized labor and the power of Eusebio Mujal, secretary general of the Confederation of Cuban Workers (CTC). In a parody of labor activism, Mujal deployed CTC leaders around the country "to organize worker resistance to the impending strike." In Havana, the CTC took "similar steps . . . to thwart a general walkout," such as full-page newspaper advertisements condemning the "political" strike as against worker interests, "instigated by non-labor classes and designed to destroy the institutions of the country." Though the U.S. embassy reported on the opposition's confidence that port workers, transport workers, bank employees, and other professional groups "would lead a fairly effective shutdown," business continued as usual in a matter of hours on the day of the strike.[14]

But for the revolutionaries, the strike had not been a complete failure. Some bank, bus, and textile workers did strike, and there were power outages and strikes in American businesses such as Sears, Roebuck and F. W. Woolworth. Though Batista remained in power, the wave of strikes around the country and widespread protests throughout Oriente had destabilized the regime, leaving the "middle ground between Government and revolutionary opposition . . . rapidly eroded," the American embassy reported.[15] Indeed, Faustino Pérez wrote País's long-time comrade Léster Rodríguez, then in Miami, that while "we were still not sufficiently prepared . . . it has been a great event, the consequences of which the tyranny will not recover from. We believe that in a short time we will have the conditions for the final shock."[16] Fidel Castro also viewed the August strike as a dry run for the future, not "as a failure at all, but rather a rehearsal, an unmistakable proof, a lovely explosion of Cuban dignity in a well-deserved homage to our Frank." He wrote Celia Sánchez that to "prepare the strike on a very large scale, an organized, overwhelming strike . . . that is the people's weapon." Castro speculated that "those who did not support" the first strike would "feel ashamed and will serve vigorously in the next one. So the army of the Sierra has to be prepared to advance resolutely to the cities and conquer them."[17]

Between the August 5 strike and the naval mutiny, which, with M267 participation, took place only in Cienfuegos on September 5, neither significant sabotage in the cities nor conflict with the army in the Sierra Maestra occurred.[18] After the Cienfuegos mutiny, the regime prosecuted dozens of suspected conspirators, formed a joint military command, and cracked down further on anti-regime activity. But unencumbered itself by the state of siege and suspension of civil liberties prevailing in the country, the Batista government continued campaigning for the June 1958 elections. From the vantage point of the 26th of July, the elimination of remaining reformist officers would "close down for quite a while . . . any chance that [the Batista regime] will crack from within." In the city and province of Havana, the M267 also faced "a real disaster," as police and military intelligence repression had caused "major breakdowns" within the 26th of July, including the loss of "safe houses, cars, many jailed and some ten deaths." In Las Villas province, where the city of Cienfuegos was located, the movement, whose activists had conspired with the mutineers, faced a "huge crisis," as its own militants alleged that the "directorate was responsible for the Cienfuegos massacre."[19]

For the surviving members of the National Directorate and for the leader of the *sierra*, the partial successes of the strike provided evidence of the mobilizing capacity of the 26th of July, however limited at the time. With few allies remaining in the Cuban armed forces, the National Directorate in Havana abandoned the notion that the end of the revolutionary struggle was close at hand. Indeed, the Cienfuegos mutiny liberated the movement from the risk of being marginalized by a coup and allowed the revolutionaries to focus entirely on the national strike plan that Frank País had set forth to Fidel just days before his death.

All of these events had left the National Directorate in disarray, with the organizational plans that Frank País had initiated still barely off the ground. Most of its living and unincarcerated members met for the first time in more than six months to devise a work plan for fall of 1957, clarify the National Directorate's membership and division of labor, and jump-start the strike plans. País's surviving comrades did away with most of the geographical representation that he had wanted, leaving slots in the new National Directorate only for Havana and Oriente, the *sierra* liaison, and the individuals responsible for organization, action and sabotage, propaganda, labor, and finances. Vilma Espín, the daughter of a wealthy Santiago family, who had once been a graduate student at MIT, became chief of organization for Oriente, while Celia Sánchez became the 26th of July's official liaison with the Sierra Maestra. Faustino Pérez remained in Havana to oversee all aspects of the movement's activities in the capital. Marcelo Fernández, also educated in the United States, remained as the movement's propaganda man, and Haydée Santamaría managed fund-raising. René Ramos Latour continued as head of action and sabotage, now not only in Oriente but in the entire country. Armando Hart—the son of a leading judge and legal scholar—transferred posts from the capital to Santiago de Cuba, where he became national chief of organization, a position that gave him oversight for all of the movement's work in the underground and in exile.[20]

The Santiago-based members of the National Directorate attempted to fill the void left by País's death and organize the strike that he had begun planning in July. They scarcely had time to recover from his loss when Fidel Castro began sending emissaries to Santiago and around the country to upbraid the *llano*—in particular, Latour, Sánchez, and Hart—for their putative neglect of the *sierra*.[21] Just after the Cienfuegos uprising, for example, Castro sent Jorge Sotús from the Sierra Maestra to Manzanillo, Santiago, around the country, and eventually to Miami to find out why the underground had apparently failed to send the rebel army sufficient money, weapons, and equipment. With over two hundred men to outfit, feed, and arm, Castro was beginning to feel Frank País's absence. His desperation quickly turned into distrust of País's successors in the underground.

Latour tried to assuage Castro's anxiety with an optimistic account of the movement's plans to continue País's strategy through a "complete organization of the movement in every province; putting into practice a plan of directed action and sabotage that will progressively intensify, culminating in a state of great agitation; declaring the Revolutionary General Strike once we've organized the provinces and perfected the labor and resistance cadre; and selecting, strengthening, training, and indoctrinating the militia, which will be the determining factor in sustaining the Strike and the stage that follows the overthrow of the regime."[22] But such explanations failed to reassure Fidel that the new crew in Santiago understood, as País had, the need to satisfy all of the demands of the *sierra* simultaneously. Nor could letters alone demonstrate that Latour was capable of filling Frank's shoes back in the *llano*. To straighten out matters directly with Fidel, Latour left Santiago on October 18, 1957 for what would become an eighteen-day stay in the Sierra Maestra.

Latour brought Fidel correspondence from Miami and Costa Rica as well as new documents outlining the National Directorate's organizational and strategic plans. These plans were intended to cause "the tyranny to fall to pieces in a few months under the weight of our action," Hart wrote Fidel. "Thanks to your heroism and the sabotage, agitation, and a whole series of tasks carried out outside of the Sierra . . . now in reality we really have become the Revolution." He explained that the underground had already begun to put into practice an action plan that "will, in our judgment, precipitate the General Strike." Soon, wrote Hart, they would release a spate of propaganda about the sugar harvest, alerting the sugar mill owners and cane growers first nicely, and then violently, to leave the country by the first of December, "after which date we will unleash greater and greater violence and revolutionary action," burning cane fields and refineries carried out by the militia.[23] The strategic plans under way for a general strike to drive Batista out by the end of the year also depended upon the movement's successfully organizing its political affairs. Though the Civic Institutions would not denounce the dictator publicly, privately they engaged in a dialogue with the insurgents, who pursued the Sierra Manifesto's formula for establishing a provisional government composed not of individuals from Cuba's traditional political parties but of representatives of civil society untainted by Cuban *politiquería*. This endeavor was an extraordinarily ambitious challenge for a group of men and women in their twenties and early thirties. If the 26th of July was successful in brokering a deal with the Civic Institutions, there would be immediate political, psychological, and international benefits to the entire movement.

After Enrique Oltuski's transfer from Havana to Las Villas, Armando Hart took the lead in discussions with the Civic Institutions about forming a provisional government, a prospect he regarded as more politically viable than on the eve of the August strike. The Cienfuegos mutiny had obliterated the option of a reformist military coup, prompting the Civic Institutions to reconsider the Sierra Manifesto—and thereby opening the door for the 26th of July to gain the support of substantial segments of civil society, while further isolating Cuba's traditional political parties. In addition, the movement's own members pressured the national leadership to assert more forcefully an identity distinct from the Ortodoxo Party and to clarify the movement's relationship to other anti-Batista groups. Internationally, a consensus had developed within the National Directorate that the movement needed to maintain an image of moderation to avoid provoking the United States. A tactical alliance with the Civic Institutions would strengthen the 26th of July domestically and reassure the Americans.

During their discussions, the Civic Institutions gave Hart a document that seemed to respond directly to the Sierra Manifesto's appeal. The "Civic Revolutionary Action Plan" proposed restoring the 1940 constitution and forming a provisional government abroad "that will assume official representation of the State." Hart praised the proposal and congratulated its authors for taking a stand against the dictator; he also pledged his movement's support for a government formed by the Civic Institutions. He believed that such an arrangement would avoid the chaotic, and for the M267, politically risky alternative of having a transitional government that would result "from the piecing together of this or that opposition sector, the moral standing and focus of which regarding the national problematic" was "very diverse," and "would make internal unity very difficult." In the short term, Hart believed that unity within the opposition and a new government would require support from "the people of Cuba, international public opinion, *las clases ecónomicas*, and the armed forces." While he expressed confidence that the "representative organizations and institutions of national life" would back the Civic Institutions in their bid to form a provisional government, he also insisted that only the 26th of July could deliver the support of the Cuban people, or the popular opposition, because it was the movement alone that "after one year is carrying out an open and frontal fight against the tyranny." Only a provisional government completely free of ties to political parties or revolutionary sectors, reasoned Hart, could remain aloof from and immune to "militant sectarianism." Still, Hart also recommended that once the Civic Institutions had formed the provisional government, its members should remain receptive to the views of any "representative sectors of the country (revolutionary, political, labor, financial, military)" that agree to the terms set forth by the post-Batista transitional government.[24]

Hart agreed to all but one of the platforms that the Civic Institutions had proposed for the new government. The one item he rejected revealed the limitations of brokering a tactical alliance with the country's middle class and professional elite. The "Civic-Revolutionary Action Plan" proposed that the new government continue the ban on the right to strike then enforced by the Batista regime and upheld by organized labor. But Hart argued that the proposal violated the 1940 constitution, which the Civic Institutions had proposed restoring, and suggested that banning the right to strike "could be used as a red flag against the new government and make it appear anti-labor." By perpetuating one of the more egregious elements of the Batista-era status quo, the ban on labor strikes would undermine "the full exercise of democracy," the very objective of a new unity government.

Writing to the movement's own cadre on the meaning of opposition unity, however, Hart was less diplomatic and notably more direct in asserting the 26th of July's hegemony over the anti-Batista opposition. At previous junctures in Cuban history, wrote Hart, Cuba had lacked "a revolutionary instrument after liquidating the immediate obstacle, first the colony, then the *machadato*, [the Machado regime] capable of" confronting and surviving confusion and counterrevolution, whether in the 1890s, the 1930s, or the 1950s. The *llano*'s leadership believed that "after eight months we are the opposition to the regime. The 26th of July's force of action has been such that today it appears in Cuban reality as the only instrument capable of conquering freedom. It is not that we should think of ourselves as the only ones; but indeed, we are those who have the enormous historic responsibility of guiding revolutionary action."[25]

This status as the sole "anti-Batista" force in Cuba meant that with "a strategy designed for the immediate goal of a general strike and armed insurrection," the movement would be able to control the means and timing of Batista's collapse as well as the shape of the provisional government that would replace the regime. After overthrowing the dictator, the 26th of July would remain a "revolutionary instrument" to "assure compliance with the revolution's program through the people's action, which is not the same as simply creating another party."[26] The National Directorate had staked out for itself the objectives of destabilizing Batista, controlling the timing of his collapse, and insuring the permanence of a revolutionary program through popular democracy under a new regime. Alluding to a vision of a mass-based revolution from the bottom up, Hart predicted that the 26th of July would become the guarantor of "political cleansing, economic rights, and social justice."[27]

If by October of 1957 the 26th of July had become *the* "anti-Batista," preparing its militants for their organization's post-Batista conversion into a "revolutionary instrument," what then was the meaning of unity with the other insurgent forces and opposition parties? At the time, the leadership of the Student Revolutionary Directorate (DRE) was either dead or in exile, the Organización Auténtica (OA) was tiny and virtually inactive in Cuba, the moderate opposition parties had also been driven into exile, the reformist military had been crushed, and the Communist Party, which repeatedly called for a united front against the dictator, did little toward that end but complain about being excluded by the opposition and criticize the tactics of the insurgent forces.[28] Unity under these circumstances, Hart explained, meant that

> (a) We will respect any unity formula that retains the Civic Institutions at its axis. They should assume the principal responsibility for this unity and for the provisional government. (b) We are ready to work jointly with any revolutionary sector to carry out specific actions that we consider useful to the process. We are ready to cooperate with any effort that will be undertaken on the basis of specific deeds to be carried out. (c) We call upon workers of every militancy and of no militancy to join strike committees at their work centers or industrial sectors with a definite objective: to prepare for the Strike.[29]

Though the 26th of July distributed a broad-based call for all political and economic sectors to join the M267-dominated strike committees, Hart stipulated that his organization would cooperate with other insurgent groups only "based on concrete deeds and not pompous and high-sounding declarations" in specific actions on the ground, making no commitments regarding future political arrangements.[30]

Until this moment, the 26th of July had needed to associate itself loosely with the prestige of the Ortodoxo Party and had thus deliberately avoided publicly staking out an independent place for itself in Cuban revolutionary politics. If the 26th of July had identified itself as only an insurgent force, and publicly broken with the nation's weak but nevertheless genuine reformist political party, it might have jeopardized negotiations with the Civic Institutions and alienated the political figures whom it had so assiduously cultivated during and after the release of the Sierra Manifesto. But the movement seemed to harbor no such diplomatic concerns in its relationship with the other insurgent forces or opposition parties. For Armando Hart and most of the National Directorate, opposition unity did not mean consensus, but rather implied creating tactical alliances to overthrow Batista. For these militants, the 26th of July had to control the timing, tactics, and politics of the entire effort. For the moment, everything appeared to be falling into place, with plans for the strike under way and the Civic Institutions poised to form a provisional government largely on the movement's terms. The country seemed on the verge of taking what Hart considered "the strongest step taken in five years in favor of opposition unity."[31]

5 | Fear and Loathing in Miami

Every day I see how much Cuba needed this revolution. We conceived of a revolutionary consciousness and we have attained it. You know this country has always been enamored of caudillos and this is how Fidel was made. I was always afraid that he would be killed, and that besides losing a great asset, that people would abandon us in the Revolution; these fears are now history, and now the people have a real sense of their own feelings and the revolution is above all else.

Celia Sánchez to her father, September 26, 1957

IN MID-SEPTEMBER 1957, WITH POLITICAL debate once again suppressed under a blanket of censorship following another forty-five-day suspension of constitutional guarantees, the venue of revolutionary politics shifted to Miami, where the 26th of July became embroiled in the Batista opposition's attempt to unify against the dictator. This episode in Cuban history has never before been explained. Before this study, we could "only speculate as to the real course of events"; now we have the documentation to show what really was happening behind Fidel's "cryptic silence."[1]

In the last weeks of Frank País's life, as he had indicated to Castro, he launched an operation abroad to obtain significant stocks of weapons for the rebel army, for the new fronts he planned, and for the sabotage militia around the island. Keeping an open channel with the American consulate in Santiago paid off when, on July 8, 1957, a consulate official there loaded Léster Rodríguez into the trunk of his car and drove him to the U.S. naval base at Guantánamo Bay, where he was given proper papers and safe passage to Mexico City. País had negotiated Rodríguez's departure from Cuba in exchange for an agreement that the 26th of July's sympathizers employed at the base would stop smuggling weapons.[2]

Rodríguez, or "Bienvenido," had worked closely with País throughout the 1950s and understood the weapons needs of both the Sierra Maestra and the underground. So he seemed like a natural choice for what the movement loftily titled "chief of military affairs in exile." He arrived in Mexico City with credentials signed by País and Fidel, as well as letters of introduction to Castro's half-sisters Emma and Lidia, to the 26th of July patriotic clubs that Castro had begun organizing during a 1955 fund-raising tour to the United States, and to former president Carlos Prío Socarrás.

Rodríguez's mission had two parts. His first responsibility was to establish clear lines of authority over the chaotically organized and competitive patriotic clubs, whose purpose was to raise money to purchase arms and equipment for the rebels. He found that in almost every city with Cuban exiles, whether Mexico City, Chicago, Bridgeport, New York, or Miami, there was not one but two and sometimes three separate 26th of July groups operating as the "official" representative of Fidel Castro. Though each in some way sought to support the revolution, in most cases they competed over which had a closer relationship to Castro and over the use of the money they raised. Rodríguez's job was to "end the anarchy of the Movement in Miami and in nearly the entire exile," as well as unify all of the groups in each of the most important cities. This step would help finance the second component of his mission: amassing as many weapons and as much ammunition as possible for shipment back to Cuba.[3] With wealthy contributors in Mexico City and Carlos Prío in Miami, Rodríguez concentrated his energies on those two cities. But neither his revolutionary credentials nor experience in the underground, dating back to the November 1956 strike attempt in Santiago, had prepared Rodríguez for the *politiquería* of exile, where his zeal for weapons began to overshadow his political judgment.

In Mexico, Rodríguez quickly got in touch with two longtime comrades, *moncadistas* Pedro Miret and Gustavo Arcos, who at the time were conspiring to send more men and weapons back to Cuba. Rodríguez reported that the "political mess of the division between Pedro and Gustavo and Fidel's sisters [was] continuing in all its splendor."[4] Though Emma and Lidia successfully raised money for their brother's cause in Cuba and could easily have financed Miret and Arcos to organize and equip new reinforcements for the rebels, they consistently withheld funds and seemed to go out of their way both to disparage publicly the two and to distance themselves from the 26th of July as a revolutionary organization. They were loyal to their brother, but they made life miserable for his deputies. They appointed and expelled representatives of the 26th of July at will and sowed mistrust and bad morale in exile circles.[5] País had ordered Léster to expel Fidel's sisters from the movement because their faction, known as the "pedregal" for the upper-class Mexico City neighborhood where they lived, was hurting the cause.

Instead, Rodríguez played all the angles in financing and arming the rebels. He quickly found that Emma and Lidia's connections with finance and weapons contacts were too valuable to pass up. Rather than risk greater damage by expelling them, Léster chose to keep the sisters close at hand, putting them in charge of the fund-raising for the 26th of July in exile.[6] He wrote País that with their help he had already purchased on the open market "60 Czechoslovakian 30.06 rifles and 30,000 American bullets that I hope to place in your hands as soon as possible."[7] In addition, Emma's fiancé, one of the movement's "most important financial supporters," had donated $43,000 and was dangling before him a tantalizing supply of material to the rebels: as a sort of matching grant he would put up $100,000 if the 26th of July could raise an additional $50,000. The offer, wrote Rodríguez, included "one million 30.06 bullets, an amphibious plane that can carry 70 men and with which we could carry out any operation without risk at all . . . 500 M-1 rifles, seven 55 mm anti-aircraft cannons, 200 boxes of grenades and a bunch of other things" on the condition that the M267 "not have an understanding with anyone."[8] Given the quantity proposed, Léster decided to "keep some distance to gain some time and see if things work out with this gentleman, and if not reach an agreement with Prío."[9]

But País died before reading Rodríguez's first report from Mexico. In fact, by the time anyone from the 26th of July had taken stock of the movement in the aftermath of the assassination, the general strike attempt, and the Cienfuegos mutiny, it was several weeks later and Rodríguez was already heading from Mexico to Miami, having given up on Emma's fiancé and his empty promise of a plane full of weapons. Since the massacre of members of the Student Revolutionary Directorate (DRE) and Organización Auténtica (OA) at the palace assault in March and the *Corinthia* disaster in May, exile had become the obvious option for what remained of these insurgent forces, and their leaders in particular, such as Faure Chomón and Carlos Prío. No sooner had Rodríguez arrived in Miami than Faustino Pérez heard a rumor back in Havana that "Prío and the Directorio's people are insisting that they have reached an agreement (pact) with the 26th of July, the organization that you represent." Echoing Hart's guidelines about the limits and possibilities of unity proposals, Faustino reminded Rodríguez that the movement would consider "useful any agreement based on coordinated action that brings with it the chance of deeds of greater resonance; but without compromises that go beyond the deeds themselves." What, Pérez asked, was really going on?[10]

The instructions Rodríguez did receive from the National Directorate lacked specifics; he was left to decide the benefits to the movement of successfully navigating through Miami's ambiguous political atmosphere and emerging with weapons for the revolution. Indeed, he diligently, if not recklessly, explored all manner of alliances, from the possible to the implausible. For example, at one point he pursued a tip that pro-Batista Eusebio Mujal Barniol, who was notorious for strike-breaking, had "apparently proposed coordinating a general strike with us and he assures that this would be definitive," particularly if the National Directorate were willing to meet directly and "agree on a defined plan."[11] A deal with the devil perhaps, but Rodríguez was well aware of the movement's deficit in labor organizing. Having experienced the benefits in Oriente from greater worker participation in revolutionary activities, he passed along the proposal.

Though Rodríguez was intimately familiar with and shared País's view of both Prío and the OA's rivalry with the 26th of July, he was equally committed to exploiting the former president and student leader's financial resources for the movement's advantage—just as País had been when planning for the *Corinthia*'s arrival in the Sierra Cristal earlier that year. Initially, Prío dismissed Rodríguez's proposals to escalate the insurgency as "crazy" and refused to help. Rodríguez reported to Havana that "there definitely does not exist any commitment with these men and I believe that neither in the future is it advisable to have contact." But after several more rounds of talks with Prío and the DRE, not only "to coordinate military plans," but also to do so "solely and exclusively until forming a provisional government that would be guaranteed and respected by the three forces," he assured the National Directorate that he would insist that the Civic Institutions, not the existing political parties, appoint a provisional government.[12] Apparently Prío had begun to come around and was willing to help the revolutionaries.

Weeks passed without a response from Cuba. Rodríguez wrote "regarding unity with the Auténticos" to "clarify that we have not reached any agreement here and we would only reach an agreement of a tactical type, for the hour of combat, as long as we see in it guarantees and benefits for our cause." He apparently understood the line he needed to walk in brokering a deal.[13] Still, he received no answer to his request for further guidance. Tiring of the hustle and endless discussions, he asked to be replaced so that he could return to Cuba to work on "whatever jobs the movement assigns me."[14] The pressure of demands to arm both the guerrillas in the Sierra Maestra and the militia everywhere else had embroiled the movement in a web of intrigue surrounding ex-president Carlos Prío —despite every effort not to compromise its independence in the process of asking for or accepting his help. Rodríguez's frustration and anxiety intensified, as did the rebels' impatience with him back on the battlefield.

Referring to the Czech weapons and American ammunition that he had purchased in July, Celia Sánchez alerted Fidel that "it appears [Rodríguez] doesn't know the urgency for arms and at the rate he's going when they arrive they will no longer be needed."[15] Rodríguez had been away from Cuba for two months, but he had yet to send even one bullet back to the island. He wrote that because of "a series of indiscretions and mistakes we lost the torpedo launch . . . the man who was going to donate it became a coward at the last minute."[16] And with FBI surveillance and seizures of the movement's weapons stocks in Miami, Rodríguez and País's brother Agustín began stockpiling weapons in Houston. After hitting a dead-end in Mexico, Rodríguez established "contact with a NATO agent in Europe who will guarantee [weapons] at negligible prices, but the smallest operation they will carry out starts at 50,000 pesos." Rodríguez's comrades in Cuba began to doubt his efforts as well.

The pressure of the war, the distance from the real fight, and the alienation of opposition politics also took their toll on the 26th of July's political affairs abroad. It was no secret that the opposition was attempting to find a consensus presidential candidate. Even the rebels isolated in the Sierra Maestra learned from Celia that the Miami press was "reporting on Javierito's father's [Felipe Pazos's] exile, . . . and he was making a play at holding court to show his presidential aspirations. One of his perennial visitors was Tony Varona, who also went into exile. Another with the same aspirations is Miró Cardona," president of the Havana Bar Association and of the Havana Civic Institutions.[17] As the smoke of *politiquería* thickened in exile, Rodríguez and Mario Llerena in Miami and Pedro Miret and Gustavo Arcos in Mexico recommended to the National Directorate that Felipe Pazos become the "Official Delegate of the 26th of July Movement in the United States," representing the movement in political negotiations with the opposition. In their view, the choice of Pazos was logical: he had signed the Sierra Manifesto with Fidel and, having lived and worked for years in Washington, he knew how to operate there and could provide a face of moderation for the revolutionaries. The alternative candidate, Raúl Chibás, was in jail.[18] But did they intend for Pazos to be regarded as the 26th of July's presidential candidate? Who would Pazos think he was representing? His own political party or the revolutionaries?

The movement's comrades in exile soon began to doubt their choice. Mario Llerena, a language professor from the University of Havana who became the movement's "chief of public relations in exile" from June 1957 until August 1958, reported that Pazos had come to Miami to situate himself for a position in a post-Batista provisional government. In his view, Pazos would represent both the histórico and abstentionista wings of the Ortodoxo Party in talks with Carlos Prío and with "politicians of every sector . . . aimed at a possible 'solution' to the Cuban problem, entering into the themes of 'military junta,' 'coalition cabinet' et cetera, et cetera, precisely the political outcome the Movement hoped to avoid."[19] Llerena worried that Pazos, who reportedly believed that "Fidel Castro has never stopped being an Ortodoxo," would play to the sympathies of the movement's members and supporters in Miami by promoting the notion that the 26th of July was merely the armed wing of the Ortodoxo Party. That prospect jeopardized the movement's efforts to forge an identity separate from Cuba's traditional opposition political parties and prompted a discussion of when it was appropriate for the M267 to separate openly from the Ortodoxos.

When Llerena confronted Pazos about the contradiction between the public commitments in the Sierra Manifesto and his presence in Miami as a consensus candidate of the Ortodoxo Party, Pazos claimed that the National Directorate had yet to give him a specific role—which was technically true. Indeed, the movement had yet to make him their official representative or candidate because they were unprepared to break openly from the Ortodoxo Party. Pazos informed Llerena that he intended to participate in the Miami alliance talks on his own accord because "of the possibility," reported Llerena, that "they will offer him and he will accept an important position (president or minister) in the provisional government that emerges."[20] Pazos agreed in principle to represent the movement in the United States, but he wanted to preserve his own options because there was no guarantee that the 26th of July would succeed in overthrowing the dictator, especially given a rumor at the time that Carlos Prío had recently met with Secretary of State John Foster Dulles. Though the rumor later proved false, the revolutionaries interpreted the alleged meeting as a sign that unless they staked out an identity independent from the Ortodoxo Party, the apparently inescapable *politiquería* of exile could draw the movement into "a process of abandoning its revolutionary thesis in order to enter into political or mediationist forums."[21]

Armando Hart responded directly to Llerena's argument about the need to break publicly from the Ortodoxos. Just as Pazos arrived in Miami, Hart was writing Llerena, Rodríguez, and the others that Fidel had largely given up on Miami as a source of weapons, explaining that "Fidel doesn't expect anything to come from the Príos', months have gone by, and he's tired of waiting." Nor did Hart have high expectations for the Ortodoxos, whom, because of their internal divisions and lack of leadership, he regarded as having contributed to the moral and political crisis that had led to the coup of March 9, 1952. While Fidel had given up on weapons from the traditional opposition, Hart likewise made it clear that with respect to the Ortodoxos,

> it is better to keep them as our best allies; for when some of them have joined the organized cadre of the Movement, they have not yielded as much as they would have, had they remained only a sympathizer of the organization. In any case, we are pointing out to you that at no time can the 26th of July regard itself a part of the Ortodoxos Históricos, instead we regard it as the political zone closest to us for a series of reasons that you know as well as I. But in the end it remains just one political zone more, and our main duty is to liquidate all of the political zones as of March 9 in order to create a new politics in line with the ideals of our revolutionary generation.[22]

In short, the 26th of July would neither join united fronts nor accede to opposition alliances unless, in accordance with the Sierra Manifesto, the Civic Institutions appointed the members of a new provisional government. Hart's guidelines required his comrades abroad to balance the tactical needs of a revolutionary organization that was just beginning to capture the hearts and minds of all Cubans (but was neither hegemonic within the insurgent opposition nor replete with material and financial resources) with the movement's strategic goals of revolutionary, financial, and political independence. Managing these competing demands would have been difficult even for the most experienced career politician. Given the stakes and the youth of the players, most of whom were under thirty years of age, the challenge was at times overwhelming. As for Pazos, who by comparison was a seasoned diplomat, whatever his appeal in the United States and among the opposition, the former national bank president was unfit to represent the 26th of July in talks of any nature.

Still, there was countervailing pressure on the movement to maintain a moderate face in dealing with the American government. Hart had recently received a report summarizing the mood in official Washington. Written by Ernesto Betancourt, a young accountant who traced his political lineage to the abstentionist wing of the Ortodoxo Party and who had been sent to Washington by Fidel's sisters Emma and Lidia to represent the 26th of July, the report reinforced the preoccupation with the movement's image that had partly motivated the Sierra Manifesto.[23] Betancourt was registered as a foreign agent with the Justice Department, and his style, the substance of his communications, and his sensitivity to American Cold War culture served the movement well in the United States. For example, he openly displayed his discomfort with the use of violence by the 26th of July and took pains to assure his American interlocutors of the anticommunism of the M267.[24] Hart did not know Betancourt personally and sensed that his views might not "correspond completely with the thinking of" the National Directorate. Yet despite Betancourt's disagreements with the 26th of July's tactics, Hart found his reports from Washington valuable.[25]

Based on conversations in the State Department and the Central Intelligence Agency, Betancourt reported that the "American national security agencies" expected violent change in Cuba and were scrutinizing every statement coming out of official and opposition circles to "try by all means possible not to become involved in the whirlpool of Cuba's bloody internal politics."[26] The U.S. government was apparently determined to avoid a replay of its 1933 mediation efforts and had decided that if events in Cuba endangered American economic and strategic interests, the "Department of State would turn to the Organization of American States and not to more or less open intervention like that which occurred in Guatemala in the case of the Arbenz regime."[27] The Americans had concluded that the June 1958 elections would be possible only if Batista succeeded in "liquidating the insurrectional *foco* of the Sierra Maestra and bringing to an end the systematic and constant campaign of sabotage and terrorism around the entire island" carried out by the insurgent forces.[28] While Washington preferred Batista's succession to transpire via the electoral route rather than a military coup, the United States would not oppose as a first step "other solutions, such as a military junta or a provisional civil government that would take the country, in the briefest period possible, to constitutional normalcy via free elections." Betancourt's interlocutors struck a familiar chord, conveying the same message as the consular officials in Santiago had to Frank País months earlier. "What the Department of State fears is a state of anarchy," he wrote, that could be taken advantage of for whatever ends by a small but organized Communist Party, if Batista falls as a consequence of the disintegration of the Armed Forces, particularly the army, without first a prior agreement existing among the insurrectionist groups to comply at least with a civil provisional government that would, in the most orderly manner possible, make the transition from the dictatorship to a constitutional government born of free elections. Washington is worried, and with reason, that out of an anarchic state, like that from which Haiti suffers, could emerge a new Batista or another left-leaning demagogue who could take the country toward an ultranationalism that might seriously affect the political, economic, and strategic interests of the United States on the island.[29]

In light of such fears, Betancourt reported that the transition scenario outlined in the Sierra Manifesto had played well in Washington. Of course, that would remain the case only if the post-Batista provisional government could prevent chaos and refrain from exercising "legislative authority over socio-economic matters," limiting its activities only to providing a stable climate "favorable to the early celebration of general elections."[30] Betancourt argued that the American allergy to instability and the distinct possibility of a military coup made it incumbent upon the 26th of July to quickly back a provisional government and president that reflected a consensus of the entire opposition—revolutionary and political. His analysis reinforced Hart's urgency to have the Civic Institutions put forward a provisional government before the opposition in Miami preempted the movement with an alternative.

But on October 15, 1957, culminating weeks of secret negotiations, fifteen opposition figures from two political parties and three insurgent forces culminated weeks of talks with the announcement of the Pact of Miami, which created the Junta de Liberación Cubana, or Cuban Liberation Junta. Among the signatories were Roberto Agramonte, Sr. and Manuel Bisbé for the Ortodoxos-históricos, Tony Varona for the Auténticos, Carlos Prío for the Organización Auténtica, Alberto Mora and Faure Chomón for the Student Revolutionary Directorate (DRE), and Angel Cofiño, the dissident CTC organizer, for his newly formed Directorio Revolucionario Obrero, or Revolutionary Labor Directorate. Despite their prior statements to the contrary and instructions from Havana cautioning otherwise, Felipe Pazos and Léster Rodríguez signed the pact on behalf of the 26th of July Movement.

On the surface, the Pact of Miami appeared to be the Cuban revolutionary and political opposition's response to the July 1957 call by the Sierra Manifesto for civic-revolutionary unity against the Batista dictatorship. The pact announced that the groups had achieved a "unity of ideals and purpose" and exhorted all Cubans to "reject the crude electoral process" under way in Cuba. Its ten-point platform stated that the Cuban Liberation Junta would "unify moral and material forces" to oversee the transfer of power from Batista to a "constitutional and democratic order."[31] Unfortunately, the exile alliance surfaced just when the 26th of July's *llano* had begun to recover from Frank País's death, define itself to its membership, appeal to Cuba's professional elite, clarify its combined strategy of strike and insurrection, and redress the *sierra*'s complaints of neglect. By joining the Cuban Liberation Junta at that moment, Pazos and Rodríguez not only had agreed to share material, financial, and human resources with the political and revolutionary Cuban opposition but also had undercut Hart's ambitions to orchestrate a post-Batista transition in Cuba that would satisfy the 26th of July Movement. In Hart's view and that of many other members of the National Directorate, the *sierra*, and the *llano*, the M267 as a whole had become *the* "anti-Batista," the only revolutionaries who had earned the right to salvage Cuba from its tortured past.

Though the junta also called for "the constitution of a provisional government" to preside over elections, and stipulated that the "provisional president cannot appear in any elected post in the elections," unlike the Sierra Manifesto, "ministers, governors and mayors" serving under the Batista regime needed only to step down from their posts for six months before running for the presidency or any other elected positions. The junta assigned no formal role whatsoever to the Civic Institutions, the core element of the Sierra Manifesto, and instead called upon civic, professional, religious, fraternal, cultural, labor, and economic organizations merely to support the junta and oppose Batista.[32] The Cuban Liberation Junta advanced a reformist social agenda that paralleled that of the Sierra Manifesto: embracing civil liberties, releasing political prisoners, ceasing embezzlement, establishing a civil service, improving education and natural resource conservation, cleaning up corruption; promoting monetary stability and import substitution industrialization; instituting agrarian reform; democratizing the trade unions; and creating industrial and agricultural jobs.[33]

In international affairs, like the Sierra Manifesto, the Pact of Miami supported public protests against the Batista regime's human-rights violations at the Organization of American States and the United Nations and announced plans to protest American arms shipments to Cuba that were part of a 1951 mutual assistance program. But unlike the Sierra Manifesto, the Miami agreement was silent on the prospect of foreign intervention.[34] And contrary to the Sierra Manifesto, which explicitly rejected the prospect that a military junta would play a role in a Cuban transition, the Miami Pact remained ambiguous on this point. On the one hand, its platform indicated an intention to "separate the Cuban Armed Forces from political struggles." But on the other hand, the junta called upon on the military to "join together with the nation in the objective of freedom from tyranny, to bring about the end of violence, hatred, blood and death that is engulfing the Republic."[35] The platform implied that while the armed forces should play no role in politics under a democratic regime, they were welcome to insert themselves into the process of destabilizing Batista.

The junta's public statements lacked specifics regarding which members of the new alliance would direct the insurgency on the ground, the tactics they would employ, the financing for the war effort, or the powers of a post-Batista government. But secret documents did began to address these questions. "Secret core agreements" revealed that the anti-Communist junta had created a central committee comprised of the Ortodoxos, Auténticos, 26th of July, Student Revolutionary Directorate, and Federation of University Students. The central committee was empowered with "leading the struggle against the tyranny, unifying the efforts of its members, naming the President of the Republic to exercise the position in the Provisional Government, . . . approving or disapproving . . . the Cabinet named by the President . . . as well as any changes in it in case of a total or partial crisis; . . . determining legislative functions under the Provisional Government; and determining how to designate provincial governors and mayors for the provisional period."[36] In short, from its headquarters in Miami, the junta would oversee the anti-Batista struggle and hold veto power over all aspects of the provisional government to follow.

Three secret subcommittees were formed as well: "joint revolutionary operations," "finances," and "public relations." Representatives from the OA, the DRE, and the 26th of July were to have equal representation on the "operations" subcommittee, and "complete autonomy in the direction and execution of insurrectionist activities, . . . agreeing to and carrying out the General Revolutionary Plan and the emergency plans," which entailed "strengthening operations in the Sierra Maestra, sabotage and other operations of similar nature, interrupting the electoral process, and blocking the sugar harvest." Each of the junta's member organizations was to contribute human and material resources to carry out the war and to promote the cause publicly. Finally, unlike the Sierra Manifesto, which called for the new Cuba to purge the military from politics, the junta's secret documents proposed that after the war, "the revolutionary forces will incorporate themselves into the regular armed forces of the Republic, with their arms; and those of their members who do not wish to do so will turn in their arms, and return to civilian life."[37]

A *New York Times* editorial described the Miami alliance as "a severe blow to the regime," praising the opposition for taking a step toward allaying the fears of "the business community and of many Cubans in ordinary life who are afraid of the chaos that normally follows the expulsion of military dictators in Latin America." The *Times* predicted that the government-in-exile would "bring some reassurance to the timid and give heart to the courageous people who have faced arrest, torture and death in the past year of Cuban turmoil."[38] Perhaps. But even if the *New York Times* had helped resurrect the 26th of July from near obscurity earlier that year, its spin on the Cuban Liberation Junta was far from welcomed by the revolutionaries back in Cuba. Because of the news blackout on the island, Armando Hart was in the dark about the Miami pact until a few days after its announcement. At that point, the young attorney tuned into the OA's clandestine radio, which reported that "Felipe Pazos was representing the 26th of July in unity talks in Miami."[39]

Indeed, well before the news reached Cuba, the American government learned about the general outline and who's who of the exile alliance from Jules Dubois, a retired lieutenant colonel from army intelligence reporting for the *Chicago Tribune*. Dubois, who shuttled regularly between Miami and Havana, told the State Department that with "no Communist participation in the plan," the Cuban opposition in exile had settled on Felipe Pazos to take over "as the first president under a rotation system" after "Batista leaves the scene." Dubois also believed that the new junta would make "every effort to coordinate and control all revolutionary activities in order to avoid useless disturbance and bloodshed."[40]

Once the new junta was public knowledge, Dubois suggested that Tony Varona (who spoke for Carlos Prío), Felipe Pazos, and Roberto Agramonte, Sr. make their case in Washington at a meeting of the Inter-American Press Association, a sympathetic audience that had just approved a resolution condemning press censorship in Cuba. Publicly, the group put on a convincing show of unity before the Latin American newspaper editor. But privately, Tony Varona "was surprisingly pessimistic" when he briefed State Department officials about the alliance. Belittling the insurgent forces' plans to topple Batista via a general strike, sabotage, and cane burning, Varona suggested such tactics had "little chance to overthrow Batista," and that instead "a successful revolution would have to come from within the armed forces."[41] Apparently Varona supported opposition unity in public only to quiet the clamor for such unity.

In part because of Cuban rumors alleging that Dubois was a CIA agent, it remains a widely held—but unsubstantiated—view that the Cuban Liberation Junta was created by the United States to undercut the 26th of July's growing popularity. To be sure, State Department documents show that the signatories to the pact sought U.S. sympathy and requested that Americans halt weapons shipments to the island. But neither the junta's public and secret statements nor its members' conversations in the State Department suggest a call for American mediation.[42] It is true that *after* the Pact of Miami was signed, State Department officials did briefly consider mediation between Batista and the opposition, represented by the junta. The significance of the Miami junta in the story of the Cuban insurrection, however, lay not with how the American government perceived it but with its effect on the 26th of July's wartime tactics and on the movement's relationship with the anti-Batista opposition.

6 | Taming the *Politiqueros* in Exile

NOVEMBER–DECEMBER 1957

> *Politiquería* has done much harm in Cuba and will do so again outside of Cuba. But we have succeeded in sending *politiquería* into exile, and that is at least one step forward.
>
> Fidel Castro to Mario Llerena, October 30, 1957

RATHER THAN EITHER PRECIPITOUSLY OR publicly ending the 26th of July's involvement in the Cuban Liberation Junta, Armando Hart took a pragmatic approach and first attempted to shape the new alliance to better promote the movement's interests. Unable to leave his clandestine base in Santiago, Hart sent Luis Buch, a member of the Civic Resistance Movement, to Miami to find out why Léster Rodríguez (who had stopped reporting back to Cuba in September) and Felipe Pazos had signed the pact. He asked Buch to explain "the movement's thinking regarding unity" and return to Cuba to brief the National Directorate.[1] Buch, who practiced law in Havana, was already in his forties and practically a senior statesmen compared to the youngsters in the 26th of July's inner circle.[2] He caught a ferry for Miami on what would be the first of several trips designed to bend the Pact of Miami into a shape the movement might be able to accept.

Léster Rodríguez explained to Buch that since Prío had at long last agreed to give the movement money to purchase arms, it had become politically necessary to work jointly with Prío's Organización Auténtica (OA)—that is, it had become important to accept the terms of the Pact of Miami in order to demonstrate the 26th of July's commitment to unity and to maintain the movement's credibility within the opposition. Indeed, Rodríguez had become so successful in stockpiling weapons that his activities had alerted local police, whose surveillance and raids on weapons caches in Miami had forced Rodríguez to transfer most of them to a safe house in Houston and a boat, the *Buddy Dee*, at a nearby harbor in Galveston, Texas.[3] Buch reported that for Rodríguez it was "indispensable to count on sufficient matériel to carry out the war" and agreeing to the pact "was the only means within his reach to get it."[4] According to

Faure Chomón, who signed the pact on behalf of the Student Revolutionary Directorate, Rodríguez convinced him to join the junta as well, saying that the promise of Prío's weapons made suffering the political stench of opposition unity worth the revolutionaries' while. Léster also convinced the Ortodoxo Manuel Bisbé to join the pact for similar reasons.[5] Finally, Prío's own terms for financing the insurgency and joining the junta stipulated that Pazos become provisional president, a condition Rodríguez felt the movement's political strength could withstand, particularly if that meant its military weakness would be overcome.[6]

As for the presidential aspirant, Pazos, he explained that had he refused to sign the pact, he would have jeopardized opposition unity and the *sierra*'s survival. "When I arrived in Miami," he wrote Faustino Pérez, "the Ortodoxos had accepted joining together in unity with the FEU, the PRC [Autenticos], and the Democrats, if the 26th agreed. The Directorio would attend the meetings only if the 26th went too. Whether unity would be produced or broken depended entirely on the 26th of July. . . . Rejecting the pact would have "put in danger the survival of our men in the Sierra, who urgently need the help unity can give them, and risk[ed] the very triumph of the Revolution."[7]

Pazos readily acknowledged the fundamental differences between the Cuban Liberation Junta and the declaration that he had partially authored and signed with Fidel Castro and Raúl Chibás, but he found the Miami pact to closely resemble "all of the proposals in the Sierra Manifesto except its [position] against intervention, against a military junta, and leaving open to discussion the form of electing a provisional government."[8] Under the original terms of the pact, before the junta was made public, each member organization was to have forty-eight hours to confer with their colleagues on the island. Pazos had neglected to do so, succumbing instead, Buch reported, to pressure from Jules Dubois to fly to Washington and publicize the unity accords with the Latin American press corps then assembled in the capital.[9]

After hearing the initial explanations of the gaffe, Armando Hart scolded Pazos and Rodríguez for misrepresenting the 26th of July's views and for joining the junta without the consent of the National Directorate. Had it not been for the *New York Times* editorial, which inaccurately stated that each signatory was "authorized by their organizations in Cuba," and other foreign press coverage of the Miami pact, which "presented us with a fait accompli," Hart wrote that he would have immediately withdrawn the 26th of July Movement from the junta.[10]

But press coverage of the agreement was only the first problem that Hart had with the new development. Far more serious was the role of

Felipe Pazos, whom the National Directorate, unaware of the Miami machinations, had indeed confirmed as the 26th of July's "delegate" in the United States (a decision that appeared in the traffic of letters during October). With Pazos now positioned as a government-in-exile's provisional president, it looked as if the 26th of July had intentionally inserted itself into the mix of opposition *politiquería,* appearing as venal as the likes of Carlos Prío and Tony Varona. As *the* "anti-Batista," the 26th of July was born to overturn politics as usual in Cuba. "The strength of the 26th of July Movement," wrote Hart, "is not in the votes it may have in this or that Assembly or Governing Junta, but rather in the historic reason and collective need that it can and knows how to defend among the majority of the people." In negotiating the Sierra Manifesto over the summer, Fidel had pointedly rejected direct participation by the 26th of July in a provisional government, not only to gain the moral high ground, but also to establish

an intelligent policy of equi-distance from a government that because of being one of transition can by nature neither have a revolutionary character nor avail itself of the strength we will need for the enormous social and political transformations the country requires. The 26th of July will demand of this provisional government only the freedom to express its transformative thinking and aspirations. Let the opposition politicians and their followers keep the ministries and bureaucratic positions, and give the Movement the right to mobilize the people and the facilities to organize its strengths in the clear light of day.

At its core, wrote Hart, the Miami unity agreement "reflected . . . able political maneuvers of discredited opposition political leaders in order to contain the Revolution." A provisional coalition government that would give every opposition political force a seat at the table, one "destined to inefficiency" and transitory by definition, would occupy but a fleeting moment in a broader historical, revolutionary process.[11] And the 26th of July did not want to spend its political capital by participating directly in governance during Cuba's transition.[12]

More concretely, Hart wrote that the national Civic Institutions, absent from the junta's transition plan, had begun to "be accountable to us," referring to their privately expressed disposition to form a provisional government. The local affiliates were beginning to adapt and mature to "the idea that the time has come to switch from their merely cultural, charitable, religious, et cetera, function, to—call it what you will—a political mission." Although some provinces were ready to demand Batista's resignation publicly, there was still no national consensus. Hart believed that with time the national leadership of the Civic Institutions would begin to reflect their local constituencies and eventually "subscribe to a private document assuming the principal responsibility for opposition unity and the future provisional government," a document that the movement would publicize at a "propitious moment." Hart hoped to have the Civic Institutions's political support lined up by December, to coincide with the general strike planned for the end of the year.[13] Instead, the Miami development had compromised the revolutionaries' claim of disinterest and threatened to damage their credibility with both the Civic Institutions and the Cuban public.

But Hart stopped short of abruptly withdrawing the 26th of July from the junta; instead he used the movement's leverage as the only functioning insurgent force on the ground to bend the opposition alliance to the movement's demands. He instructed Pazos and Rodríguez to persuade the other signatories to amend the junta's platform to reflect the Sierra Manifesto's original formula for constituting the provisional government. The new revolutionary generation was trying to overthrow not only Batista, wrote Hart, but also the "political machinery that supported the regime through its lack of morals and vision." He thus insisted that no elected official holding office during the term of the provisional government could run in subsequent elections. (The Pact of Miami had proposed that current officeholders could run for election. Hart feared that this could recreate the Batista political machinery, which would only again "absorb and disorient public opinion.") If Rodríguez and Pazos failed to deliver on this demand, Hart wrote them, they would "endanger our support for the Junta, and thus for unity."[14] In a sign of how much the anti-Batista opposition needed the 26th of July Movement, the group unanimously approved the change.[15]

Next, Hart insisted that the junta directly petition the Civic Institutions to appoint the entire cabinet of the provisional government-in-exile. All junta members, both political and revolutionary, would then recognize explicitly the exile government's legitimacy, back its decisions, and appoint a delegate to the provisional government who would have a "voice but no vote." Knowing in advance from Raúl de Velasco, president of the Civic Institutions, that there was still no guarantee that his organization would accept this role, Hart included an alternative method whereby the junta itself would select the cabinet members from a pool of nonpartisan individuals similar in prestige to the Civic Institution leadership.[16] Hart also demanded that the 26th of July terminate its participation in the provisional government, a step that would immediately force Felipe Pazos either to pull out of the junta or break with the movement in order to preserve his presidential aspirations. "Even though we are aware of his identification with the Movement," wrote Hart, since "the 26th of July cannot form part of this [provisional] government, but only support it, Pazos cannot appear as our representative."[17]

Indeed, Hart soon learned that Pazos, who had been a student revolutionary in the 1930s, had never been eager to give the Civic Institutions center stage in a post-Batista transitional regime; he had only reluctantly accepted the idea while in the Sierra Maestra with Fidel earlier that year. On November 3, René Ramos Latour returned to Santiago from his eighteen-day stay in the mountains, where he had arrived just one day before Hart learned about the Miami pact. Though the timing of his arrival in the Sierra had prevented Latour and Castro from "specifically address[ing] the unity problem," they had discussed the general theme of the movement's ties with the opposition. As Latour reported, Fidel's views reinforced Hart's instructions to the Committee in Exile:

> I do want to alert you that Fidel analyzed the possibilities of a public denunciation of Prío, a formal break with everything he represents. His frame of mind regarding the Auténticos and the question of relations with the politicians can be appreciated in his letter to Llerena, but in addition we want you to know that he is thousands of leagues away from accepting proposals like those that Pazos and Léster accepted. We have even come to learn that Fidel talked with Pazos about the Civic Institutions formula. Pazos was fairly reluctant to accept it though in the end he did. All of this is strictly confidential so that you are aware of the material and human situation with which we are working. All of this is because we want to tell you that the Revolutionary 26th of July Movement, its National Directorate, and all of its combatants are in no way prepared to accept in any way the agreed upon Pact if unity does not take the course that we have pointed out in previous documents. We know that this Committee is not responsible for unity as such . . . But since you are now the maximum authority in exile with plain and absolute powers from Fidel Castro and the National Directorate, we trust you to get us out of this mess as quickly as possible.[18]

Mario Llerena confirmed Hart and Castro's doubts about Pazos's full commitment to the Sierra Manifesto formula. Apparently Pazos had "confessed" that "he won't accept the presidency if it is the Civic Institutions that appoint the members of the government." Both Pazos and Llerena doubted that a loose grouping of nongovernmental organizations could govern the country. Pazos had made it clear that if the 26th of July succeeded in imposing the formula laid out in the Sierra Manifesto onto the Cuban Liberation Junta, he would back out of the presidency. And that step stood to jeopardize Prío's commitment to fund the insurgency and to undercut the movement's negotiations with the Civic Institutions, the leadership of which was clearly reluctant to move forward without full opposition backing.[19] Under those circumstances, there were fewer and fewer reasons for the movement to maintain the facade of unity, and Pazos's voluntary withdrawal would make it that much easier for the 26th of July to embrace complete political independence.

When Réne Latour returned from the Sierra Maestra, he and Hart sent Fidel the details of the Miami unity pact, as well as Hart's correspondence and instructions regarding the matter. Hart wrote Fidel that despite progress with the Havana Civic Institutions, which had finally agreed to form a provisional government, the "false unity" in Miami had "paralyzed these efforts" because the Civic Institutions wanted the backing of not only the 26th of July but also the entire junta.[20] Latour, who believed that the M267 was the only revolutionary group to have sustained the war against Batista, had also concluded that the "extraordinary sympathy in public opinion, the foreign press and even" the New York Times editorial had tied the movement's hands, leaving it to try to "get the best results possible" as "we can in no way reject it straight out."[21] In the Sierra Maestra, Fidel and Celia, who had transferred from Manzanillo, agreed that the positive publicity to the pact had placed the movement in a difficult position. In the first indication that Fidel and his colleagues knew anything about the Miami pact, Celia wrote to Latour about the "undesirable unity," hoping that "that Dario [Hart] in his letter to this duo will ban them from any such agreement without first advising us; it would be unpleasant to have to publicly refute Pazos and Rodríguez. The politiqueros have some nerve in making the Movement subordinate to them."[22] Only Luis Buch thought the 26th of July might derive some benefit from upholding the unity accords. He recommended that the National Directorate take advantage of the opportunity to finally obtain the quality and quantity of weapons that had long eluded the movement. The revolutionary and political opposition, wrote Buch from Miami, had finally "achieved the unification of command, war matériel, and finances in a general staff that for the moment is functioning admirably well."[23] Buch counseled Rodríguez to remain in the junta for the time being.[24]

DURING HIS three weeks in the Sierra Maestra, René Ramos Latour and Fidel Castro discussed the National Directorate's strategy to organize professionals, workers, and students and to arm an urban militia for the end-of-the-year general strike. Fidel endorsed this long-term plan, the immediate burning of sugarcane in order to interrupt that year's harvest, and other *sierra-llano* coordinated actions. By early November 1957, the rebel army had torched ten sugar mills around the perimeter of the Sierra Maestra. By the middle of the month the rebels had burned some 44,000 short tons of sugar from 20,000 acres, more than half of which belonged to sugar magnate Julio Lobo.[25] Recognizing the strategic connection between economic sabotage and advancing the general strike plans, Celia, who authored much of the correspondence to the National Directorate on Fidel's behalf, wrote Latour that the quick success in damaging the local sugar crop averred well for targeting rice production, given the rice-cutters' demands for a salary increase: "The environment is ripe to attack the rice, in our zone we're sure it will work, but for your part you must quickly extend the rice burning across the island, especially to Pinar del Río, the heaviest rice zone; this has to happen quickly because the cutting lasts only 3–4 weeks. This action, together with the cane burning, can accelerate the strike."[26]

Without País to maintain the balance and consensus between the *sierra* and *llano*, Fidel may have hoped that Latour's visit would convince the National Directorate of the primacy of the guerrilla war and the rebel army in the battle against Batista. But while Latour's stay in the Sierra Maestra gave him an understanding of the guerrilla army's dominance in the region, his experience did not change the movement's basic priority of urban insurrection. In fact, quite the opposite was true: precisely because Batista's forces had been unable to dislodge the now consolidated guerrilla *foco* from the Sierra—and with the rebel army quintupling in size since the summer and "the revolutionary army govern[ing] throughout the region and the peasants organized militarily in order to stabilize the region's revolutionary force"—the National Directorate had concluded that the army would "concentrate its terror" and counterinsurgency campaign in the cities around the Sierra Maestra, including Manzanillo and Bayamo. In other words, the movement, in what would later prove to be a significant strategic error, was to respond by confronting the regime directly in the cities. Heightened repression by Batista would not stop, Hart wrote to the movement's committee in exile and provincial coordinators, "that which is already unstoppable: the process leading toward the General Strike."[27]

By November 1957, the 26th of July had begun organizing clandestine cells among students, workers, and the middle class. In order to attract groups and individuals who did not openly support the armed path, Hart charged the Civic Resistance Movement, itself not yet publicly identified with the 26th of July, with organizing heterogeneous strike committees that would report to the newly created National Strike Committee. Hart chose not to reveal even to the movement's own top militants that the Miami junta had undermined the 26th of July's autonomy and credibility with the Civic Institutions. He also kept quiet his intention to break from the junta if its members rejected the movement's demands regarding the selection and composition of the provisional government.

Whether it was a bit of youthful bluster meant to rally the troops, or whether he truly believed his own rhetoric, Hart predicted to his comrades that "the decisive stage of the revolutionary triumph" was imminent.[28] The urban underground was planning a "week of resistance" for the first week of December that involved extensive cane burning, nationwide student protests, commemorations of the one-year anniversary of the landing of Castro's yacht, *Granma*, and international protests against the regime's human rights record. Hart and his comrades believed that sabotage against the island's lifeblood, sugar, would again politicize Cuban sugar workers to provoke a strike as in 1933 and 1955. This strike, it was hoped, would incite the police into more forceful repression against the urban population, priming the Cuban people to shut down the country and force Batista's resignation.[29]

Hart feared that the appearance of opposition unity in Miami, however flawed, would diminish the force with which the M267-controlled National Strike Committee would be able to control the timing, plans, direction, and participation by other opposition groups in the general strike. The Pact of Miami had announced that all of Cuba's revolutionary groups would jointly plan and carry out operations on the ground, but Hart had every intention of preserving complete control over the strike committees and their members—whether from the Student Revolutionary Directorate, the Organización Auténtica, and though it was not part of the junta, the Communist Party. He warned the movement's members that the 26th of July would "work together with the other opposition organizations to produce this or that insurrectionist action" but "with respect to the strike, the 26th of July should make clear with the Liberation Junta its thesis that only via the Civic Resistance Movement and the Strike Committees is it possible to coordinate all of the isolated efforts in order to make the strike a beautiful reality." A highly political conspirator, Hart stressed that the opposition "will achieve unity with . . . the Civic Resistance Movement," which, he wrote, "brings together the opposition from every militancy and from no militancy."[30]

Wishing to control the strike without appearing to do so, Hart sought a rather convoluted balance between unity Miami-style and "the anti-Batista's" desire to take charge of the insurgency. Newly recruited students and civic resistance members, for example, were to form "student revolutionary committees" that would appear nonsectarian but remain in the movement's control.

> However it is done, in any case, it should be attempted so that even though they may outwardly appear to have a cover that has nothing to do with the "26th," there should always be students from the Movement who guide this type of Directorate or Revolutionary Student Committee . . . People outside of the Movement can belong to these committees, but they must prove they are sincerely driven to promote rebellion in the high schools in order to paralyze classes in every school.[31]

A similar principle applied for labor organizing. Hart instructed the movement's militants to recruit "union elements from within and outside of the Movement as long as they guarantee their sincere work on behalf of the General Strike . . . but making sure that the 26th of July takes the leadership positions."[32] In a leaflet distributed more widely, the movement explained its rationale for crafting an independent labor committee outside the traditional domain of existing labor organizations:

> The 26th of July's labor militants neither recognize nor receive directions from any other national proletarian force other than the Movement's own labor section. In accordance with this, our militants will not reach any unity that is not through the Strike Committees in work places or in industrial sectors . . . The Strike Committees will be organized with the country's clean labor elements and will form a powerful National Labor Front (FON) that will assume responsibility for legitimate representation of the Confederation of Cuban Workers. When the 26th of July forms these Strike Committees it is not interested in being considered because of its public prestige nor for the fact that it is the revolutionary group that has initiated the greatest number of battles against the tyranny, and whose principal leaders are in the Sierra Maestra or in underground life. We don't want respect for these facts though we have the right to it. The 26th of July's working-class militants want to be regarded as a work force by the workers it already has organized, and not for whatever merits the 26th of July has garnered outside of its union-related work. Likewise, when the time comes to form the Strike Committees, the 26th of July's working-class militants will not give consideration to this or that opposition workers' group, but rather will do so with the true proletarian forces in the country and at its work places that are sincerely ready to strike and that have a history of service in the cause of liberty . . . As a consequence, the labor section of the 26th of July . . . out of principle and with the complete support of the National Directorate, which has given the identical directions to the other branches of the Movement, rejects any accord

reached at the top, because it is only at the base that the revolutionary and political sectors can launch the noble task of organizing the people and especially . . . the workers.[33]

Thus, although before the Pact of Miami the 26th of July had sought to organize a general strike with as many workers of as many stripes as possible, even Communist Party workers, with the unity alliance looming in Miami the National Directorate became more partisan.

Had the National Directorate unequivocally embraced the Miami alliance, it might, in practice, have promoted a more genuine, broad-based unity on the ground, one that encouraged greater democracy within the strike committees. Hart wanted to have and eat the proverbial cake, controlling the strike committees but making them appear as broad-based and diverse as possible. Moreover, he wanted the 26th of July strike leaders to function so that "militants and other organizations that are wholesome and usable for the Revolution do not believe that we think of ourselves as the 'only ones.'"[34] The timing of all of this was crucial. For the strike plans to succeed, Hart's negotiations with the Civic Institutions in Havana and with the Liberation Junta in Miami would have to yield a suitable outcome *before* a national strike began. Otherwise, the 26th of July risked expending its resources and political capital for the sake of a "false unity" that might deliver power back to the old-guard politicians and marginalize Cuba's true "revolutionary instrument."

7 | With Friends Like These, Who Needs Enemies?

NOVEMBER 1957–JANUARY 1958

> You know perfectly well that . . . the strike is a process in which we are moving forward in gigantic steps and that it will unfold at a given moment without our being able to force it or slow it down . . . The coming weeks should be of great importance for the revolutionary struggle . . . This is possibly the most important moment for the struggle against the tyranny.
>
> Armando Hart to Mario Llerena, November 19, 1957

DESPITE HIS APPARENTLY OPTIMISTIC vision of revolutionary victory, Hart harbored serious reservations about the 26th of July's prospects for wresting control from the Cuban Liberation Junta. Under the best of circumstances in Miami, the Civic Institutions would agree to appoint the members of an interim cabinet and Felipe Pazos would withdraw his candidacy for provisional president. In Cuba, by the middle of December a successful "week of resistance" would force Batista to intensify repression against the population and again renew the suspension of constitutional guarantees, polarizing the climate to such a degree that a general strike would force the dictator out by the end of the 1957.[1] If the two initiatives—a government in exile and a successful insurrection—did not coincide, Hart wrote Fidel Castro that the Batista regime might respond to the "week of resistance" with a crackdown of such magnitude that the general strike would not be ignited, but rather would have to be delayed by the movement for several months.[2] It was vitally important that the opposition reach a consensus regarding the composition of the new government before mid-December, when Batista was to renew or withdraw constitutional guarantees that had been suspended in mid-September after the Cienfuegos mutiny.

Consolidation of the movement's hegemony over the opposition was not Hart's only motivation for insisting that a provisional government be established. Fulgencio Batista had recently strengthened his control over the Cuban military by creating a *mando único*, or unified command—a joint chiefs of staff that brought the army, navy, and police, including the intelligence services, under the command of one man, Francisco Tabernilla Dolz. A new law guaranteed Batista the highest-ranking military post in the country even after the end of his presidential term. These steps increased speculation that Batista had no intention of respecting the outcome of elections scheduled for June 1958, after which he would bear permanently the title of commander-in-chief of the armed forces.[3] Hart believed that just as Batista had consolidated his power under a joint military command, it was imperative that the opposition take the equivalent political step. Moreover, the very act of forming a government-in-exile would significantly weaken the regime. Hart alerted the M267 Committee in Exile that unless the Cuban Liberation Junta accepted all of the movement's demands by December 10, he intended to withdraw the 26th of July from the Miami alliance unilaterally and publicly.[4]

In a final effort to form a credible government-in-exile and undercut the Miami alliance, Hart proposed that the junta designate a five-member government with "legislative and executive powers . . . to assume in effect the direction of public authority when the tyranny is overthrown."[5] Based in Jacksonville, Florida, the new government, which the 26th of July would publicly embrace, was to honor "any legitimate national or international commitments contracted by the Cuban State and recognize those which the tyranny has contracted prior to the first of January 1958," but "will not regard itself obliged to comply with national or international obligations contracted by Fulgencio Batista and his government after the 31st of December 1957."[6] Under this scenario, the Cuban Liberation Junta would devolve into a purely deliberative body, one open to the original signatories and to "other opposition organizations that currently remain outside of it."[7]

But in truth, Hart's final offer for "unity" constituted, as René Ramos Latour wrote to Celia, "the basis for [the junta's] complete disintegration," since the new government would depend for its legitimacy upon the "anti-Batista's" successful conduct of the war at home "as a revolutionary organization, before and after Batista's overthrow."[8] After consultations back in Cuba, Luis Buch returned to Miami to make this final proposal, suggesting that the new five-person government be composed of consensus candidates: Judge Manuel Urrutia Lleó, Felipe Pazos, Raúl de Velasco, Justo Carrillo, and José Miró Cardona.[9]

The junta flatly rejected the idea of a Jacksonville-based government-in-exile, opting instead to accept Hart's original proposal that the Civic Institutions appoint the new cabinet. Despite Hart and Buch's efforts that fall, only the Oriente and Havana chapters of the Civic Institutions agreed to take on the role; as Raúl de Velasco had predicted, the national Civic Institutions would not step forward to endorse the Sierra Manifesto formula. The 26th of July Movement was headed for an outright break with the opposition.[10]

Hart briefed Fidel on his attempts to steer events in Miami.[11] When Castro received documents tracing the negotiations with the Cuban Liberation Junta and the Civic Institutions, he sent the material to his brother Raúl and Che Guevara for their opinions. Both men adamantly protested Hart's management of the opposition imbroglio. Raúl charged that Hart's belief that foreign press coverage of the junta had tied the movement's hands proved that the urban underground lacked sufficient revolutionary ardor.[12] Che Guevara, too, was fed up with the *llano*. He thought that Latour in particular was deliberately sabotaging him by failing to send adequate supplies, while Latour believed that the Argentine interloper had violated security protocols by accepting supplies from locals of dubious reputation.

Guevara seized upon the National Directorate's preoccupation with unity politics and elevated bickering over tactics and resources into an ideological polemic between the *sierra* and *llano*.[13] The National Directorate was not the only target of Guevara's suspicions: Fidel's "cryptic" silence on the junta matter had left Guevara wondering about the political and philosophical limitations of the man he later called "the best thing to come out of Cuba since Martí."[14] Moreover, Guevara warned Fidel to break his silence on the question, suspecting that Uncle Sam was most certainly pulling the strings behind the junta.[15]

GUEVARA'S SENSITIVITIES about possible U.S. manipulation of the exile's power play were not entirely unwarranted, though his suspicions were fueled by political instinct and a sense of history rather than concrete evidence. After the junta's formation, Washington did briefly consider it as a possible player in a solution to the Cuban crisis. In the middle of November 1957, two State Department officials, William Wieland and C. Allan Stewart, respectively the director and deputy director of what was then referred to as the Office of Middle American Affairs, drafted a memorandum to the assistant secretary of state proposing that the United States act "as a discreet middleman" between Batista and the Cuban opposition. Warning that "a breakdown of the democratic process in Cuba" would set a bad example for the hemisphere and expose the island to a "resurgence of communism," they attempted to stake out a middle ground in Cuban politics, fearing that without an imminent solution,

Batista would soon be replaced by a "military or civilian junta or the Batista forces will seek to perpetuate themselves in power."[16]

To avoid such an outcome, they suggested that the United States might "permit Batista and the opposition to retreat from their intransigent positions" prior to elections. The first step in such a process would be for the United States to convince Batista to permit both the radical right and "Fidel Castro and his followers in the Sierra Maestra to leave the country until elections are over." With the right and the left sides of the political spectrum out of the country,

> the next move would involve talks with opposition groups, including the Junta de Liberación Cubana group in the United States. It is suggested that our role must be as discreet as possible. Batista, for example, might be persuaded to reach a direct agreement either to send an emissary to the rebel groups, or to receive a delegation from them to negotiate. Eventually, however, our role as middleman would probably become known. There are many who think that the opposition does not want free and fair elections, since it is divided into so many groups. Confronted with the possibility of a truce and honest elections, the opposition would be placed in a difficult position if it failed to go along, especially if word of the negotiations were made public. Although the bulk of the opposition is banded together at present in the Junta, it would require considerable persuasive talent to get them to agree with each other and with the groups in Cuba on terms of a settlement with Batista, since they are jockeying for political advantages. However, it might be persuaded beforehand to settle on a slate of three or four presidential possibilities, [with] the opposition candidate to be chosen from among them once an agreement with the Government were signed.[17]

Who was the State Department's candidate of choice? Felipe Pazos. Having given audience to virtually every member of the Miami junta, Wieland and his staff recommended renewing Pazos's American visa, suggesting that unlike some of the opposition's "real reprobates," Pazos was to "be given preferential treatment as [in] the United States' interest . . . [and] known to be pro–United States and one of the leading candidates for Provisional President being forwarded by the opposition Unity Movement."[18]

Wieland, who as editor of the *Havana Post* in 1933 had observed the American attempt to mediate between the opposition and Gerardo Machado, felt skeptical that the United States could successfully orchestrate Batista's exit from the Cuban political stage and proposed three alternatives.[19] First, the United States could "return to its policy of aloofness from Cuban internal affairs," in which case a unified opposition might intensify its "revolutionary campaign" and via a "general strike or some other means, overthrow Batista." Second, the United States could back a coup against Batista or try to weaken him by threatening to suspend arms sales unless the dictator curtailed "widespread excessive brutality, marked by torture and murders." Third, rather than withdraw support from Batista, the United States could instead press the opposition to negotiate satisfactory conditions for elections. If the opposition refused, the United States could then "adopt harsher measures to curtail their revolutionary activities here. This would have as a corollary more positive United States support for the Government of Cuba."[20] Thus, one potential result of the 26th of July's withdrawing from the Pact of Miami would be an American crackdown on the revolutionaries' weapons purchases and fund-raising activities in the United States.

To corroborate his judgment about developments on the ground, Wieland spent ten days in Cuba talking to individuals in and out of government, among the foreign press corps, and in the opposition. Among those he spoke with were *New York Times* journalist Ruby Hart Phillips, Jules Dubois, the Canadian headmaster of a prominent Havana private school, and a "former policeman . . . now in the hills with Castro."[21] Wieland's conversations convinced him to discard his earlier recommendation that the United States either orchestrate a mediation or promote a coup d'état. Meanwhile his colleagues at the American embassy had conceived of a solution to the Cuban crisis under Batista's watch. Though Wieland encountered universal skepticism that Batista would actually allow a clean electoral process to unfold, he nevertheless echoed the view of his colleagues and recommended that the United States support the June 1958 elections with Batista at the helm.[22]

Back in Havana the M267 quickly learned that the Americans were reevaluating their support for Batista. Not only did Luis Buch act as a liaison with the opposition, but he also frequently engaged American officials, directly and indirectly, in Havana and Santiago. In early December 1957, an intermediary gave Buch a two-part message from the American embassy indicating that the United States had "sounded out the possibility of making contact between the Movement and a government figure . . . and was even considering that Alex [Castro's nom de guerre] and this individual hold a meeting on a boat of the American fleet." Serious or not, the suggestion coincides with Wieland's exploration of how the United States might discreetly mediate between the opposition and the government. Buch quickly dismissed the gesture and "the manner in which it was transmitted as nothing more than" a test "to measure our reaction and study our thinking."[23]

But Buch was far more concerned by the second part of the message—that despite growing evidence Batista was negotiating in bad faith, the United States planned to back the electoral process then under way. Jules Dubois, whom Buch believed was an American intelligence agent, had recently intimated that Batista was wavering on holding elections the following June.[24] After meeting with Batista, even Ambassador Earl E. T. Smith warned of a "strong possibility elections will be postponed for several months" beyond their June 1958 date. Moreover, cautioned Smith, the Cuban government had "no intention of restoring constitutional guarantees in the near future," and Batista "will make every effort to make sure his own candidate is elected."[25] Buch felt strongly that the movement should maintain a moderate posture regarding elections—that it should back a provisional government so the Americans would not think it was further polarizing the Cuban political climate. Buch thus counseled Hart to immediately "set up a government that, in the name of all sectors, should drive home the point" that elections held by a ruler bent on remaining in power were simply unacceptable.[26]

The "week of resistance" had not produced the shockwaves the National Directorate had hoped for. Its keystone, caneburning, succeeded only in Oriente. Bad weather, limited resources, and poor organization in the western provinces severely limited the militia's effectiveness.[27] The 26th of July was simply too weak to play Carlos Prío for his money, thwart his power over a government-in-exile, and maintain an image of moderation for the Americans, all while contriving to make sure that any new government would be transitory enough to guarantee that after the revolution the movement would be able to govern, in a sense, from below. Worst of all, tensions that were to polarize the movement itself were flaring again within the 26th of July.

Writing on Fidel's behalf, Celia Sánchez accused Hart and Latour of botching the movement's affairs both at home and abroad. Hart's reply to the still-classified letter provides clues to the source of Fidel's ire at the time. Sánchez insinuated in two of the "three points that have assaulted *Alejandro* [Castro]," first that the *llano*'s failure to set fire to substantial tracts of sugarcane fields had allowed Batista's troops to penetrate the Sierra Maestra and kill two rebel captains, and second, that Hart had mishandled the Cuban Liberation Junta.[28]

These accusations came as a major blow to Hart, who felt his actions and beliefs had been distorted in the Sierra Maestra. In Hart's view, he had behaved as a dutiful soldier, attempting to finagle the opposition into lining up behind the 26th of July's Sierra Manifesto program. But his comrades in the *sierra* had a more narrow outlook: they needed weapons, had not received them, and saw no further reason to maintain a tactical pretense of unity. Hart wrote Celia that after learning of the *sierra's* mistrust he "better understood the reasons for the failure of the two great revolutions, that of '95 and '33" (the war of independence from Spain and the popular movement to topple Gerardo Machado, respectively), when internal divisions had undermined and weakened earlier revolutionary movements. Hart defended himself against the suggestion that his effort to navigate the riptides of opposition politics and arm the rebels, however fruitless, made him or the National Directorate somehow less revolutionary. He replied to Celia,

> I regard myself as the most radical of all of us . . . in the political aspect of revolutionary thinking, and I take historic responsibility for what we did and I'll request of Alex [Castro] that if [the opposition] doesn't accept the Movement's proposals we should begin a brutal barrage of propaganda against the Príos and the whole group . . . If we choose to go one step beyond the Sierra [Manifesto] formula, we should discuss a broad-based strategy that for weeks I've been thinking about regarding the revolutionary struggle and proposals for programmatic and economic and social transformations . . . I don't know if you've read the reports about the workers, but I think we have the requisite organization to begin a real social revolution. If Alex is ready to take this step it would be one of the happiest days of my life because he has an extraordinary ability to understand when politically we should put forward proposals of a radical nature. We are ready to move beyond the Sierra Manifesto and return to the programmatic points of "History Will Absolve Me." I must say that only by doing that can we free ourselves of the errors like those Pazos and Bienvenido [Rodríguez] have committed.[29]

What the *sierra* rebels either did not comprehend or refused to acknowledge was that over the last two months of negotiating and cajoling Hart had reached the same conclusion they had about Prío and the opposition. Embittered by their accusations, disappointed by the movement's failure to intensify the urban insurrection, and ready to abandon the Miami opposition, Hart ventured up to the mountains to explain himself face to face.

Hart brought along a written proposal that he hoped would untether the movement from the political constraints of the Miami "unity" dynamic. "I believe," he wrote Fidel, "that the time has come to assume the formal responsibility of stating who we are and where we are going." Five months had elapsed since Castro, Pazos, and Chibás had called for a broad-based Civic Revolutionary Front. But the M267 no longer needed to work with the militant or moderate opposition in order to overthrow Batista, he argued to Castro. Like Frank País before him, Hart believed that the movement should articulate and publicize its economic, social, and international program for a new Cuba in order to assuage the doubts of the "middle sectors" of public opinion. It would be a "grave error" and a sign of "political immaturity" to remain "in a vacuum . . . now that the Movement has consolidated its position in its organization outside of the *sierra* and especially in the Sierra Maestra." The 26th of July, wrote Hart, "cannot aspire to power while doubt prevails regarding essential aspects" of the movement's program. Since the Civic Institutions had proved to be "inefficient in overthrowing the dictator," the 26th of July, he argued, "should stake out its independence once and for all."[30]

Despite his skepticism, Hart suggested a final round of talks with the Civic Institutions to propose they nominate for provisional president Judge Manuel Urrutia Lleó, the Oriente judge who had ruled in the trial of the captured *Granma* expeditionaries that insurrection was a right protected under the 1940 constitution. Hart acknowledged Fidel's desire for the 26th of July to "provide further proof of its disinterest" in attaining power, but he believed that if the Civic Institutions rejected the Urrutia proposal, the movement had grown strong enough to put forward its own presidential candidate. In this case, Hart declared that he would nominate the thirty-two-year-old Castro, whom he described as "the only figure with the capacity and force to substitute Batista." Whomever they chose as a presidential candidate, Hart was convinced that the moment had come for the movement to abandon the Sierra Manifesto's objective of cultivating the Civic Institutions as key allies; they should instead "take on in this moment the formal leadership of the entire opposition" and "immediately withdraw from the Liberation Junta."[31]

Though there was no agreement to make Castro the movement's presidential candidate nor to articulate publicly a political or social vision for Cuba after Batista, there was consensus within the National Directorate, *sierra* and *llano,* for breaking with the exile alliance.[32] With input from Celia Sánchez, Raúl Castro, Che Guevara, and René Ramos Latour, Castro and Hart drafted a lengthy and later widely publicized letter to the Cuban Liberation Junta members explaining the 26th of July's resignation from the Pact of Miami. They outlined five procedural and substantive reasons for the rupture: Léster Rodríguez and Felipe Pazos had not adequately consulted with the National Directorate before joining; the pact did not explicitly reject the option that a military junta replace Batista, or directly denounce the possibility of American intervention; it made no sense for a joint military operations committee to run the insurgency from Miami; and the proposed provisional government augured perpetuation of politics as usual after Batista.[33] The letter reflected Raúl Castro's view that the pact was a "trap of *politiquería*," demonstrated by "the simple fact that while the leaders of the organizations signing the agreement are abroad carrying out an imaginary revolution, the leaders of the 26th of July Movement are in Cuba making a real revolution."[34] Echoing Guevara's suspicion of American involvement, Castro wrote that the 26th of July would have accepted the Pact of Miami "due to the positive value of unity" and the promise of "aid offered to us" if not for the junta's "evidence of lukewarm patriotism" regarding foreign intervention and its "self-evident act of cowardice" toward the prospect of a military junta replacing Batista. Reflecting Hart's view, Castro attacked the junta's agreement that its members retain power to approve or veto cabinet members in a provisional government because the agreement implied "the establishment of two executive powers within the state." Granting power to "organizations lacking the support of the masses" might be satisfactory "within the canons of traditional politics," but such a practice was "at variance with the high revolutionary and political goals of the 26th of July Movement."[35]

Nor would the movement countenance the junta's secret agreement that after Batista's collapse the rebel army and all revolutionary forces would be incorporated into Cuba's standing armed forces. Instead, the 26th of July Movement would alone assume "the function of maintaining public order and reorganizing the armed forces of the Republic." Castro, like País before him, attacked the Auténticos, who had joined the Student Revolutionary Directorate in the March 1957 suicide assault on the presidential palace, for hiding their weapons and taking comfort in exile, watching idly as their compatriots died in Cuba's cities and mountains. Though silent about the Directorate, Castro nevertheless alluded to Faure Chomón's organization when he rhetorically asked whether the Auténticos had given up their focus on "a putsch in the capital" and instead accepted the movement's "thesis of a general strike." Cuban exiles had no right, he wrote, to "tell us from abroad what peak we should take, what sugarcane fields we should burn, what sabotage we should carry out, or at what moment, in what circumstances, and in what form we should call a general strike." The 26th of July would not "offer the Republic as a booty to gain their aid." The insinuation? Neither the exiled opposition—political or revolutionary—nor their colleagues on the island had the right to power after Batista's overthrow.[36]

Loftiness of purpose prevailed over Hart's pressure to provide specifics on the movement's programmatic outlook for the country. Castro noted only that the 26th of July Movement would "provide substantive solutions" for Cuba's "major problems" by relying on the "formidable support of the masses," whom the movement would direct and guide from "the underground, from the Sierra Maestra, or from the graves of our dead." After nominating Judge Manuel Urrutia as the movement's candidate for provisional president, Castro closed the letter with the celebrated admonition, "To die with dignity does not require company."[37]

DESPITE HIS earlier recommendation that the movement stick with the junta, Luis Buch dutifully returned to Miami just after Christmas 1957. This time his wife, Conchita, accompanied him, concealing the letter to the junta in her beehive hairstyle.[38] Buch brought Léster Rodríguez, Mario Llerena, Raúl Chibás, and Jorge Sotús (whom Fidel had sent to hunt for weapons over the summer) together in a hotel room and presented them with Castro's letter. "Tears streamed down his cheeks" when Rodríguez finished reading it, wrote Buch.[39] Despite the letter's strident reprimand, Rodríguez and Sotús insisted that Buch wait one week before publicizing what in essence would mean the collapse of the junta. They were expecting Carlos Prío to make a major weapons delivery to them any day and did not want to jeopardize many months of effort for the cause. Sotús invoked the weight of his military credentials, assuring Buch that he would "accept all responsibility with the Commander for not releasing the letter . . . because if he spoke with the Chief he'd convince him of the" value and quantity of weapons. Buch felt intimidated "by the presence of a military officer, Capitán Jorge [Sotús], who should know the military advantages of the aid," and feared, as Sotús had threatened, "one day . . . being held responsible for the *sierra* not receiving aid that was ready to go . . . because of maintaining a strict order and the Revolution had lost because we weren't flexible with received instructions." Therefore, Buch sent his younger nephew Tony Buch back to Santiago to double-check with the National Directorate before publicizing Castro's letter.[40] In Santiago, Tony Buch explained his uncle's hesitation to René Ramos Latour. But Latour had received instructions from Hart via his fiancée Haydée Santamaría to deny Sotús's request to hold out for weapons and to instead immediately publicize the letter.[41]

The champagne in the 1958 New Year's glasses had hardly bubbled before news of Castro's démarche had spread through Miami. The Ortodoxos, Auténticos, and Student Revolutionary Directorate responded publicly to the movement's break from the junta. The Ortodoxos immediately withdrew from the junta as well and reiterated their support for the 26th of July and insurrection. Tony Varona condemned Castro, reminding him that Prío's money had come in handy to the rebel leader in the past. Felipe Pazos insisted that he had never betrayed the 26th of July and had operated at every step with the National Directorate's approval. But the harshest response came from Faure Chomón, secretary general and military chief of the Student Revolutionary Directorate. Chomón felt manipulated by Rodríguez and stung by Castro's public rebuke. He castigated Fidel for his "sectarian arrogance" in suggesting that the 26th of July was the only revolutionary organization spilling its blood in Cuba.[42] Within one month, Chomón was to set up his own front in the Sierra del Escambray in a direct challenge to Castro's claim of primacy in the fight against Batista.

Following a recommendation by the State Department, the United States seemed to crack down on Cuban revolutionary activity within U.S. borders. In February 1958, a New York grand jury indicted Carlos Prío and eight other Cuban exiles for violating U.S. neutrality laws in launching the *Corinthia* expedition from American territory.[43] Days later off the Gulf Coast of Texas, the Coast Guard intercepted the *Orion* in an expedition led by a *fidelista* Ortodoxo party member Arnoldo Barrón.[44] Also within days of the Prío indictment, the FBI seized the *Buddy Dee* in Galveston and a safe house in Houston, Texas, where Léster Rodríguez, with Prío's financial and material assistance, had stashed weapons, medical supplies, armbands, and other materials to be used in a joint OAM267 expedition to Cuba.[45] Fearing arrest, Rodríguez and Jorge Sotús left Miami for Central America. After a brief stint in a Costa Rican jail, they crossed the border to Nicaragua, where the founder of the Sandinista National Liberation Front, Carlos Fonseca Amador, picked them up, gave them a place to stay, and later helped them return to Miami. In July of 1958, they returned to Costa Rica and flew a planeload of weapons to the Sierra Cristal, in northeastern Oriente province. When they arrived, Raúl Castro, who in an earlier fit of rage had suggested executing Rodríguez for his role in getting the movement into the junta mess, rewarded Rodríguez with the rank of captain of the "Frank País" second front.[46]

The life and death of the Cuban Liberation Junta has heretofore been treated as a relatively minor episode in the history of the Cuban insurrection.[47] But the 26th of July's involvement with the junta is significant because it illustrates the scope of the urban underground's decision-making autonomy and authority with respect to the *sierra* and to Fidel Castro. The National Directorate's attempt and failure to establish hegemony over the militant and reformist opposition demonstrates the limits of coalition-building faced by a revolutionary organization. We now know that even though Fidel let the urban underground try to amend the unity accord to the 26th of July's advantage, the National Directorate's tactical tolerance for Cuba's political opposition exacerbated problems that were already brewing between the *sierra* and the *llano*. Che Guevara seized upon the Miami affair to build his case with Fidel against the National Directorate, accusing its leadership of treason for conspiring to sell out the revolution to the United States. Eventually, the *sierra* and *llano* did reach a genuine consensus to break with the Pact of Miami. But the sting of Raúl Castro's and Che Guevara's charges of betrayal endured. Indeed, the legacy of their accusations combined with the practical implications of such a public break from the entire Cuban opposition significantly amplified the 26th of July Movement's partisanship. Overall, this experience made the National Directorate less inclined to join forces on the ground in any way that might imply sharing power after Batista's collapse.

FOR THE National Directorate, and for Hart in particular, the movement's break with the exiled opposition was a liberating step that permitted the organization to focus exclusively on the war at home. Hart had not been to the Sierra Maestra for nearly a year, since February of 1957, when a handful of poorly armed combatants had convinced Herbert Matthews of the *New York Times* that Castro then led a bona fide guerrilla army. Nearly one year later, with over two hundred rebels divided into various platoons based throughout the Sierra Maestra, Hart found "a veritable military-agrarian State" that had succeeded "beyond the bounds of what my imagination allowed," he wrote his fiancée, Haydée Santamaría.[48] He also wrote her that the break with the Cuban Liberation Junta represented

> a momentous step in the history of the Movement. Because of Fidel's attitude and willingness, we are ready to once and for all set forth the most intransigent political line to which any sincere revolution could aspire at this time. We've also talked a lot about the future, as we have drawn up precise plans for it in every sense. We've talked about organization. In that respect we should be working hard outside [of the Sierra Maestra] so that our efforts are felt more each day. We've reached certain strategic points in the development of the struggle against the dictator in which Daniel [Latour] and Pablo [Alonso Hidalgo] completely coincide . . . The theses of the (total war I believe should be developed).[49]

"Total war?" Santamaría was dumbfounded by Hart's instructions to move forward with the "thesis" of a "total war," a strategy that Latour supported. Santamaría wrote Latour that her fiancé was "insisting that we have to launch the slogan of total war [*guerra general*]. I don't understand this well, I thought he meant strike *(huelga)* and instead of putting *huelga* he had put *guelga,* though I am tremendously surprised by this mistake, but the thing of *guerra general* I don't understand."[50] This was no mere typo and Santamaría was correct. Hart's instructions, which because they were written from the Sierra Maestra certainly had Fidel's endorsement, appeared to represent a significant tactical departure from the strategy of the general strike. Confusion between "total war" and general strike prevailed within the National Directorate, which at the time was poised to execute what was to be the final stage of the anti-Batista war effort. Nor could Hart be much help in clarifying what he meant by *"guerra general."* On January 10, 1958, as Hart returned from the Sierra Maestra to Santiago, the police arrested Hart, Javier Pazos, and Tony Buch in the town of Bayamo. Fearing that the three faced certain death at the hands of the Santiago police chief Salas Cañizares, the M267 generated enough domestic and international attention to the arrests to save the young men. Tony Buch was released within months, while Hart and Pazos spent the rest of the year in jail.[51]

Because of the direct contact and time for conversation with Fidel and others in the hills, Hart's month-long stay in the Sierra Maestra repaired some of the damage that the Liberation Junta had caused the movement. It also drove home to him the scope and requirements of the rebel army. But just as the 26th of July was to shift into high gear for a general strike, his removal from the fray of insurrection again forced the National Directorate to regroup from the loss of the individual who, like Frank País before, had begun to provide cohesion between the *sierra* and *llano.* Ironically, though, the attempt to insert the Civic Institutions into the center of a post-Batista solution, a gesture Hart hoped would prevent "militant sectarianism" from dominating a transition government, contributed to a similar divisiveness within the 26th of July as well as between the movement and other anti-Batista opposition groups.

Don Cosme de la Torriente and José Miró Cardona (far right, second from right) of the Sociedad de Amigos de la República following a meeting with deposed Auténtico Party leaders—former prime minister Manuel Antonio de Varona and former president Carlos Prío Socarrás (far left, second from left), August 16, 1955. Office of Historic Affairs, Cuban Council of State.

Frank País (center, in white suit), Carlos Chaín (far left), and others stand trial in Santiago de Cuba court, March 1957, accused of participating in events related to the Santiago de Cuba uprising of November 30, 1956, and the *Granma* landing of December 3, 1956. Office of Historic Affairs, Cuban Council of State.

Taras Domitro Terlebauca, son of Russian immigrants, at home in El Caney, outside of Santiago de Cuba, in 1956. First a co-conspirator and friend of Frank País—Domitro's sister América was País's girl-friend—Domitro later worked with René Ramos Latour as the militia's quartermaster in the western provinces. Office of Historic Affairs, Cuban Council of State.

Celia Sánchez bandages Fidel Castro's finger at the beginning of the rebel insurgency, January 1957, in Los Cocos, Sierra Maestra. Office of Historic Affairs, Cuban Council of State.

Rebel Army and National Directorate members gather during the visit by *New York Times* journalist Herbert Matthews to El Jíbaro, Sierra Maestra. Seated are Haydée Santamaría and Faustino Pérez; standing, left to right, are Raúl Castro, Vilma Espín, Fidel Castro, Armando Hart, and Universo Sánchez. February 18, 1957. Office of Historic Affairs, Cuban Council of State.

Faustino Pérez, Armando Hart, and their defense attorneys at trial in Havana, April 1957. The two had been arrested after the Student Revolutionary Directorate's assault on the presidential palace on March 13, 1957. Office of Historic Affairs, Cuban Council of State.

Raúl Chibás, Felipe Pazos, and Fidel Castro work to create the Sierra Manifesto in July 1957. Julio Martínez Paez, the first Cuban physician to join the rebels, sits behind Pazos and Castro. Office of Historic Affairs, Cuban Council of State.

Javier Pazos and Armando Hart incarcerated at Boniato prison after their arrest on January 10, 1958, in Bayamo. They were captured as they returned from meeting with Fidel Castro in the Sierra Maestra, where Hart had traveled to sort out the misunderstandings generated by the Pact of Miami and begin plotting the movement's next steps, both political and military. Office of Historic Affairs, Cuban Council of State.

Manuel de Jesús "Nene" Leon Ramirez, a member of the Cuban congress, went to the Sierra Maestra in February 1958 to ask Fidel Castro to engage in peace talks with the Batista regime. Fidel Castro is reading a publication either by or about the right-wing militia group Los Tigres, led by another congressman, Rolando Masferrer. Office of Historic Affairs, Cuban Council of State.

Alonso "Bebo" Hidalgo (far right), another comrade of Frank País and René Ramos Latour, during his venture to Miami, March 1958, to buy weapons for the general strike in April. Office of Historic Affairs, Cuban Council of State.

During the National Directorate's prestrike planning meeting of March 8, 1958, Haydée Santamaría watches while Fidel Castro examines a new scope in El Naranjo, Sierra Maestra. Office of Historic Affairs, Cuban Council of State.

Vilma Espín, Haydée Santamaría, and Celia Sánchez (left to right) at a break during the National Directorate's prestrike planning meeting at El Naranjo. Fidel Castro, Marcelo Fernández (with beret), Faustino Pérez, and others are in the background. March 8, 1958. Office of Historic Affairs, Cuban Council of State.

Mapping their strategy during the prestrike planning meeting with Fidel Castro at El Naranjo, March 8, 1958, are (left to right) Marcelo Fernandez, Haydée Santamaría, Vilma Espín, René Ramos Latour, Fidel Castro, David Salvador, Celia Sánchez, and Faustino Pérez. Office of Historic Affairs, Cuban Council of State.

In July 1958, Raúl Castro (left), with his fiancée, underground operative Vilma Espín, negotiates the release of captured American and Canadian hostages with an unidentified American in Calabaza, the Sierra Cristal. Espín, who had studied at MIT, served as translator. Office of Historic Affairs, Cuban Council of State.

Cuban rebels Oriente Fernandez, Raúl Castro, Manuel Piñeiro (one of the architects of "Operación Antiaérea," designed to force the Cuban air force to stop bombing Raúl Castro's area of operations in the Second Front), and Vilma Espín discuss the release of hostages with an unidentified American, July 1958. Office of Historic Affairs, Cuban Council of State.

René Ramos "Daniel" Latour (standing, second from right) and comrades in the Sierra Maestra during the summer 1958 offensive, just weeks before his death at the end of July. Office of Historic Affairs, Cuban Council of State.

Léster "Bienvenido" Rodríguez (right), made captain by Raúl Castro and wearing American army surplus gear, poses with others in the Second Front, October 1958. Office of Historic Affairs, Cuban Council of State.

José Llanusa, Luis Buch, and Haydée Santamaría return from New York, Caracas, and Miami, respectively, and are greeted by Armando Hart (right) at the airport in Camagüey, January 1959. Office of Historic Affairs, Cuban Council of State.

At the presidential palace in January 1959, newly inaugurated president Manuel Urrutia Lleó (center) holds a press conference with Che Guevara (second from left) and Camilo Cienfuegos (far right). Office of Historic Affairs, Cuban Council of State; AP/Wide World Photos.

Civilian politicians in the new revolutionary cabinet, as well as rebels from the Student Revolutionary Directorate (DRE) and 26th of July, hold a press conference at the presidential palace in January 1959. Seated from left to right are newly appointed prime minister José Miró Cardona, foreign minister Roberto Agramonte, president Manuel Urrutia Lleó, and Faure Chomón Mediavilla, chief of military affairs of the DRE. Enrique Rodríguez Loeches, who signed the Pact of Caracas for the DRE, stands at center in the plaid shirt. Office of Historic Affairs, Cuban Council of State.

Down from the mountains and back in their street clothing, Celia Sánchez, Vilma Espín, Haydée Santamaría, and her sister, Aida Santamaría (left to right), attend an official send-off at the airport in Havana, 1960. Office of Historic Affairs, Cuban Council of State.

As minister of communications in the new revolutionary cabinet, Enrique Oltuski, who during the insurgency managed the movement's clandestine operations in both Havana and Santa Clara, became host of the television program *La Revolución Explica Su Obra* (The revolution explains its work). Here the twenty-eight-year-old Oltuski (left), the youngest cabinet member, appears in 1959 with his guest on the show, the twenty-nine-year-old Armando Hart, then minister of education, to discuss the new government's literacy campaign. Courtesy of Enrique Oltuski.

8 | Total War?

> We needed to achieve a more complete integra-
> tion of leadership, more systematic direction, and
> a more complete and precise doctrinal and pro-
> grammatic body of work . . . Our hope rested in
> the extraordinary capacity of Fidel, in your insis-
> tent ability to achieve such objectives, and in the
> magnificent opportunity to propose, define, and
> carry them out . . . But the worst happened at the
> best moment. We were left again with a leadership
> vacuum.
>
> Faustino Pérez to Armando Hart, October 3, 1958

THOUGH THE *LLANO*'S HANDLING OF exile politics did generate significant conflict within the 26th of July Movement, the National Directorate in the urban underground retained substantial political and tactical autonomy from Fidel Castro's forces in the Sierra Maestra. As Batista's ability to hold onto the presidency grew increasingly tenuous during the first quarter of 1958, the urban revolutionaries came to believe that the tide of public opinion had finally turned and the Cuban people were finally ready to overthrow the dictator through a nationwide general strike.

On January 25, 1958, Batista, to prepare for elections the following spring, restored constitutional guarantees throughout the island and lifted press censorship except in Oriente, the province that harbored his strongest opposition.[1] Batista's sudden announcement was not welcomed by the revolutionaries. Ever since Castro had arrived from Mexico in December 1956, and except for a brief reprieve the previous spring, the rebels had grown accustomed to operating under a near total state of siege, without the writ of habeus corpus, constitutional liberties, or a free press—a climate they welcomed to polarize the population and escalate the conflict with the regime. Cuba's legal opposition and government coalition parties responded to the move by immediately announcing party conventions to select candidates to run in the elections. Even the Communist Party, which had been excluded from the machinations in Miami, lauded the opening as a triumph for the country's popular forces and an opportunity to agitate publicly for democratic elections.[2] But the

26th of July wanted to prevent any pretense of normality in the country, particularly elections, and viewed the restoration of constitutional liberties as a "double-edged sword that can be the kiss of death for the regime or for us."

> We find ourselves compelled to take action to demonstrate the impotence of the regime in containing the revolution. We cannot vacillate for one instant in the eyes of domestic and international opinion. We must avoid at all cost the government moving forward in its pacification . . . via the electoral farce. We're developing an offensive that will force the regime to . . . suspend guarantees again and re-impose press censorship, that is, to make clear to the Cuban people and the rest of the world that the regime is incapable of returning the island to normalcy.[3]

To fill the void left by Hart's arrest and to develop their response to the renewal of civil liberties, the National Directorate met in Santiago for the first time in over three months.[4] Just as they had after Frank País's assassination, the National Directorate again restructured its membership and revised and redrafted plans to increase outreach among students and organized labor. Marcelo Fernández, who like Vilma Espín had also studied at the Massachusetts Institute of Technology, had been running the movement's public relations efforts and taken over Hart's role as national coordinator. With Celia Sánchez to remain permanently in the Sierra Maestra, René Ramos Latour replaced her as the *llano's* liaison with the rebel army.[5] Most importantly, the underground militia known as "Action and Sabotage" (also under Latour's direction) became the center of the urban strategy to overthrow Batista. Why was it necessary to remake plans that País and Hart had already set to paper and begun to implement? Had the "total war" strategy changed things?

Elected to the Federation of University Students (FEU) from the University of Havana's engineering department, Fernández described a chaotic mess among anti-Batista organizers at Cuban universities. On the one hand, since the relaxation in repression, "communist students and others who are not [communists have been] proposing the possibility of opening universities and returning to the tactic of protests, street acts, etcetera." The movement's own sympathizers had also returned to class, while at the same time its action and sabotage brigades were arbitrarily bombing schools, presumably to prevent attendance and thereby demonstrate student opposition to the dictator.[6] Fernández supported the militia's goal of shutting down the schools and proposed creating the National Student Front or FEN to organize a nationwide boycott of all high schools and universities. He also suggested attempting to bring members of the long-standing Federation of University Students (FEU) into FEN ranks to distribute propaganda, sell bonds to families, and even provoke "repressive police action by throwing rocks or shooting at patrol cars from schools, in order to force the [police] to storm the schools themselves, right in the middle of classes, and beat up students and professors."[7] Though Cuban students had been the de facto turf of the Student Revolutionary Directorate (DRE), which viewed itself as an offshoot of the FEU, the FEU remained independent from the DRE. After the split from the Liberation Junta, the National Directorate's members saw little reason to maintain the veneer of unity, and thus set their sites on students as a constituency that the 26th of July had not yet fully organized. Indeed, while the DRE had drawn many of its members from the FEU, many FEU members were also active in or sympathized with the 26th of July. Indeed, beneath the top tiers of leadership in both organizations, there was considerable crossover among students associated with the FEU, the DRE, and the 26th of July—especially after the death of DRE founder José Antonio Echeverría following the attack on the presidential palace.[8]

"If the 26th wants to win over labor, we have to do it defending their interests. Remember," wrote Fernández, "that the magazines *Time* and *Life* have called our revolution 'a middle-class revolution.'"[9] Fernández set forth few guidelines to the movement's activists for reaching out to Cuban workers. The National Workers Front (FON) must "intensify work in each of the thirty-three industries and federations, especially transportation and electrical workers" and distribute propaganda to 26th of July workplace cells calling upon "workers to struggle for the specific demands" of each sector. The movement's organizers had begun to realize that if they wanted to expand their base among the agricultural and industrial working class, they needed to demonstrate a connection between the conditions that Cuban workers faced and the broader struggle against the dictator. This was a difficult challenge because the 26th of July was extremely reluctant to work with any of the existing *mujalista* labor federations or any other labor group associated with an existing political party, such as the Communists. Though there were independent labor organizers throughout the country, and a steady stream of labor-driven and labor-focused anti-regime actions throughout the decade—a strike of 500,000 sugar workers in 1955 and significant activism in the sugar-producing province of Matanzas, for example—the 26th of July had not yet made substantial inroads with the individuals or organizations leading these efforts.[10]

Fernández also proposed two departures from the model that Armando

Hart had recently implemented. He wanted to shift the movement's headquarters from Santiago to Havana, "the most strategic location of the nation and the best place to convene meetings."[11] That the new national coordinator regarded the Cuban capital, with a population of over one million, as the strategic nerve center of the insurrection suggested an underlying tension between the Havana- and Santiago-based urban cadres, one that would have a direct effect on the plans for and outcome of the national strike. And like Frank País, Marcelo, or "Zoilo," believed that the composition of the National Directorate should reflect the demographics of the island, with participation in strategic decisions opened up to each province, not simply Havana and Oriente, as well as to the movement's leaders in prison, in exile, and in the Sierra Maestra. But the militia chief, René Ramos Latour, prevailed at the meeting, arguing for Santiago to remain the organization's headquarters and for the National Directorate to limit its membership.

Latour's jurisdiction and influence over decisions and strategy expanded at this time. He became responsible for recruiting, training, and arming the militia in every province of the country; supplying the *sierra* and *llano* with arms; and acting as a "link with the General Staff of the Revolutionary Army."[12] Of the urban underground's six "sections" (finances, labor, propaganda, organization, civic resistance, and action and sabotage), Latour's militia emerged at the center of the movement's plans in an apparent reflection of the "total war" scenario Hart had come down from the Sierra to activate before his arrest. "To convince the country that we're at war," Fernández wrote, the top priority was fomenting

> armed action across the island's territory, not by opening combat fronts, which would be impossible, but rather through the militia. We can even organize special militias comprised of workers and peasants who work normally during the day and carry out actions at night; such efforts have proved to be very effective in Cyprus, Indochina, Algiers, and Ireland . . . Bombs should be set off for three reasons: (a) to sabotage means of transportation, electricity, water, etcetera; (b) in locales for parties and recreation to dramatize the fact that we are at war; and (c) in the homes of government officials and snitches, to execute them. Bombs in stores, businesses, and thrown in the middle of streets, are counterproductive.[13]

Had Fidel approved of this strategy? When Hart was arrested, the Oriente police confiscated his documents, leaving Latour unsure of whether Fidel had endorsed his proposal to expand the underground's sabotage teams in Oriente and throughout the island. Latour knew that Hart supported the new strategy of total war, but he wrote Fidel asking him to clarify whether he endorsed the new plan.[14]

Instead of an explicit answer, Fidel sent Latour a long inventory of materiél required to manufacture weapons in the Sierra Maestra, and a polite but impatient request that Latour send arms and mortars from the *llano* to the guerrillas.[15] Fidel also issued orders to the militia in several Oriente towns to send the *sierra* rebels all rifles in their possession. But the militia of Holguín, Niquero, and Manzanillo ignored the order, a defiance Castro viewed as a "criminal act" no different than Carlos Prío's refusal months earlier to provide arms to the movement. And Celia reported to Latour that in a fit of pique, Castro had toyed with making an object lesson of one militia member then holding four Garand rifles: "Fidel says why not execute him, that it has been criminal to detain the arms like Prío, that you teach them a good lesson so that news circulates to all of the militants so that no one else keeps weapons, they don't use them but [instead] turn them in."[16]

In the clearest exposition yet of the National Directorate's strategy to derail the government's peace plan, stop the elections, and drive Batista out, Latour responded to Castro's rather troubling threat. He wrote that the National Directorate considered the restoration of constitutional guarantees a response to American pressure both to restore a climate of normality in Cuba and to move forward with elections. Though the Cuban population might, in large measure, see through these tactics, the Directorate feared that the government's "propaganda apparatus in some measure may influence some sectors of the population" to see the elections as a viable solution to the Cuban crisis. While the end of press censorship might allow the "traditional press" to cover the revolutionary process temporarily, the National Directorate had concluded that

pseudo-freedom does not benefit us at all, because in the end it will be an indication that the government is trying via the press to give off a sense of strength, that action and sabotage within and outside of the Sierra Maestra affect its stability very little, and that in the extreme it is capable of governing even with constitutional guarantees and press freedom. This impression will begin undermining and weakening the faith the people have put in the revolutionary movement, especially since the period that began the day of Frank País's assassination.[17]

To derail the government's "pacification" plan, which had surfaced after Hart's arrest, the National Directorate decided to force Batista to reimpose censorship and suspend constitutional liberties in order to demonstrate to the "Cuban people and to the United States and the whole world" the regime's inability to "contain the booming revolutionary struggle." The longer-term goal was a national general strike, the catalytic step toward overthrowing the dictator. Thus, "action and sabotage" would seek first to halt the electoral process by "attacking meetings, burning offices of election boards, carrying out assassination attempts against government figures and the 'loyalist opposition,' . . . slowing down the harvest with sabotage of sugar mills and cane . . . and sabotage to major, especially foreign industry, . . . to create a climate of insecurity and lack of normalcy in the country to make felt the consequences of the civil war."[18]

Latour wanted the llano's militia to soak up a number of independent, roving bands of men, who, inspired by the rebel army, were wandering from village to village randomly attacking government targets. To do so, the militia had begun to form guerrilla units outside of the Sierra Maestra. "We cannot allow," wrote Latour, "these elements to begin to operate on their own . . . In the majority of the cases these elements would be taken advantage of by ill-intentioned want-to-be leaders . . . until degenerating into delinquent bands that assault and destroy in the name of the revolution, harvesting discontent and provoking hostility toward the revolutionaries." Since the rebel army, he wrote, had not been present in those areas to counter "the outbreak of banditry," Latour concluded that the "Movement should assume absolute control over the insurgents' activities, utilizing ideologically and militarily capable commanders as the only way of preventing these forces from slipping from our hands." The militia would "create various fronts . . . that had already begun attacking small army contingents and guard posts. Sabotage plans were already under way, involving cane burning, attacks on sugar mills, blocking bridges and trains, etcetera," he wrote.[19] In a departure from the National Directorate's conception and from Frank País's model for the militia to create highly trained, armed, and disciplined but numerically small action and sabotage units in the towns and cities alone, Latour appeared to be encroaching directly on the traditional terrain of the sierra.[20]

In addition, together with the M267's labor activists, the militia were to play a key role in mobilizing Cuban workers during the general strike. He wrote that the FON was organizing strike committees and recruiting workers to the 26th of July "across the island and in the principal work places." But neither abstract revolutionary ideals nor a burning need to express opposition to the dictatorship would prompt workers to join a general strike, argued Latour. Indeed, FON coordinator David Salvador persuaded the National Directorate that "workers are ready to strike, but under the condition that there is an insurrection." The movement's strike committees could mobilize workers only "WHEN THERE IS A CLIMATE OF ABSOLUTE ABNORMALITY IN THE COUNTRY and only if armed insurrection is maintained in the streets as the only means to sustain the strike,"

Latour insisted.[21] Sabotage against industries, utilities, and transportation would provide cover for workers otherwise unwilling to risk losing their jobs by defying standing no-strike orders. A massive display of firepower by the militia would prevent workers from going to work and eventually force them out of their jobs, after which time they would naturally join the national strike.

Thus, the militia was made the center of the underground's strategy and given three objectives: to force the government to suspend the constitution and call off elections, to convert roving bandits in Oriente into a militia force that could execute "total war," and to assure a massive turnout of Cuban labor during a general strike. Fidel's own demand for the militia's weapons took on quite a different light in the context of these other demands, which were, Latour wrote, "in large measure the reason for the minimum success we've had in getting the Chiefs of Action of the various municipalities to deliver the few arms that you have requested. We require them to keep up sabotage, armed action, and agitation; we tell them that it is they who will have to provoke and sustain the strike and they know they cannot do this with their hands or with rocks. There have been many victims already."[22]

Latour agreed to "try to lend a hand" with uniforms, backpacks, and bullets. But as for the mortars that Fidel wanted the militia to turn over, Latour held off, countering that "half or more of the mortars will be a determinant factor in consolidating the strike. They can be used against barracks and against electrical plants. Don't you think we should leave some of them around here?"[23] Not only would the strike require weapons already in the movement's possession that Fidel intended for the guerrilla war, but Latour also announced that he intended his militia to keep for itself the weapons "we have been awaiting for so long from abroad."[24] Was this a bold-faced challenge to the *sierra* or did Castro concur, at least in principle, with the new *llano* strategy?

Immediately after Hart's arrest, Latour had begun dispatching agents to Miami, New York, Georgia, California, Haiti, Costa Rica, Honduras, and Venezuela to buy all manner of arms and matériel.[25] A comrade of País's and Latour's from the Santiago militia, Alonso "Bebo" Hidalgo (also known as "Pablo"), went to Miami in January to replace Léster Rodríguez as the movement's military affairs coordinator in exile. Unbeknownst to Latour, Fidel also sent his own men abroad to finalize plans for a second, long-prepared expedition by Moncada veterans Pedro Miret and Gustavo Arcos.[26] At first, Latour mistakenly assumed that Hidalgo would easily get his hands on the weapons that Rodríguez had amassed the previous fall. But he learned quickly that Rodríguez and Jorge Sotús had joined forces with the Organización Auténtica (OA) and after preparing to launch a joint expedition to Cuba, skipped town to evade arrest.[27] Even without that equipment, with the militia now the strategic priority of the National Directorate, if not Fidel, Latour had leeway to send Hidalgo all the money he needed. In turn, Hidalgo found that the American arms market offered a near endless supply for the right price.[28]

Latour needed a deputy across the country in the capital, so he appointed Taras Domitro, a longtime comrade, as the militia's quartermaster based in Havana. The son of Russian immigrants, Domitro, a Santiago militia captain first recruited by Frank País and member of Latour's thwarted attempt to open a second guerrilla front in the Sierra Cristal, faced the daunting task of recruiting, training, and arming militia in the western provinces of Matanzas, the outskirts of Havana, and Pinar del Río.[29] He became Latour's go-between for orchestrating weapons deliveries from Miami and Mexico, determining in what proportion to distribute new weapons among the militia in the western provinces and even as far east as Fidel's guerrilla column in Oriente. Initially, Domitro was confident of prospects for arming the revolutionaries and optimistic of the movement's ability to implement a "a national action plan that will bring us to the general strike and final blow" in a matter of months.[30] He even welcomed a promise conveyed by Carlos Prío before his arrest in Miami that OA forces operating in the Sierra del Escambray mountains of Las Villas province since November 1957 would share their weapons with the M267.[31] But in subsequent months leading up to the general strike, Domitro wavered between certainty of victory and certainty of demise, between believing a revolution was possible even without weapons, and being convinced that the movement was doomed without them. He was plagued by self-doubt and ambivalent about Latour's instructions for him to distribute weapons throughout the western part of the country, as opposed to concentrating them in Havana, where Batista's police and military intelligence forces were most heavily concentrated. Once in the capital, it became clear to Domitro that the Cuban population might well support a popular reformist coup similar to that which had toppled the Venezuelan dictator Marcos Pérez Jimenez in January 1958. He thus pushed Latour to "launch the uprising in the next (two or three) months; and I am sure that the people will respond even though we have almost no weapons."[32]

The 26th of July Movement faced the overwhelming challenge of simultaneously gearing up for "total war" in Oriente, supporting new guerrilla columns in the Sierra Maestra, and intensifying urban action in the cities. In order to pin down the army on both tips of the island, the movement also decided to create a new guerrilla front in the province of Pinar del Río.[33] In early January 1958, the province's militia coordinator, Jesús Suárez Gayol, traveled to Mexico, where Pedro Miret helped him purchase a boat and several thousand dollars' worth of weapons.[34] Domitro shuttled between Pinar del Río and Havana recruiting new militia and preparing for the arrival and transport of men and arms from Suárez's "Operation Fishermen" to the Sierra del Rosario mountains.[35] By the middle of February 1958, he had written Latour that the militia in Pinar del Río had only fourteen rifles, no ammunition, and not one bullet from abroad.[36] Domitro began to fear that the climate of revolution was building and implored Latour to "send more people abroad to solve the problem of bringing in a minimum amount of equipment. I believe that events are about to overtake us and I hope we can actually get the basic materiél we've sought to obtain, because it is evil to prolong this situation that has cost so many lives."[37] Two days later, Latour sent Frank Fiorini, an M267 gun-runner and American ex-marine known as "García," to New York to help Hidalgo find weapons.[38] Still fuming over the "the huge failure" from Rodríguez's Miami operations, which had cost the movement $200,000, Latour did not hide his aggravation at spending even more money abroad. These were funds he felt the Committee in Exile could easily raise in the United States or Venezuela, rather than from Cuba itself, to "sustain the Organization in Cuba and above all the Sierra Front and others of recent creation." He reluctantly sent $20,000 to Pedro Miret in Mexico for another scheme known as "Operation Butterfly."[39] But Miret soon left his men and arms with Suárez Gayol in Mexico and headed for Costa Rica, where a more promising plan was in the works.

9 | The Golden Age of the *Llano*

FEBRUARY–MARCH 1958

> Every day sabotage is more intense, every day more young people, children killed. Today the Civic Resistance's protests against the assassination of the seventh grade boys in Santiago de Cuba are in the news. The demonstrations are widespread in every school, even the private ones. It must be that all these events make this meeting necessary. But analyzing other problems that have emerged in the National Directorate and the *sierra* I think it has been planned . . . for everyone to come and fix the bad impression they've brought with their arrival in the Sierra.
>
> Celia Sánchez, diary entry, March 4, 1958

BACK ON THE ISLAND, THE MILITIA carried out a series of rapid-fire attacks in the capital that appeared to intensify opposition to Batista and gave members of the National Directorate the impression that the Cuban population was ready to join a protracted general strike. In early February, "action and sabotage" teams commanded by militia commando Sergio González, or "El Curita," set fire to 400,000 gallons of jet fuel stored in Regla, outside of Havana, at the "Belot" oil refinery owned by New Jersey–based Esso Standard. The fire burned for over three days, forcing the oil company to form an air bridge and fly in chemicals from the United States to put it out.[1] Three weeks later, on February 24, the rebel army began short-wave broadcasts from Radio Rebelde, carrying the voice of the Sierra Maestra throughout Cuba. On the same day, Faustino Pérez, Oscar Lucero, a militia captain from the Oriente town of Holguín, Arnold Rodríguez, an advertising executive who also worked for the underground, and others staged a high-profile kidnapping of the Argentine race-car champion Fangio during a race along the Malecón, Havana's seaside drive. The abduction drew widespread press coverage in Cuba and abroad for the 26th of July, Fidel Castro, and the revolution. Obliging as the grateful hostage, Fangio referred to his captors as "my friends the kidnappers," telling Mexican journalist Manuel Camín that though he regretted not racing in the Gran Premio de Cuba, "if my capture can serve a good purpose, as an Argentine, I support it."[2] The U.S. embassy predicted that the "widespread publicity" in the United States, Europe, and Latin America "will probably cast the government in a bad light as incapable of maintaining order in its own house."[3]

For the *llano*'s leaders, the period initiated by the Fangio kidnapping marked the "golden age" of the urban insurrection, when the U.S. embassy reported that "rebels and terrorists continued to harass the Government from one end of the island to the other," rendering "the incidents . . . too many to attempt to catalogue."[4] Indeed, the goal of the underground's harassment campaign was to force the government to cancel the elections, again suspend the constitution, declare a state of emergency, increase repression by state security forces, and reimpose press censorship. Of course, the rebels took advantage of press liberties while they could for free publicity. For example, just two days after the kidnapping, in "another daring raid," El Curita's militia entered the central clearinghouse of the National Bank of Cuba, held employees at gunpoint, and set fire to the previous day's checks and bank drafts delivered from all over Havana—to demonstrate the inability of the Cuban state to manage the country's economic affairs.[5] In the same week, political prisoners in Havana's El Principe prison started a widely publicized hunger strike to protest the absence of habeus corpus and judicial norms.[6]

On the other end of the island in Oriente, Fidel Castro expanded his guerrillas' base of operations. He promoted Juan Almeida Bosque and his brother Raúl Castro Ruz to the rank of *comandante,* and formed two new columns under their command: Almeida's "Mario Muñoz" Column number three, located in the Sierra Maestra east of Santiago de Cuba, and Raúl Castro's "Frank País" Column number six, located in northeastern Oriente's Sierra Cristal, where Frank País, René Ramos Latour, Jorge Sotús, Taras Domitro, and thirty-eight other men had unsuccessfully tried to open a new front nearly one year earlier.[7] Instead of waiting for the Oriente militia under Latour's command to deal with the roving bands of unaffiliated armed men, Almeida immediately started to bring them under his command, weeding out the criminals among them, at times, through executions.[8] At the same time in Santiago, the murder by local police of two seventh-grade boys sparked an extended school boycott by high school and college students.[9] By the beginning of March 1958, students organized by the 26th of July and the Student Revolutionary Directorate (DRE), often with the collaboration of school administrators and teachers, had shut down virtually all of the public and private (including Catholic) primary and secondary schools, as well as colleges and universities, across the country.[10]

But even by enthusiastic standards of the revolutionaries, not every province in the country was ready for the final push to topple Batista. Pinar del Río, a tobacco-growing region known to be conservative, for example, had little revolutionary activity, despite the attempt to open a new guerrilla front there. Matanzas, on the other hand, a sugar- and textile-producing province, boasted an impressive history of labor activism aimed at the regime and the Confederation of Cuban Workers (CTC), as well as a wide antiregime underground that the M267 had gradually been able to become part of throughout the decade.[11] In the adjacent province of Las Villas, massive arrests of movement activists in the crackdown that followed the Cienfuegos mutiny forced the 26th of July to reorganize its underground network almost from scratch. After the shakeup of the National Directorate that followed Armando Hart's arrest, Enrique Oltuski was given a transfer from his employer, Shell Oil, and relocated to his home town of Santa Clara, the provincial capital, to become the M267 coordinator for the province.[12]

Las Villas, located in the center of the island, presented an extremely complicated challenge to the 26th of July. By February 1958, three separate guerrilla groups were operating in the Sierra del Escambray mountains: one under the command of 26th of July captain Victor Bordón outside of Sagua la Grande, another under the command of Organización Auténtica (OA) militant Eloy Gutierrez Menoyo outside the colonial city of Trinidad, near Cienfuegos, and a third in the same area under the command of Faure Chomón Mediavilla. Menoyo began operating in the Cienfuegos-Trinidad area in November 1957. After the Cuban Liberation Junta debacle, Chomón led an expedition from Miami that landed in the province in early February, ready to join forces with Menoyo. By the end of the month, however, the two forces had split, accusing one another of banditry and double-crossing.[13] From a military and political perspective, having the center of the island contested by three rival factions heightened the vulnerability of the insurgent forces as a whole as they prepared to take on the Cuban army directly. Moreover, with Las Villas several hundred miles closer to Havana than Oriente, even if the 26th of July were eventually to control and even establish a provisional government on the eastern end of the island, it would still have to race against the DRE and the OA to reach Havana were Batista to fall.

When Oltuski first arrived in Santa Clara, he found little more than a bare-bones version of the underground structure that País and Hart had attempted to erect. Only the local militia under what he described as Latour's "praiseworthy" direction was in shape, having carried out assassinations and the sabotage of cane fields and sugar mills. Expanding his command further, Latour had even managed to place under his direct orders the movement's local guerrilla column commanded by Victor Bordón. Oltuski began to rebuild the underground first by recruiting individuals to raise money and distribute propaganda. But quite beyond his control was the disappointing news that David Salvador, who had been working as the movement's coordinator for the National Workers Front (FON) since the fall of 1957, had yet to appoint a deputy there. Oltuski believed that conditions in the province left "a lot to be desired" and that his region had "a long way to go before it is ready for the definitive action."[14]

In Havana and Matanzas, however, the FON and other dissident labor activists were making enough noise to force the CTC to hold an extraordinary session of its national council, where "the most important question" on the agenda, reported the U.S. embassy, was "the tactics to be used in counteracting renewed and intensified efforts of revolutionary elements to bring about a general political strike."[15] Warning that the CTC's Eusebio Mujal's "days are numbered," *Bohemia,* during a rare break in censorship, reported that workers around the country had inundated the magazine with letters repudiating the repressive tactics of the CTC and revealing their membership in the FON.[16] Indeed, "persistent rumors of an impending general strike" had forced general secretary Mujal to seek renewed support from the 240-member national council for the CTC's long-standing opposition to politically motivated strikes. Compared to the state of affairs in Las Villas, the American labor attaché reported that in Havana, where "workers [are] dissatisfied both with Mujal's leadership and with the Batista regime," the FON posed a credible threat to the CTC. The official reported that during "the abortive attempt at a general strike on August 5, 1957," the electrical plant workers, telephone workers, bank employees, and several bus lines went on strike. The FON was again rallying these groups and some members of the traditionally conservative Catholic Youth Workers, or Juventud Obrera Católica. By convening an emergency session of the national council, the CTC leadership had exposed its anxiety about its ability to enforce discipline and unity against strikes and other anti-regime political activity.[17]

Indeed, Mujal was rumored to have acknowledged privately to Batista and to U.S. embassy sources his "difficulty in maintaining discipline over the workers" and concerns about being able to prevent Cuban labor from joining a general strike.[18] As David Salvador had predicted, underground sabotage of the railroads in Camagüey and Oriente had already forced the government to discontinue evening service, prompting laid-off workers to defy the CTC and go on strike. By the first of April, Batista had issued a "decree-law" announcing that "workers who fail to show up for work will lose jobs and all rights" and that "employers who interrupt or suspend activities in their establishments" would be sentenced to thirty days to six months in jail.[19] Full-page ads such as those published in the conservative *Diario de la Marina* warned that "mistaken and cowardly" CTC members who "failed to go to work" in the event of a "abnormal and counterrevolutionary" general strike "will lose their jobs" and the CTC's benefits.[20] The effectiveness of this and other such government measures would soon be evident.

From the perspective of the revolutionaries, an expanded rebel army in the mountains, successful sabotage in the plains, and growing support from Cuban labor meant an ever more favorable climate of insurrection and seemed to portend Batista's imminent collapse. Thus it was incongruous at best when the *New York Times* published an article by Homer Bigart at the end of February reporting that Fidel Castro had agreed to participate in the government's peace initiative, which had been drafted by Batista in January when he restored constitutional guarantees. Bigart also reported that in exchange for the withdrawal of the Cuban army from Oriente province, Castro would support an OAS-sponsored election and back a presidential candidate other than Judge Manuel Urrutia Lleó, the movement's candidate of choice.[21]

Adding to the public clamor for peace, Cuba's two archbishops and five bishops published an appeal directed at "all those making war in antagonistic camps" to drop their weapons and for Batista to establish a "government of national unity."[22] Four opposition parties in addition to several private groups, including the Civic Institutions, Catholic Action, Catholic Youth, and the Society of Friends of the Republic—which earlier in the decade had tried to mediate a solution to Cuba's political crisis—publicly supported the appeal. Anti-Batista politicians and pundits such as José Pardo Llada and columnist Luis Conte Agüero chimed in with their support for peace talks. And most of Batista's cabinet resigned, not in protest of the regime, but to run in the June elections.[23] Batista responded to the peace initiative by creating a short-lived Harmony Commission of church and government officials to consider the Catholic hierarchy's proposal.[24]

In light of the underground's escalation of the conflict and increased popular mobilization around the country, Fidel Castro's apparent will-

FEBRUARY–MARCH 1958 | 109

ingness to join the public momentum and participate in a peace process represented a formidable challenge to the M267's strike plans, prompting questions about whether Fidel had made a "fundamental change in the Movement's strategy" without consulting the organization's leadership.[25] If so, the new stance directly challenged the focus of activities in the underground, where the revolutionaries were attempting to completely halt all momentum toward elections. The public demands for peace and Castro's apparent readiness to end the civil war had created an urgent "demand for a radical and transcendental statement by" the 26th of July Movement and clarity from the commander in chief of the rebel army.[26] Thus in early March nearly the entire membership of the National Directorate, René Ramos Latour, Marcelo Fernández, Haydée Santamaría, Faustino Pérez, Manuel Ray (secretary general of the Civic Resistance Movement), David Salvador, and Vilma Espín, headed for the rebel army's base at Santo Domingo in the Sierra Maestra.

Fidel and his closest comrades had some idea of why the National Directorate was bringing so many of its members from around the island to the mountains for a meeting with their *sierra* comrades. Writing in her diary, Celia Sánchez anticipated that their agenda would include the brewing internal tensions that continued to burden the 26th of July:

> What a surprise! . . . I tell Fidel that this meeting with representatives from the Labor Movement and Civic Resistance strikes me as reaching definitive plans. That's what the mood is they're bringing from [the] Batista [regime] . . . They have always regarded the struggle here as something symbolic of our Revolution and not as a decisive factor of this war; that's the root of our disagreements. I'm only sorry that Raúl won't be at the meeting—he's wanted one so much.[27]

Castro, Sánchez, and their underground comrades met for four days without Raúl Castro, Juan Almeida Bosque, or Che Guevara, whom they had stopped to see at Guevara's base in El Hombrito outside of Bayamo, where he commanded column four of the rebel army. According to Marcelo Fernández's subsequent report, Fidel defended his comments to the *New York Times* as a tactical gesture meant to demonstrate that despite harmony commissions and promises of free elections, the dictator was not genuinely committed to a peaceful resolution of the crisis. Fernández reported to the movement's militants that Fidel had indeed acknowledged, "and the other members of the National Directorate also believe[d]," that "it was an error to make such a proposal at the moment he did it, given that the radicalization of the citizenry invalidated any even apparently pacifist proposal."[28] Indeed, the Central Intelligence

Agency, which had managed to station one of its informants—possibly a foreign journalist—with the rebels in the Sierra Maestra at the same time, reported that "Castro hoped to achieve his purpose of forcing Batista to abdicate through a campaign of intensified terrorism in Oriente Province and a nationwide general strike. This was scheduled to begin in early April 1958, inasmuch as Castro's plan called for the collapse of the Batista regime by 12 April. Castro declared that he would not negotiate an agreement with Batista."[29]

Quashing any lingering doubt that the 26th of July would even flirt tactically with peace talks, Latour wrote Hidalgo in Miami that after "long and often heated arguments," the revolutionaries had agreed "by unanimous vote" that Fidel would publicly reject the Catholic Church's peace offer and any proposals by Batista's Harmony Commission, and would issue a public call for a national general strike. As a result of this newly reinforced consensus, the movement was now "at the height of current circumstances in accord with the radical attitude that the Cuban people now display—circumstances that allow no other strategy than the Revolutionary General Strike and Armed Insurrection." Fidel may well have harbored doubts about the strategy of a general strike, but to the National Directorate members, the meeting had produced "absolute integration between *sierra* and *llano* and we were able, in the end, to bring to the minds of those who have remained in the hills for over one year . . . the importance of the struggle in the *llano,* the need to arm and strengthen the militias. In the end we got Alex [Fidel] to change his opinion entirely."[30] Latour's enthusiastic report was not that of an overzealous commander looking for a consensus that did not actually exist. Faustino Pérez later confirmed that Fidel had given his blessing to the *llano* to initiate the national strike in a matter of weeks from the meeting: "We all agreed that the degree of organization we had reached and the climate in the country suggested the moment had come to unleash the final outcome, the general strike."[31]

As a result of the *sierra* meeting held on March 12, 1958, the 26th of July publicized the "Manifesto of Twenty-One Points, a plan for 'Total War against Tyranny.'" Signed by Fidel Castro and Faustino Pérez, the new manifesto articulated the "total war" strategy that Armando Hart and René Ramos Latour had been advocating since January, signaling to the regime and the public that the 26th of July intended to initiate a nationwide general strike after the first of April. "Due to the visible disintegration of the dictatorship, the growth of the national consciousness, and the belligerent participation of all social, political, cultural, and religious sectors of the country, the struggle against Batista has entered its final stage," they wrote. The call to arms reiterated the movement's selection of Judge Urrutia as president and announced, "The strategy of the final blow is based on the general revolutionary strike, to be seconded by military action" by the rebel army.[32] The American embassy described the manifesto as "the most confident and combative statement which Castro has issued to date," correctly noting that it "was drafted with an eye to creating the impression that the 26 of July Movement has a great reservoir of strength which is awaiting only to be triggered into action."[33] Castro's statement rejecting both the Catholic Church's call for a government of national unity and the Batista Harmony Commission, reported the embassy, was a "blow" that "resulted in the collapse" and "dissolution" of the peace process—thereby fulfilling the objective of the urban underground since the restoration of constitutional guarantees three months earlier.[34]

A cascade of developments favorable to the opposition followed the new manifesto's publication. The document also called upon the Cuban judiciary to denounce the regime's obstruction of the judicial process. Shortly after its release, a group of eleven federal judges in Havana did just that, and shortly fled to exile or underground, among them Enrique Hart Ramírez, father of Armando Hart Dávalos, then in jail, and Enrique Hart Dávalos, an M267 underground organizer in Matanzas. Marcelo Fernández credited the movement with having emboldened the judges to come out publicly against the regime and later paid a visit to several Santiago judges to encourage them to follow suit.[35] At the same time, a particularly brave Havana superior court judge indicted the notoriously sadistic police chief Major Esteban Ventura Novo and Navy Lieutenant Julio Laurent Rodríguez of the Naval Intelligence Service, linking them with the torture and murder of prisoners taken during the naval mutiny in Cienfuegos.[36]

The next day, Batista handed the 26th of July a major victory by suspending constitutional guarantees and reimposing censorship. On the same day, the Communist Party (PSP) reversed its earlier support for peaceful elections and published in *Carta Semanal* a statement of support for guerrilla war and the general strike. The PSP vowed to organize strike committees across the country, calling the next day for a "patriotic united front" to overthrow Batista in a general strike.[37] On March 14, the United States suspended weapons sales and shipments to the regime.[38] On March 15, the Civic Institutions, representing 200,000 Cubans in forty-six organizations, at last took the step that Armando Hart had been unable to persuade them to take earlier by calling publicly for Fulgencio Batista to resign and hand power to a provisional government.[39] The night of March 16 became known as the "Night of One Hundred Bombs" because the Havana militia exploded close to that many across the city, from Old Havana to the commercial district of Vedado.[40] By the middle of the month, the National Student Front (FEN) had orchestrated a complete shutdown of schools across the country. Delivering another victory to the insurgents, Batista canceled the June elections.[41]

By the end of the month the National Association of Mill Owners and Cane Growers (*Hacendados* and *Colonos*) withdrew their support from the dictator, whose forces had been unable to protect sugar refineries and cane fields from the militia's sabotage. Indeed, throughout February and early March of 1958, the U.S. embassy reported that the revolutionaries continued "unabated" arson, bombing, assassination attempts, and the targeting of public transportation, schools, sugar and tobacco warehouses and crops, oil refineries, police and military officers, and CTC officials, noting that "sources within the revolutionary opposition are talking aggressively of growing power in the cities and among labor and predict that a general strike, accompanied by violence, will take place within the next few weeks."[42]

By setting for themselves a deadline of April 1 to initiate the final stage of the insurrection, the 26th of July had set in motion the militarization of the strike. There was simply no time for more protracted organizing. Almost as an aside, the movement's activists were instructed to build more workplace strike committees, appoint a national labor council, and publish slogans voicing "proletarian demands," all with the goal of placing the National Workers Front at the center of the struggle.[43] But the National Directorate's reports and instructions to the movement's militants unambiguously show that "action and sabotage" teams were to lead the uprising by "unleashing total war in the province of Oriente," "opening war fronts" in Las Villas and Pinar del Río, "perfecting the organization" of urban militias, and "opening up armed action patrols in every province, thereby provoking a state of national war."[44]

Whereas during the August 1957 strike attempt the 26th of July had lacked "sufficient citizen organization," by March 1958 the movement's top leaders believed success was at hand. Marcelo Fernández wrote to organizers around the country that their challenge included the tall order of "maintaining sabotage and armed action, to weaken the regime militarily; intensifying labor organizing nationally, to weaken the regime through trade unions; creating conditions for the resignation of judicial and executive branch officials, to weaken the regime institutionally; and undertaking measures such as blocking transportation, tax evasion, asking the Civic Institutions to call for Batista's resignation, etcetera, to weaken the regime psychologically and give it the final blow." Finally, wrote Fernández, though "we still lack some part of the necessary military supplies," with enough weapons, "the month of April" would be "decisive for the Revolution."[45]

10 | The Arms Race

MARCH–APRIL 1958

> The people, workers and owners, are still desperate to take an active part in the final battle against the dictatorship. The militias in every province, though lacking all the necessary military equipment, maintain an unbreakable and necessary decisiveness and are ready for the final battle unaware of their inferiority in arms, and they think that their high morale will arm their efforts, confiding also in the strength of the people.
>
> René Ramos Latour to Juan Almeida Bosque,
> March 27, 1958

FIDEL'S EXPLICIT AND PUBLIC CONSENT for a general strike, as well as the expansion of the militia from Oriente to the island's strategic midpoint of Las Villas and beyond to the far western province of Pinar del Río, allowed René Ramos Latour to intensify the drive to equip the militia and guerrillas for the final push against Fulgencio Batista. Indeed, across the country there were growing, visible signs of rebellion and repression. In Oriente province insurrection was in the air, not only in the Sierra Maestra and outlying towns but also in the provincial capital, Santiago, where the army posted armed patrols on downtown rooftops and regularly paraded its tanks through the streets. Over a thousand miles away, clear across the country, Latour believed that by unleashing "total war in Pinar del Río . . . we will be creating another Oriente there."[1] He tried to convince his deputies around the country that even with far fewer weapons and explosives than they had hoped for, a strategy of "total war" would "pin down the army at both extremes of the island, and squeeze the rest of the island into submission, including Havana."[2]

By its own estimates, the 26th of July would have to bring sufficient materiél from abroad to equip three hundred militia members in Pinar del Río, as many as three thousand in Havana, some 150 each in Las Villas and Camagüey, two hundred in Santiago de Cuba, another three hundred in the Sierra Cristal, as well as an estimated three hundred men then under the command of Fidel Castro, Raúl Castro, and Juan Almeida.[3] Latour worried about whether the underground could control the growing crescendo of popular insurrection long enough to smuggle in sufficient weapons for all of these combatants. He confided to the *comandantes* in the rebel army that with sabotage, forced layoffs, student boycotts, and more repression, the movement was "running the risk that some event—a murder, a demonstration, a sabotage—will be the spark that sets fire to the island and makes the strike unfold" before they were ready.[4]

The underground would have to contain an "anxious population" in order to "bring in the minimum amount of weapons and organize the armed insurrection to support the strike." Otherwise, Latour wrote to Juan Almeida, the regime would "drown the strike and insurrection movement in a bloodbath."[5] Yet having succeeded in convincing his comrades to adopt his militia-driven insurrection plan despite its obvious vulnerabilities, Latour committed the militia to a direct confrontation with the regime, weapons or not. He believed that Havana would take the brunt of the regime's repression because it was the capital, the symbol of the Batista regime's control over the country and home to the highest concentration of state security forces. But he had concluded with his closest collaborators in Oriente that there was little chance the organization could sustain a protracted uprising. In his view, Havana already harbored more weapons than the rest of the country and would have access to more from abroad, especially after the first of April, when the militia would shut down train and highway routes to the eastern provinces. Thus, he concentrated on getting arms to Raúl Castro and Juan Almeida in Oriente, the new militia in Pinar del Río, and the urban militia in Havana, in that order of priority. He instructed his Miami agent Alonso Hidalgo to first send a major air delivery to Raúl Castro in Oriente's Sierra Cristal by March 30.[6] Despite a certain bravado in his correspondence, Latour was not at all convinced he could accomplish such ambitious goals in so little time. After nearly three months in Florida, "Bebo" Hidalgo had sent back little more than a few pistols, leaving Latour with the excruciating realization that "with the materiél we've received we can't sustain [the strike] even for half an hour."[7] Once a passionate advocate of an urban strategy, Latour was beginning to shift his horizon to the hills, as it became clear that the movement would be unable to initiate a general strike according to the calendar agreed upon between *sierra* and *llano* when they had last met.

By the end of March 1958 only one shipment of weapons—unrelated to the National Directorate's initiatives—had reached the island from Costa Rica. Earlier that month the spouse of a Camagüey rice farmer exiled in Costa Rica, Huber Matos, had notified Fidel that her husband was putting together a shipment of weapons from Costa Rica, with the aid of President José Figueres. On a plane piloted by Pedro Luis Díaz Lanz, Pedro Miret arrived in the Sierra Maestra on March 30 with "fifty-something weapons and some 100,000 shots," concluding an odyssey from Cuba to Mexico to Costa Rica and back to the island.[8] Miret had left another stash of weapons and some twenty-five men back in Mexico waiting for a militia captain, Jesús Suárez Gayol, to bring them to Pinar del Río to open the front in the Sierra de los Organos. But by the end of March, nothing but a trickle of pistols had arrived in the western provinces. Even if the delivery from Costa Rica had contained the massive amounts that Figueres later reported, the rebels would have had no way of transporting them out of the Sierra to distribute to militia around the country, especially those as far away as Havana or Pinar del Río. Taras Domitro begged Latour to postpone the strike because of the lack of arms.[9] With just days to go before the M267 would officially call the national strike, Miret's delivery was more significant than anything that had come from Miami.

Fearing that the volatile climate on the ground would soon moderate, the National Directorate met in Santiago at the end of the month to decide on a firm date for the strike to begin. Their debate split along geographic lines. The Santiago-based cadre, Latour and Fernández, insisted on waiting for more weapons from abroad before calling the strike. The Havana-based cadre, led by Faustino Pérez, insisted the strike begin on March 31 lest they risk weakening the capital's revolutionary fervor and expose the city's militia to more devastating police crackdowns.[10] Indeed, unlike Latour, Pérez felt passionately that Havana was the key to Batista's collapse. After one of their periodic meetings, the New York Times reporter Herbert Matthews, who weighed in with the State Department in support of the rebels, wrote that in Pérez's view, "Miami no longer counts; not even Oriente or Pinar. It is recognized on all sides that the decision will be in Havana and that the decisive moment is approaching . . . Oriente's function and [that of] the other provinces is to keep up their activities so as to pin down troops and permit seizure of the entire island at once, but the key is Havana."[11] Pérez sent a colleague from the Civic Resistance Movement to Santiago to state his case:

This thing is losing its intensity with every day that goes by and the repressive apparatus adjusts and perfects its operations. If we wait beyond the fifth [of April] for something big to happen, things will cool down here again. Triumph is a process wherein the people are the principal factor; it can't be conditioned by "hierros" alone, rather by the sum of all concurrent factors, and there is no doubt that in the success we've had to date arms have not been the decisive factor. To sum up, I believe it is a mistake to further delay our final decision . . . Everyone is asking why we didn't call the strike in the last few days . . . Delaying it again would be foolish.[12]

Taras Domitro, the other Havana voice to weigh in at this crucial moment, vacillated between wanting to call the strike immediately and believing it worthwhile to wait for weapons. By the end of March, police had killed at least four of the Havana militia's top captains. Holding out longer would endanger the lives of more activists. "Any equipment that may reach us," Domitro wrote, "won't compensate for what we're losing by delaying the date." Two days later, Domitro changed his tune, declaring that he was prepared to hold off the strike even if it risked allowing Batista "to break us down little by little."[13] But in the end, the Havana- and Oriente-based members of the National Directorate chose, reluctantly, to delay the strike until more weapons arrived from abroad.

By April 1, the militia had successfully halted transportation along the central highway between Oriente and Camagüey by placing its patrols along the road. The action paralyzed some economic activity, but it also reduced the chances that any weapons entering the country east of Camagüey would make it to the capital by ground transport.[14] Still, holding off the strike initially appeared to be the judicious decision because Latour's weapons dealers in Miami finally had put together two separate shipments, one for Oriente and the other for Pinar del Río.

The Oriente delivery was earmarked for Raúl Castro, whose militia patrols in the Sierra Cristal planned to surround and lay siege to five small towns on the day of the strike.[15] His men cleared a landing strip to prepare for the plane's arrival. But in Miami, "Bebo" Hidalgo had only one pilot available to make the trip because the pilot with most knowledge of the area, Pedro Díaz Lanz, was still in the Sierra Maestra after making the trip with Pedro Miret from Costa Rica. The remaining pilot, Frank Fiorini ("García"), made the flight despite insisting that he was unfamiliar with the terrain around the Sierra Cristal.[16] But by the time Hidalgo and García were ready to move the equipment out of Florida, the army had discovered the airstrip. Raúl's men prepared a second strip. Days passed with no delivery. Where was the plane? At first, Latour, Taras Domitro, and Raúl Castro thought Fiorini had landed in Fidel's zone of operations. If so, they assumed Fidel would distribute the weapons in Oriente.[17] But if instead the plane had been diverted to Pinar del Río, Domitro wrote Fidel that given the "scarcity here especially of light arms, automatics, and machine guns," he would keep whatever arrived with the new delivery in the western provinces, where arms were scarce. No one in Cuba ever laid eyes on the weapons. After one week, Latour sent word to Raúl that he "deeply apologized" but had "lost all hope" that

Fiorini would get to the airstrip.[18] The Cuban air force and navy's surveillance of both the north coast of Oriente and the coasts off of Pinar del Río had twice forced Fiorini back to Miami, foiling the movement's plans to pin down the army on both ends of the island.[19]

Prospects for the strike were dim in Pinar del Río. Police had arrested the movement's coordinator there five days before the strike. The last vestiges of hope lay with the Suarez Gayol expedition from Mexico and a final delivery from Miami to equip the militia in the province's fifteen counties. Four days before the strike, Suarez Gayol departed from Mexico on the *Corojo* carrying twelve men, the infamous seventy-four Czech rifles that Léster Rodríguez had purchased nearly one year earlier, two thousand pounds of dynamite, 45,000 bullets, thirty-one pistols, four machine guns, and one anti-tank rifle. The rebels landed on the southern coast of Pinar del Río the day before the strike.[20] A separate guerrilla column commanded by the obscure figure Juan Palacios had already begun operations in another region of the province, the Sierra del Rosario. Movement activists in Pinar del Río believed that Fidel had sent Palacios because of his reputation for "noble intentions in favor of the cause," prompting Domitro to divide the *Corojo* materiél equally between Suarez Gayol, Palacios, and the provincial militia.[21] But his evenhandedness was to no avail. Suarez and his men were quickly stranded without guides or packhorses on their way to the Sierra de los Organos; they were forced to bury their weapons and split up into two groups to avoid discovery by the army. Five of the twelve men deserted and the army soon uncovered the hidden arms. The remaining seven men reached the Sierra, where they remained until the end of April before abandoning the venture. The Palacios column in the Sierra del Rosario eventually totaled some sixty armed men but the Cuban air force bombed the column out of existence in late April 1958.[22]

With the Oriente and Pinar del Río prospects clear, it was Havana, where the "climate had transformed into a climax," that appeared to hold out some prospect for success.[23] One week after the originally agreed upon strike date, the National Strike Committee moved the date to April 9. Domitro took advantage of the extra time to send one of the capital's militia captains on a separate weapons mission to Miami. But three state and federal raids soon quashed any remaining hope for the rebels. In New York, police arrested some of the movement's "best weapons merchants" just as they were about to deliver to Havana thirty-three machine guns and ten automatic rifles. In Miami, police seized a thousand hand grenades and thousands of dollars' worth of explosives. Finally, the U.S. Coast Guard seized a boat headed for Havana containing 250 pistols, 16 rifles, 35 Italian carbines, 45 machine guns, some 40,000 bullets,

1,900 feet of explosive fuse, four rolls of electrical cable, 59 pounds of TNT, and 1,500 detonators. The interdiction of this boat spelled disaster for the Havana underground.[24]

One of the most outwardly expressive of the underground's leaders, Taras Domitro, reproached himself as a "failure," lacking in "revolutionary qualities," and in letters to both Latour and Fidel despaired of the "cruel blow" dealt to the movement by these last-minute disasters.[25] Not so Marcelo Fernández or Faustino Pérez. Neither openly expressed such a bleak prognosis for the insurrection. "In the capital," Fernández wrote to Fidel, "the climate for the strike could not be better. The news reaching us from the other provinces is very encouraging . . . as you will see, the situation looks very good for the cause."[26] Despite the lack of arms, Faustino Pérez insisted that favorable conditions overall would soon bring victory for the revolution:

> I am working incessantly, at the vortex of a whirlwind. Everything is moving forward toward the final moment, though with an infinite number of problems. Also, the situation here is tense, with everything turning on the expectation of something that at the moment appears imminent. Each sector is showing its readiness to support or favor the strike, in greater or lesser degree. Workers look okay, the Institutions already came out, as you know, with the document demanding the tyrant's resignation and they've complemented it especially with organization and preparations in the professional schools for the strike. We've had to slow down the press and journalists and the graphic arts workers. The Mill Owners and Cane Growers want contact and are showing a positive attitude toward paralyzing sugar processing . . . The upper classes are beginning to panic, and today formed long lines at the banks, because people are withdrawing their money . . . a result of a Civic Resistance campaign of telephone calls . . . In terms of equipment, we've received some in small quantities recently and they've hit us very hard in the United States . . . Despite all of this, with the sum of all of these factors I think we can carry out the battle for Victory. The regime knows it is about to play its last card and is using all of its resources to repress with barbaric methods. They refuse to acknowledge they have lost.[27]

Considering the underground's failure to equip the nascent militia and guerrilla group in Pinar del Río, Raúl's column in Oriente, or the Havana militia, on the day of the strike the 26th of July risked virtually all of its resources but refused to acknowledge the extremely limited prospects for success. The stakes at this moment were enormously high for the National Directorate, the movement, and the entire country. To complement and compensate for the military component of their plans, the underground leadership attempted to overcome its distaste for "unity" and reach out to other revolutionary groups for help with the national strike.

11 Politics and Popular Insurrection

MARCH–APRIL 1958

> In no way can one underestimate mass struggle, and it is the most important . . . but one must not forget the presence of the guerrilla movement, which can bring to an end such an action. The fundamental issue is not tactical difference but rather the intention of the tactics, and this is proposed as a means to be able to put a break on the masses when they choose, and it will probably be when the Embassy wants, and we must fight against this with all of our strength to avoid it. I don't think Fidel's last manifesto clarifies every point, but it does fix a bit the worker problem, the one that frightens me most of all.
>
> Ernesto "Che" Guevara to Calixto García, March 30, 1958

THOUGH THE REVOLUTIONARIES OFTEN used the word "huelga" or strike to refer to their plans for urban insurrection, they did not intend the term to refer only to labor-driven work stoppages. Rather, like their predecessors in Joven Cuba and the ABC of the 1930s, the urban underground—especially once Latour took over the militia—believed that by orchestrating a crescendo of walkouts, industrial and agricultural sabotage, violence, selective assassinations of government figures, attacks against symbols of the regime, and generalized mayhem, they would expose the Batista regime's inability to maintain public and economic order, destabilizing it sufficiently to drive the dictator out of power.

Among the differences between the ABC and the M267, however, was that with the exception of its Student Left Wing faction (and the student revolutionaries at the time), the ABC approved of and assisted Sumner Welles's efforts to mediate a solution to the standoff between the opposition in Cuba in 1933 and the dictator, Gerardo Machado.[1] The 26th of July certainly factored in how the American government would interpret their insurgent activities. But despite suspicions to the contrary, the movement had no intention of pursuing urban insurrection in order to provoke American involvement in the Cuban crisis; instead, its members sought to demonstrate to Washington and of course to the Cuban public that Batista could not govern the country. Moreover, in the 1930s there had been widespread participation in opposition strikes—by sugar, transportation, and tobacco workers, whereas in the 1950s—at least after the sugar strike of 1955, which involved 500,000 or more workers—massive labor mobilization was simply unknown until January 1959.[2] Indeed, a debate continued throughout the insurgency within the M267 over whether workers would be more likely to strike as a way of making economic demands or as a way of demonstrating their opposition to the regime. Eusebio Mujal's banning of political strikes, backed by the threat that those participating in them would be fired, was a significant deterrent to unionized workers who openly opposed the regime and wished to express that sentiment by walking off the job. But economic strikes were problematic as well. With the exceptions of its Oriente and Matanzas branches, where grassroots, worker-based antiregime activity existed well before the M267 became a national organization, the 26th of July did not have the capacity or experience to organize workers into economic strikes.[3]

One of the reasons that the insurgents' definition of "strike" began to be supplanted by the more comprehensive "total war" strategy was the National Directorate's awareness of these constraints and of difficulties with both the Communist Party (PSP) and Confederation of Cuban Workers (CTC): the M267 simply did not have a large enough labor base to stage a worker-driven national shutdown and came to believe that violence and sabotage carried out by the militia was the only way to spark a national uprising. Still, economic conditions in the country between 1956 and 1958 certainly contributed to the growing discontent, and by later in 1958, to the mobilization of the *clases populares*. In 1957, real national income grew at a rate of 6.46 percent. But in the 1957–1958 period, the same indicator declined by 6.3 percent.[4] The combined total of unemployment and underemployment as a portion of the labor force was always high, due in part to the long dead season of the sugar harvest, which each year left some 400,000 sugar workers unemployed for several months per year. In 1956–1957, total unemployment reached 30.2 percent, in 1957 the figure stayed somewhat constant at 20.2 percent, and in 1958, the level was 19.0 percent.[5]

By the end of 1958, declining real wages began to hit the middle and industrial working classes—concrete evidence of the Batista regime's weakness and certainly one element that contributed to the explosion of popular opposition toward the end of the year.[6] Nevertheless, the anti-Batista opposition movement, which included a very broad cross-section of Cubans, was driven less by an interest in redressing poor economic conditions—something of a subtext in the debate at the time—than by a desire for a reformist, nationalist agenda that, despite the progressive character of the 1940 constitution, had eluded the country since the repeal of the Platt amendment in 1934. The urban underground was gambling that widespread but carefully targeted sabotage, as well as massive work stoppages by organized labor, would spark a successful nationwide strike. With weapons deliveries from abroad nowhere near adequate, the movement also pursued a parallel track to secure the amount of matériel and human capital necessary for the strike. For this, the 26th of July turned to rival opposition groups, the Student Revolutionary Directorate (DRE) and the Communists (PSP). Negotiations with the DRE promised to yield desperately needed weapons for the Havana militia's sabotage campaign. And fruitful talks with the PSP offered the prospect of the two organizations merging their separately formed strike committees to bring to the streets large numbers of politically significant workers as well as other party members from the arts, professional organizations, and the university. But in the wake of the movement's withdrawal from the Cuban Liberation Junta, Faustino Pérez, who led the talks with the DRE and PSP, was in no mood to share control and decision-making power with either of the organizations. For Pérez, as for others within the ranks of the National Directorate, the long-heralded but elusive ideal of unity had come to mean that the 26th of July should aspire to hegemony over rather than consensus within the opposition.

After the failed naval mutiny in Cienfuegos in September 1957, the M267 abandoned hope that a "putsch," or armed action, without mass struggle and in particular without a concerted effort to incorporate the industrial and agricultural working class into the anti-Batista movement, would alone bring down the dictatorship. The movement thus recruited David Salvador, a seasoned insider from the Cuban labor movement who, as a former Communist and Ortodoxo party member, appeared to be in tune with Cuban workers and able to exploit the vulnerabilities of organized labor under Eusebio Mujal's pro-government leadership. And the movement was correct in its assessment of the importance of organizing workers. While the PSP still controlled the CTC, not only were the demands of the labor movement less ambitious than after 1947 when the Auténticos had taken control, but more importantly, the Auténticos had diluted the authority of the CTC through their own corruption and polarization of labor politics. The 26th of July, on its own, had made only limited inroads with labor and was from the PSP's perspective ill-equipped to represent unionized workers under a new regime.[7] But with

Salvador's help, the M267 created the National Workers Front (FON) to build Cuban worker participation in a general strike.[8]

By the middle of the 1950s Cuba boasted a workforce of 2 million people and 1,641 unions represented by thirty-three federations, all of which had been amassed under the CTC and presided over by Mujal since the Communists were purged under Lazaro Peña in 1947. By 1952, the CTC still retained some autonomy from the government, and indeed organized a general strike in March of that year to protest Batista's coup against President Carlos Prío. But Mujal called off the strike shortly after cutting a deal with Batista: in exchange for benefits to organized labor, the CTC would no longer protest the new government.

Cuba's 1940 constitution, among Latin America's most progressive at the time, guaranteed benefits for disability, old age, and unemployment, as well as other protections. By 1956 the Batista regime's ministry of labor had issued various decrees and rules covering dismissal procedures; wages and salary protections; working conditions such as hours, holidays, sick leaves, and vacation; maternity benefits; workmen's compensation; and social security. But again, the workers paid a steep price for these benefits and protections: a confederation-wide ban on strikes and work stoppages.[9] According to one report, by 1954 over half—or more than one million—of the Cuban labor force were members of unions that belonged to the CTC.[10] Throughout the decade, government interventions, often backed by the army and police, rather than collective bargaining, were the primary mechanism for dispute resolution between labor and management in industries where organized labor was present, such as sugar, textiles, sisal, manufacturing, transportation, communications, electric power, hotel and restaurant operations, and banking.[11] Unions were weak or nonexistent in small businesses, coffee and tobacco farming, cattle ranches, and small farms. And as historian Hugh Thomas wrote, "driving around in ducktailed Cadillacs, the labour leaders, many of whom were involved in the graft and gangsterism associated with all pre-Revolutionary politics, made a deplorable impression on nearly all sections of society, particularly on the often nearly starving unemployed for whom they were supposed to be responsible."[12] In addition to high unemployment during this period, some 15 percent of the Cuban labor force was underemployed.[13]

Despite the ban on strikes and the CTC's strength in Havana, home to most of the country's industrial workers, breakaway unions in outlying provinces such as Matanzas defied the *mujalista* no-strike order throughout the decade. Some labor leaders, like Conrado Becquer from the sugar industry and José María de la Aguilera from banking, joined the FON and the 26th of July as much out of ideological sympathy with the goals of the movement as disgust with the CTC and the PSP.[14] Other trades—for example, the electrical workers—defied the no-strike ban to protest Mujal's expulsion of Angel Cofiño from the CTC executive council. Cofiño was president of the electrical workers union and also a former Communist.

Despite the PSP's illegal status, the Communists could still draw upon a significant number of militants working in ports, transportation, manufacturing, and the sugar industry. Estimates vary on the number of party members. In 1951, according to one account, the party, which had already lost control of the CTC, had some fifty thousand members. By 1958, membership had declined to a still strong eight to twelve thousand, according to a CIA intelligence report. Indeed, for most of the 1930s and until 1949, the Communists, who officially adopted the name PSP that year, controlled the dominant labor federations in Cuba, first the National Confederation of Cuban Workers (CNOC), and then the re-named Confederation of Cuban Workers (CTC). The PSP worked in the Congress and with Batista-dominated, nominally civilian presidencies between 1934 and 1940, with the Batista presidency of 1940–1944, and with the Grau presidency in the early years of his 1944–1948 term to guarantee a variety of worker rights related to compensation, collective bargaining, pensions, and benefits.[15] By 1942, the height of Communist political participation in Cuban public policy, Batista had granted cabinet appointments to Juan Marinello, president of the Communist Party, and Carlos Rafael Rodríguez, a young economist and Communist leader.[16] Though many Communist union officials switched to the Aútentico Party in 1947, when, under then minister of labor Carlos Prío the party lost control of the CTC, and even more dropped out after the party was banned two years later, the Communists still boasted a significant following. PSP-associated labor committees existed for nearly three hundred businesses, in defiance of the unions officially sanctioned by the CTC.[17] As the anti-Communist climate of the Cold War set in, the party and party members—some of whom ranked among Cuba's most accomplished professionals and artists, were cast in an increasingly hostile light. Repression under Batista's second government increased in the 1950s, aided by the CIA-nurtured Bureau of Anti-Communist Repression (BRAC), and non-Communist anti-Batista activists began to suspect some PSP members of informing the BRAC of revolutionary activities.[18]

Faustino Pérez and others in the National Directorate remained suspicious of the Communists because of the party's relationship with Batista and Aútentico presidents—and perhaps most significantly, because of the behavior of the party during Cuba's struggle against dictatorship twenty-five years earlier. After initially joining students in the general strike against Gerardo Machado in 1933, just before the dictatorship's fall that August, the Communists and the CNOC tried to call off the strike and order their disciplined cadre back to work, fearing that a success might provoke an intervention or occupation by the U.S. government. In exchange, the Machado government granted the CNOC formal recognition.[19] Decades later, especially given the CTC's arrangement with the Batista regime, the 26th of July found that maintaining a practical working relationship with the Communists, difficult and historically charged as that was for a young revolutionary movement, improved its chances of capturing the support and participation of Cuban workers and other party sympathizers, not to mention the PSP's finances, in carrying off a successful general strike.

Against that background, the FON tried to build bridges with white- and blue-collar workers in such disparate industries as banking, distilling, textiles, transportation, tobacco, cattle, communications, oil, sugar, rail, graphic design hotels, and restaurants. By March 1958, FON's activists felt that they "could carry out a general strike, since [the militia's] actions and the triumphs in the Sierra Maestra had created among the working class and among the people a feeling of solidarity that was reflected in each sector."[20] Because of the Miami experience, the National Directorate's substantive and rhetorical commitment to opposition unity had faded. Nevertheless, its urban leadership came to regard the FON as a viable instrument for the 26th of July to dominate anti-Batista activism among workers. In order to do so, at a minimum the M267 would have to overcome its reluctance to work with the Communist Party. But the movement's first widely publicized call to strike, the "Manifesto of Twenty-One Points" issued in March 1958, declared that "the organization and direction of the strike in the labor sector will be charged to the National Labor Front [the FON], which will assume in turn the representation of the proletariat before the provisional revolutionary government." By this, the manifesto's authors meant that neither the *mujalista* CTC, nor the Communists, nor any other workers' group would control organized labor under a post-Batista government.[21]

Privately and publicly the PSP chafed at the idea that the 26th of July alone could possibly organize a strike and control the CTC after Batista's collapse. In the party's underground publication *Carta Semanal* the March manifesto was deemed "erroneous" and "sectarian," since "the FON is but one of many labor groups, and though it may be important, to consider it the only one would not only by unreal (and thus quite transitory), but also, moreover, would go against the workers' wishes, divide them further, and weaken the bases for the strike." This criticism made sense coming from a political organization that had successfully managed the mammoth CNOC without anywhere near the level of corruption and malfeasance that followed in the Auténtico-CTC era.[22] To make its views known directly, the PSP sent an Oriente-based member to speak with Che Guevara at his base outside of Bayamo. Guevara was not involved in the urban insurrection and he regarded the members of the National Directorate as soft, excessively preoccupied with avoiding a provocation with the Americans, and unable to break from their middle-class trappings as Guevara himself had done. His philosophical sympathies clearly lay with the Communists. After his experience in Guatemala, where he lived while Jacobo Arbenz was president, he had developed ties with the Guatemalan Communist Party.[23]

Guevara agreed with the PSP's critique of the March manifesto's exclusive designation of the FON to lead striking workers. He urged Castro to accommodate the PSP for the sake of the strike and to strengthen the guerrillas. In fact, Guevara reported to Fidel that the party had offered to "place itself unconditionally at the movement's orders without a tactical discussion of any nature. I felt it my duty to warn him about the National Directorate and the division that exists between them and the *sierra*. They are planning to work in the strike committees and infiltrate themselves anyway despite the National Directorate's opposition. They're going to form a committee to supply the *sierra* directly through their own channels."[24] Thus, both the PSP and Guevara sought to bypass the National Directorate by persuading Castro to reach out more broadly; the communists for political-strategic reasons and Guevara because he had little faith in the National Directorate and urban insurrection as a path to unseat Batista. Indeed, sometime in the second half of March 1958, the PSP sent Osvaldo Sánchez Cabrera to the Sierra to convey the party's views directly to Fidel Castro.[25]

At the end of the month Castro issued a little-circulated second manifesto intended to show his movement's capacity to "rise above political flag-waving and personal rivalries." Castro wrote that by charging the FON with

leading and organizing the General Strike in the labor field . . . our Movement makes no exclusions of any nature. All Cuban workers, whatever their political or revolutionary militancy, have the right to join the strike committees at their workplaces. The National Workers Front is not a sectarian organization; it was conceived of as an instrument to bring together and direct the workers in the struggle against the dictator. The FON's leadership will co-ordinate their efforts with the workers' sections of all political and revolutionary organizations . . . and with all organized nuclei that are fighting for economic and political demands of its class, so that no worker remains outside of this patriotic endeavor.[26]

Castro issued this much broader statement in response to Guevara and the PSP and to repair the damage the National Directorate had caused with its partisan approach to organizing workers for the strike. Even while attempting to indicate that the movement supported a broad coalition of forces against Batista, Castro respected the tactical division of labor within the National Directorate. He wrote to a Santiago contact that he personally would not be able to "give the strike order, but rather it must be the corresponding organizations that call for the strike."[27]

The response among revolutionaries to the new manifesto was different in Santiago than in Havana. In the Oriente capital, where the PSP, M267, and other opposition groups had worked together for most of the decade, Vilma Espín, the movement's coordinator in the province, reported that activists were "moved and encouraged" by Fidel's inclusive gesture and could not have been "more willing and disciplined" in preparing to strike.[28] But in Havana, David Salvador strenuously objected to Castro's new policy of inclusiveness as having "changed without justification the position we've followed to date." Because of these objections, Faustino Pérez delayed distributing the new document until Salvador could first inform other FON members of the change. It "went over like an atomic bomb," Pérez wrote Fidel. Nevertheless, Pérez and Salvador overcame their resistance and sent the new document off to the printer, where it apparently remained because it was never actually distributed in Havana.[29]

Despite the conciliatory intentions behind the second manifesto, Pérez betrayed a similar reticence in his talks with the Communists. In early April he met in the office of a Havana radiologist with two officials from the PSP's National Committee, Anibal Escalante and Ursinio Rojas. Pérez asked them to support the coming general strike. But according to his subsequent account, while the PSP concurred that the moment was ripe, Escalante insisted that the two organizations should first organize joint strike committees. Pérez felt such a task "implied months, if not years," and represented "an insolvent problem because we were working with an agreement and a date . . . that we couldn't change."

We even told them that at least each organization should support the strike, independently from whether there were committees of that group or . . . that were organized through the FON, which in some cases were coordinated [with the party], not directed at the national level but that in fact existed. But they insisted on the need to come up with an organizational plan of greater spark. And certainly, the fact that we were pressured by a date, and under more pressure than they, was the basic discrepancy. That's why we didn't even tell them the exact date [of the strike] because since we saw it wouldn't be possible [to coordinate with them] why would we go and divulge the date if we couldn't get their support?[30]

After the meeting, the PSP complained in writing to Fidel about Pérez, about the M267's strike strategy, and specifically about the FON. According to two reports they sent to Castro in early April, Pérez had refused even to share a copy of the second March manifesto, contending that "there was no time" to print it. But Oriente Party members had already obtained the text from Che Guevara's guerrilla press, *El Cubano Libre*. Offering to print and distribute it, the party cautioned Castro that "since you asked . . . we're giving you our assessment" that "it is an exaggeration to say that the FON is a very extensive organization. Based on the FON, it will not be possible to organize the strike."[31] Echoing its criticisms of Fidel's attack on the Moncada barracks five years earlier, the party complained that "the leadership of the 26th of July has decided to initiate armed actions, without relying on a [workers'] strike," and warned that pinning the success of a nationwide strike on "chance or mere spontaneity would be pure adventure."[32]

Despite these objections, the Communists reiterated to Castro and the National Directorate their readiness to coordinate strike committees with the 26th of July—among workers and "civic society"—and proposed responding together to police repression and strike breakers, organizing demonstrations, reaching out together to workers in other anti-Batista groups, and agreeing jointly to a date for the strike.[33] As if to counter the National Directorate's suspicion that such proposals intended to delay a final action to overthrow Batista, the memorandum to Castro explicitly stated, "These proposals are not meant to slow down the beginning, but rather to advance and assure it. Everything we've proposed can be done at once."[34]

If privately the Communists politely implored Fidel to correct his comrades in the *llano* and appeared magnanimous in their readiness to support the strike, publicly the party blamed the strike's delay neither on the strike-breaking threats of the CTC nor on the government's repression, but rather on "division between parties, groups and opposition sectors and the fact that at these heights they have not coordinated amongst themselves." At the grassroots level, "unity between workers and the people was growing through the formation of hundreds of strike committees," but at the top "there is no common plan." Instead, those lacking faith in the people had begun to place their bets on "isolated actions disconnected from the masses . . . with the goal, they say, of hastening an open yankee intervention."[35] The Communists provocatively attributed the militarization of the strike plans to a desire within the 26th of July to end Batista's regime through American intervention, echoing the very issue that had motivated their withdrawal from the anti-Machado strike in 1933.

Che Guevara agreed. He believed that the FON and National Directorate were unwilling to work with the Communists because of the underground's conservative antipathy toward genuine social revolution, as well as its inherent deference to the United States. After Guevara succeeded in focusing Fidel's attention on the political implications of a partisan uprising, he was almost completely cut off from strike plans, without news of the actual date of the strike and with no instructions from Fidel or René Ramos Latour other than to block highway transportation.

Like Latour, it appears that both Fidel and the Oriente *llano* leadership had intentionally left Guevara out of the loop in the days immediately prior to the strike. "Tell me," Guevara wrote Camilo Cienfuegos, who left Fidel's column on March 31 to take over the militia in Bayamo, "about everything you're doing . . . how things are going over there—from here I have no idea about anything." And two days later, Guevara insisted, "It's important that you send me news of everything you know . . . not only from a military perspective, but also with respect to the transportation shutdown and the general strike, because I have absolutely no information of any kind." Indeed, just before the strike Che's only contact with the National Directorate came in a letter from Vilma Espín. She reported that Santiago was "practically under siege" and that all of the province's electricity and telephone lines except in Manzanillo and Bayamo had been cut off by sabotage. In the middle of what would possibly turn out to be the definitive event of the revolution, Espín mused (perhaps sardonically), "Well, I hope that soon you will be able to take a hot bath and sleep on a Simmons mattress." One can only imagine how Guevara, who already opposed the strike and distrusted its advocates' middle- and upper-middle-class backgrounds, reacted to this brief lapse in concentration. On the same day, referring to Espín's letter, Guevara wrote Castro that though the "D. N. [National Directorate] sent word that the entire province is in convulsions, . . . keep me informed about how this [the strike] is going—I have no news."[36]

Despite Espín's report, Guevara believed that the National Directorate had deliberately slowed the pace of sabotage and blocked electrical workers from joining the strike to signify its reluctance to truly work with the PSP. The day before the strike, Guevara wrote Fidel that the National Directorate had exaggerated the extent of blackouts and sabotage in Bayamo, and he volunteered to go himself to shut down the town. He wrote Fidel that a M267 leader's public criticism of Fidel before the organization's militants was a "gratuitous" remark "that shows their true colors with respect to the FON, ordering a putsch once victory is achieved" in the strike.[37] Guevara's chance to convince Fidel in person of the National Directorate's flaws was only weeks away. But within days, they would become evident enough.

Indeed, Faustino Pérez did harbor genuine doubts about working with other opposition groups. He feared that they would take advantage of Castro's offer to work with all labor groups and felt the movement not only could do without the help of other organizations, but should avoid at all cost "falling again into the inoperable, fraudulent, and hollow unity thing like the Liberation Junta, which is what the majority of the so-called leaders of parties, organizations, and groups are seeking to gain."[38] He was loathe to allow adversaries in the anti-Batista struggle to steal center stage during the insurrection, or later in the race to power.

Pérez made his suspicion of "hollow unity" pacts abundantly clear in negotiating with the Student Revolutionary Directorate (DRE) for weapons to supply the militia in Havana and those in the western and central provinces. After the Pact of Miami collapsed, Faure Chomón, the DRE's secretary general, returned by boat to Cuba with sixteen others and opened a guerrilla front in the Sierra del Escambray mountains on February 13, 1958. The front quickly expanded to three columns totaling twenty-nine men. While the DRE maintained its long-held strategy of "hitting at the top," or assassinating Batista to end the dictatorship, a manifesto explained that the DRE had only temporarily adopted the tactic of guerrilla war.[39] Temporary indeed. By the end of the month, with three men killed by the army, Chomón and his men had left the mountains for Havana, hoping to carry out several military actions to commemorate the one-year anniversary of the DRE-OA assault on the presidential palace that had nearly killed Batista in March of 1957.[40]

In the capital, Chomón and Pérez met on several occasions to discuss joint military plans and possible DRE participation in the general strike.[41] Chomón even offered the M267 a large cache of weapons then warehoused outside of Havana "on the condition," Pérez told his colleagues in the National Strike Committee, "that we give [the DRE] representation in the overall leadership of the struggle and even in the subsequent direction" of the insurrection and "more strategic agreements . . . involving the problem of future government . . . [and] more complete unity agreements." Initially Pérez confessed that he was "partisan to letting them in," as he had been while discussing a unity pact in prison with DRE members in 1957.[42] But Chomón claimed that Pérez waffled, delaying his final decision until it was too late to accept the proposed arrangement in exchange for the weapons. On March 30, Cuban police raided a house in the Havana suburb of Santa Fe and, as Pérez wrote Castro, "busted almost everything the DRE had."[43] There was no longer any reason for the M267 to consider "more strategic" or "complete unity agreements" with the movement's longtime adversaries.

On the eve of the strike, the revolutionaries faced numerous obstacles: precious few weapons for the militia, the assassination of Havana's top militia captains, failure to reach an agreement to work jointly with either the PSP or the DRE, anti-Communism and partisanship within the FON, passivity in the official labor movement, and intensifying and brutal repression by Batista's security forces. Nevertheless, Marcelo Fernández, who in addition to replacing Armando Hart as the movement's national coordinator was also the M267's National Strike Committee coordinator for "organization and propaganda" in Havana, put pen to paper to develop a comprehensive "Plan for the Organization and Development of the Revolutionary General Strike"—in effect, a blueprint for the national strike that assigned tasks to the militia, labor, "civic resistance," and "propaganda" sections of the strike committee. Fernández circulated only eleven copies of the plan before the strike: to Fidel, to the five members of the National Strike Committee, and to each of the six provincial strike coordinators.[44]

At the national, provincial, and municipal levels, the strike committees comprised representatives from the 26th of July's own entities only: the militia, the FON, civic resistance, propaganda, and organization. The plan spelled out the role for each of the movement's sections. Set against the reality of the moment, the plan was very nearly literary, reflecting a collective imagination of how the national strike might have unfolded under the best of circumstances.

Under the plan, the militia's principal focus was to use violence to create havoc and chaos. On the first day of the strike, the militia was to establish roadblocks, take over nearby buildings, and lob grenades and Molotov cocktails at police motorcycles and patrol cars. Warning against direct confrontation with the army and police, the plan instructed the militia to conduct commando raids, sniper attacks, or guerrilla actions "with the goal of diffusing and blocking the concentration of repressive forces." On the first of April, the militia was to begin assassinating *mujalista* labor leaders, *batistiano* political figures, and any politician associated with Batista's recently announced campaign for the June 1958 presidential elections. The militia was also responsible for "maintaining the strike at all cost" in Cuban schools. Outside of Havana, the militia would attack small army barracks. Further, the militia was to cut off electricity, telephones, water, and transportation by blowing up bridges, burning vehicles, and barricading streets. Finally, as militia chief, René Ramos Latour would coordinate with "the commanders of our Rebel Army . . . armed actions of a major scale" to coincide with the strike.[45] "We must commit the people to become an active part in the General Strike. We will exhort them to provide safe haven to the revolutionaries, carry out street protests, manufacture Molotov cocktails, and litter the streets with garbage to block transit," the plan admonished. Before the strike, the movement's militants were to form neighborhood committees of workers and students to "lead these popular actions," because "the people should be actors, not observers, in the process of the Strike."[46] Without weapons, even with spontaneous outbursts of support from the mostly unorganized urban population, the militia faced an almost impossible and extraordinarily risky task.

The "Plan" confirmed the PSP's and Guevara's suspicion that the FON had neglected to reach out to the Communists and other organized labor groups on bread and butter issues affecting Cuban workers. David Salvador had long made his doubts known to the National Directorate that workers would join a strike *without* violence to provide them cover, given Mujal's standing and well-enforced no-strike order.[47] The assumption that the revolutionaries could not count on worker support—despite labor's antiregime activism in parts of the country—permeated the thinking of the movement's militia chief too. He believed that labor had only become willing to defy Mujal in recent months because of the M267's successful sabotage of industry, utilities, and transportation, actions that had "forced" train and bus workers, for example, "to strike because of the firings and salary reductions, a logical consequence of the [losses] in revenue for these companies."[48]

Still, in the days before the strike, M267 labor activists were to "raise the temperature" on the shop floor, distributing leaflets and hanging posters announcing the coming strike and instructing workers that the FON would "be in charge of leading the strike movement." When the strike itself was called, the 26th of July would order workers to "abandon" their jobs or be considered strikebreakers—"not to hide," but to join "popular actions" organized by "neighborhood committees." But the most important function of the FON would come after the strike, when its labor committees were to form commissions of workers "trained by and belonging principally to the 26th" to act as the "provisional leadership" of each affiliate until "union elections are convened." Indeed, if all went according to Fernández's blueprint, the 26th of July would designate eight members of each CTC-affiliate's labor commission, including the secretary general; secretaries for organization, resolutions and correspondence, propaganda, and finance; and the delegate to represent the union in talks with management and government officials. That is, the FON would become the vehicle for purging the *mujalista* order from the CTC after Batista's departure.[49]

Unlike the plans for labor, the M267 developed a far less partisan, more ecumenical design for the Civic Resistance Movement's participation in the strike. Since Civic Resistance was, by definition, a catch-all front organization for recruiting sympathetic professionals, the plan called for the creation of strike committees in each of the country's 144 counties. Each committee would include three members from Civic Resistance, one from the private sector, and one representing Cuba's professional guilds. Each individual in the five-member committee would "agitate" within their respective fields: Civic Resistance militants would shut down bodegas, hardware stores, pharmacies, clothing stores, hair salons, movie theaters, restaurants, and diners; the business representatives would run the strike in industries, banks, and other commercial establishments; and the professional representatives would take on law firms, medical and dental offices, engineering and architecture firms, public relations companies, and accounting firms. In addition, Civic Resistance members were to keep the schools closed, advocate for nonpayment of taxes, and "persuade" public officials to resign their office. If the reward for labor was control of the CTC after the strike, the payoff for Civic Resistance members was also power, because each local strike committee was to occupy and form provisional governments in city halls around the country: "Once the strike has culminated, Civic Resistance leaders from every location, accompanied by representative individuals, should make themselves present at public offices: ministries, provisional governments, post offices, customs, states' attorney's offices, etcetera, proceeding to occupy them with the support of the militia."[50]

For the "propaganda" section, if the strike proceeded as planned, one of the movement's first bulletins might read:

People of Havana: the General Strike has reached the boiling point throughout Cuba. Our glorious Revolutionary Army has come down from the Sierra

Maestra and is advancing through Oriente province in every direction. Fidel Castro has taken Manzanillo and is threatening to take over Santiago. The Nicaro mine has been occupied by the 26th of July Militia under the command of Commander Raúl Castro.

In Havana the General Strike is a success. All urban transportation is paralyzed. There is no electricity. There is no telephone service. There is no water. There are no newspapers. All industry is shut down: Modelo, Polar and Tropical Beer Companies, Esso and Shell refineries, Gancedo distillery, Goodyear, Sabates, Crusellas, Coca Cola, Pepsicola, the Materva bottling companies, the radio and television stations CMQ, Telemundo, Radio Progreso, CNC, all the maritime terminals of the Port, banks, the clothing stores El Encanto, Fin de Siglo, Ten Cent, Sears, bodegas, pharmacies, and movie theaters. Yesterday at 23rd and L, our militia set fire to six patrol cars, forcing their crews to escape.

From Miami, Doctor Manuel Urrutia has declared that he is ready to return to Havana at any moment. Doctor Alliegro, president of Congress, managed to escape through Rancho Boyeros. Batista is meeting with the ministers that remain, considering turning over the Government. *Habaneros:* not one step backwards. Six years of struggle have brought on Victory. National Strike Committee, Havana.[51]

After five days of generalized insurrection, continued Fernández, the army itself would force Batista's resignation and flight from the country. When workers, professionals, and students demanded that Judge Urrutia take over the government, the 26th of July's National Strike Committee would obligingly turn power over to the Santiago judge whose legal rulings had helped legitimize the insurrection. "Taking advantage of these moments of confusion," the militia would then "take over barracks, police stations, and navy posts," distributing weapons to unarmed militia and to "our cadre" among workers and the resistance. Next, the first post-Batista issue of *Revolución*, the movement's newspaper, would appear. Students, militia, and the resistance would form commissions to maintain order, patrolling the streets and preventing looting and vandalism. Finally, "the General Staff of the Revolutionary Army, and especially its Commander in Chief, Fidel Castro . . . will take possession of Santiago de Cuba and military command of [the army's] Regiment Number One. This will constitute a formidable obstacle to any possible counterrevolutionary attempt at a coup in the capital."[52]

But back in the rough and tumble world of revolutionary politics, progress toward this outcome was far from smooth. It is an understatement to say that things did not turn out as the blueprint for the general strike imagined. Faustino Pérez waited until April 8 to alert his own people in the FON leadership that the strike would be called the very next day, and asked the movement's top cadre not to inform their grassroots organizers until just two hours before he was scheduled to broadcast the call to strike on national radio.[53] But with 26th of July cells "at every level of the country," the FON's activists believed that the organization's "clandestine channels" of communication were sufficiently secure to accommodate "a period of 72 hours," not two hours, of advance notice.[54]

The National Directorate's strike leaders understood the risks of their late-notice military strategy, which did nothing to alleviate partisanship within the revolution. "Everything seems to indicate," Marcelo wrote Fidel, "that the regime is ready to drown the strike in blood . . . We're reaching the climax and I can smell the end. As you well note, the entire Nation is ready to be free or perish. And Cuba must not perish."[55] But on the eve of the strike, both the militia and labor, the two cornerstones of the strike, had been rendered essentially impotent. Neither negotiations with rival groups nor costly schemes to import weapons and explosives had yielded sufficient materiél to wreak havoc on infrastructure and industry across the island. Likewise, widespread police and military repression, a steady stream of threats by Mujal's CTC against those workers who dared dabble in politics, the last-minute collapse of talks with the Communists, the failure to reach an agreement with the DRE that might have produced weapons and other sorts of collaboration, and the 26th of July's decision to place its bets on violence all conspired to limit the potential of the national strike to succeed in ousting the dictator. Yet no one involved in the "whirlwind" of planning the uprising could slow the momentum or shift gears. The 26th of July had committed to a particular path and would soon watch it and its consequences unfold.

12 | "Bordering on Chaos"

APRIL 1958

> The strike in Havana was "paralyzed," and its tragic consequences have been incalculable. For it wasn't only that one more opportunity to overthrow the dictator had been frustrated, and that the streets of Havana and the ground of Cuba were again awash in plentiful blood, but it left public opinion and many revolutionary leaders—even from our own movement—the false impression that the strategy we'd been advancing of general strike and armed insurrection was no longer the correct one, which gave shape among our own to a clamor for unity and the thesis of war between armies.
>
> Faustino Pérez to Armando Hart, October 3, 1958

AT ELEVEN IN THE MORNING ON APRIL 9, 1958, the 26th of July Movement interrupted Havana and Santiago radio stations to broadcast a call for a nationwide general strike. Precious few workers walked out of their jobs in the capital, where poorly armed militia attacked an armory in Old Havana and other targets. Almost without exception, police gunfire eliminated the commandos. Sabotage to the city's main circuit board caused temporary blackouts from Old Havana to the Vedado district. By late afternoon, though, most bus routes had resumed their normal schedules, businesses and banks had reopened, and workers had completed their afternoon shifts. According to one report, not one factory or business in Havana had shut down as a result of worker walkouts, and the movement's militia took the brunt of police violence deployed to counter their sabotage. Faustino Pérez wrote to comrades in Miami that "here in Havana the strike didn't catch and, acting with absolute cruelty, the repressive forces staged a frontal attack on actions initiated with the scarce equipment available." After the strike, police repression in the capital included arrests, tortures, murders, and disappearances of almost all of the militia's captains, prominent lawyers coming to their defense, and members of the movement's propaganda and Civic Resistance cells. In all, the M267 estimated that some two hundred of its members were murdered by order of police chief Pilar García.[1]

But with Oriente province still largely shut down, local militias commanded by René Ramos Latour and Luis Clerge and rebel troops under the command of Raúl Castro, Juan Almeida, and Fidel Castro attacked targets around the province. In Santiago de Cuba workers did strike, but by afternoon, employers had already begun to replace them. In Guantánamo, local militias burned the homes of the police chief and mayor. Despite Enrique Oltuski's earlier doubts, most of the towns in the province of Las Villas joined the uprising, holding Sagua la Grande until the Cuban air force bombed commandos out of their positions the next day.[2] The provinces of Camagüey, Matanzas, and Pinar del Río had sporadic actions, but the rebels in Pinar del Río were so disorganized that even a last-minute injection of weapons failed to push the province into an uprising of any significance.[3] Fearing that striking workers might lose their jobs without having accomplished anything, on April 10 Vilma Espín issued a "back-to-work" order in Santiago and notified Havana to call off the strike.[4] American embassy staff reported banks and stores open again, electricity restored, and 80 percent of workers at the U.S.-government-owned Nicaro nickel plant and two-thirds of employees at the Moa Bay Mining Company in Oriente province (owned by the U.S. Freeport Sulphur Company) back on the job. The event around which the 26th of July Movement had staked the revolution's success had "generally fizzled," ending in "definite failure."[5]

As a result, between April and July of 1958, Fidel Castro and his entire organization faced a crisis that reverberated on several fronts: between *sierra* and *llano* within the National Directorate; within the 26th of July's labor, student, and professional front organizations; and in the Communist, militant, and moderate anti-Batista opposition. Each exerted pressure directly and indirectly on Castro to revamp the 26th of July Movement organizationally and strategically and to resurrect the previously discarded opposition unity alliance. Long before it was at all clear that the rebel army would defeat the Cuban army in the frontal assault in the Sierra Maestra (which the rebels knew would follow the strike), Fidel Castro wagered that he could convert the movement's temporary weakness into strength: he initiated unity negotiations that culminated in the July 1958 creation of the long-elusive Civic Revolutionary Front and the signing of the Pact of Caracas by eight opposition organizations.

Despite scattered militia action, then, the day after the strike workers were back on the job. In Oriente it fell to Espín to communicate the back-to-work order to national militia captain René Ramos Latour, touching off a bitter dispute over the proper tactics to pursue in the immediate aftermath of the defeat.

After speaking with Zoilo [Fernández] . . . I feel it would be useless to keep sacrificing the people from here. I gave the order to go back to work [while] remaining alert to a possible change, since they had started to send in replacement workers. Zoilo approved of sending people back to work and we left it that we should continue following Havana. People here are absolutely furious with the *Habaneros,* they want to destroy them, and they don't want to go back to work . . . I even think the people here are ready to sacrifice themselves."[6]

Espín had also given up on revolt in the capital but hoped the Santiago militia would make another go of the strike within days, even before the rebel army's takeover of the provincial capital.[7]

Latour was outraged at the order to retreat. After they attacked the Boniato military barracks outside of Santiago, Latour and his thirty-man militia had taken to the hills outside the city and formed "Column number nine."[8] Latour upbraided Espín for calling off the strike and insisted that the strike continue, claiming that even without the entire population's support, the force of the 26th of July militia would eventually bring even the most reluctant citizen into the revolutionary wave. He demanded that Espín inform Raúl Castro, Juan Almeida, Fidel Castro, and the entire National Strike Committee that he intended to shift to the strategy of "total war"—widespread sabotage against industry, agriculture, highways, and transportation, from Cuba's urban centers to the countryside.[9]

Espín refused. She demanded that Latour leave his new column and return to Santiago at once to meet and renew the plans for urban action, warning that he must not "leave vacant the headquarters of National Action."[10] Latour found Espín's request to "abandon a completed force"— that is, his new militia column—"for a broken one," the urban commando, completely "absurd." In his mind, the urban strategy was no longer a priority. He no longer served as national commander of the "action and sabotage," but instead commanded one column of men whose loyalty, discipline, and respect he had only recently undertaken to earn. After sleepless days and nights with little food and "none of the comforts of the Sierra Maestra," he had implored his men to maintain revolutionary discipline and warned them that abandoning the new column was tantamount to treason. His leaving, even for a few hours, would be devastating to the group, and he refused to return to Santiago.[11]

Moreover, to back up his position Latour argued that he had the support of the entire National Directorate in the decision to shift to "total war" if the strike were to falter. "You will recall," he wrote Espín, that during the meeting of the D. N. [National Directorate] we talked of the remote possibility that the strike would fail. I said that if that were to happen Oriente, Las Villas, and Pinar del Río should emerge with powerful revolutionary armies to maintain war in the countryside and gather strength until they've moved into conditions to penetrate the cities. That is precisely what we're trying to do here, and I'd say we've almost reached that point. Moreover, I believe we can keep Cuba in the state of abnormality or total war that has persisted in Oriente since the first [of April], or that we can do it in three provinces, or that in the worst case just Oriente. Any of these three possibilities would allow us, all the columns under arms, to gather strength, take more and more objectives, extend our radius of action, and gradually wedge cracks into the two most important pillars of support for the dictatorship: the economy and the unity of its armed forces. It is utopian in these moments to think about the militia's struggle in the cities or towns where the army has concentrated all of its power, knowing that there it can drown the entire movement.

Latour believed that the National Directorate, including Fidel Castro, had already approved plans for the militia to initiate a rural-based war of attrition, a strategy that differed substantially from the approach of the rebel army, which was planning to confront the Cuban army directly. Only those who wished to remain "enslaved," chastised Latour, would cling to the cities as the center of the insurrection.[12]

Unfortunately, Latour had to rely on Espín, who disagreed with him, to make his case among the 26th of July's military and civilian leadership. Anguished and frustrated that the uprising he had planned for almost one year had failed with no apparent sign of resurgence, Latour repeatedly demanded that Espín send his plan to Fidel, each of the other guerrilla commanders, and each civilian member of the National Directorate. Latour wrote, "If in the cities the tyranny succeeded in drowning the strike in blood, the militia everywhere should leave the cities and go to the countryside to form revolutionary armies with the goal of continuing the struggle without truce or rest and maintain throughout the country the state of total war." This state of total war, in his view, had reigned in Oriente since the beginning of the month and was starting to damage the region's economy. Indeed, the State Department also reported "considerable harassing of American citizens in Oriente Province . . . as well as appropriation and destruction of property belonging to American companies," which had resulted in losses of several hundred thousand dollars to American interests alone.[13]

Latour proposed an "Eight Point Plan of Action," or sabotage, in order to shut down the country's communications, transportation, and utilities; assassinate government officials and corrupt labor leaders; attack progovernment newspapers and radio stations; burn large industrial targets; and attack the military's barracks and convoys by staging ambushes and initiating battles against government forces in rural areas. When Latour learned that Espín had apparently sat on this proposal rather than promote it with the rebel army commanders and the National Directorate, he tried to convince—in writing—the militia members around the country that his Eight Point Plan would speed up the revolutionary process and save lives.[14] He also went directly to the rebel army. He approached Almeida first, complaining of Espín's insubordination in calling off the strike without consulting either himself or Fidel and arguing that even without the entire population's support, many workers were indeed willing to lose their jobs for the cause. "If we continue as we have until now," he wrote, "soon we will be the absolute owners of Oriente province, and from there to the liberation of Cuba, there is only one more step."[15]

Supplying this new rural militia, a departure from the rebel army's guerrilla *foco* strategy, was a tremendous and probably impossible challenge. Though with his comrades Latour gushed with enthusiasm for total war in Oriente, he also acknowledged the paucity of equipment available to conduct a war of attrition against an entire national economy and the weakened but still resilient state. Writing to "Bebo" Hidalgo in Miami, Latour was far more sober in detailing a long list of materiél needed for the new strategy in Oriente, Las Villas, Pinar del Río, and even Havana, which, in an apparent moment of fatigue-induced delirium, he announced, "we are going to invade with experienced and combative men from Oriente."[16] Since "Fidel's column received a good reinforcement before the strike"—that is, the planeload delivered from Costa Rica—Latour instructed Hidalgo to concentrate supply operations on reinforcing the new militia columns in Oriente, where the largest concentration of guerrilla columns were also based.[17]

Latour did not view the guerrilla columns under Castro's command as a secondary force that the militia would supplant. He believed that since the urban strategy had failed, the insurrection would succeed only through the combined force of the established guerrilla columns and the new "revolutionary armies" drawn from the militia under his command. "Our key force to culminate the insurrection process," he wrote, "will be the columns and guerrillas, which are the best-trained forces to achieve a victory. The militias for their part will be in charge of maintaining a state of abnormality and preventing the regime from concentrating its attention on the countryside."[18]

Latour's extraordinarily ambitious plan underestimated the effect on the movement's security and resources of intensified repression in the aftermath of the strike. In Oriente alone, the brutality and blanket repression of security forces had driven hundreds of urban commandos into the hills outside of Santiago. Their sheer number created a severe drain on the movement's resources and produced conflicts over who was in charge—the captains appointed by Latour, or Almeida, a guerrilla commander appointed by Fidel who was based in the outskirts of Santiago. Latour was advocating a significant change in strategy for the rebel army. The conflict that such a change caused, combined with the dramatically increased repression and shortfall of resources, contributed to the collapse of Latour's "Eight Point Action Plan" soon after the ink had dried.

Raúl Castro wrote Fidel to protest the plan as well. Since opening his new guerrilla front, Raúl had begun to lay the groundwork for a long-term presence in the province. Military, administrative, intelligence, legal, educational, and medical systems spanning four companies, each under the command of a captain subordinate to him, were to be distributed throughout his region.[19] Soon after his arrival in the area, local sugar mill administrators and coffee farmers had agreed to halt production and harvesting after April 1, to coincide with the general strike. But Raúl objected to Latour's plans for sustained sabotage against these industries because the rebels had brokered a deal with local producers that permitted production to continue in exchange for payments to the guerilla group. "I hope," he wrote Fidel, "that on this last point I will not be ordered to suspend the coffee harvest; that would mean ruin."[20] Raúl's guerrilla front needed the compliance, political goodwill, and economic support of the region's productive base, which Latour's plan would threaten.

Indeed, Latour's militia was already undermining the rebel army—specifically the column commanded by Juan Almeida in the hills to the east of Santiago de Cuba. Almeida echoed Raúl's concern about the impracticality of a militia-driven "total war."[21] Latour had appointed a longtime urban commando from Santiago, Luis Alberto Clerge Fabra, or "Manuel Campos" (his underground name), to command the new Oriente militia.[22] Clerge had climbed up the ranks of the militia, leading cells, companies, squads, and finally the province's rural militia. But he was not equipped to make the transition to commanding the militia for an entire province. His conduct was "not very exemplary" when given command over some seven hundred men roaming Oriente's coastal towns before, during, and after the strike. Almeida reported that Clerge's authority over troops was weak and his military skills poor. For example, during the strike Clerge decided to stage an attack of the Baire army barracks—but he announced his arrival with twenty trucks and a loudspeaker, thus eliminating any chance of an ambush. Worse, since Latour had failed to coordinate strike plans with Almeida beyond sending instructions to cut off highway traffic, Almeida's guerrilla column inadvertently selected the same targets for attack during the strike as Clerge. Since Clerge's forces traveled on trucks, and Almeida's column by foot, Clerge's group arrived first, leaving Almeida without a strategic target for the day of the strike. Instead, Almeida's column staged an attack in the town of El Cobre the day *after* the strike "with the intention of continuing to Santiago if the strike supported us."[23]

Once the uprising failed, Clerge and his men became sitting ducks in their encampments outside of Santiago, with little to do, discipline failing, and a steady stream of desertions as they came under attack by the army. Under pressure from Espín to return to Santiago, Latour asked Almeida to bring some order to the militia under Clerge, whose desperation and incompetence, not to mention a death threat from another militia captain, had convinced Almeida that the very presence of an extensive militia in the Sierra Maestra "aggravates our supply problems and creates other problems we didn't have before." In Almeida's view, Latour should never have promoted Clerge in the first place. And worse, the militia that Latour hoped would first paralyze the province and then the entire country had already proven to be unwieldy, a drain on resources, and militarily unfit.[24]

By the end of April, plans for a "total war" executed by an expanded militia had become untenable. When a defeated Latour returned to Santiago, his deputy, Belarmino Castilla ("Aníbal"), and an entire detachment of men joined Raúl Castro's Second Front with the understanding that they would "subordinate themselves under our orders," Raúl wrote Fidel. Raúl was eager to absorb Castilla's men, money, and weapons because the merger meant the militia posed less of a challenge to his base in the Sierra Cristal and would help deflect an imminent air strike and ground force attack by Batista's forces. At the same time, Raúl's fiancée, Espín, had arrived at his base to discuss some urgent issues: "what to do about Daniel [Latour]," a new plan to fly arms in from Miami by air, and the "always latent problem between the National Directorate and the Sierra Maestra."[25]

Back in Havana, Faustino Pérez's initial response to what he described as a "momentary failure for the movement" was to propose an "increase

[in] armed action as much as possible in the countryside and in the cities in order to pick ourselves up from this fall as quickly as possible." As if forgetting the difficulty the M267 had faced in getting enough arms for the strike, he wrote his comrades in Miami to send more weapons for a second strike.[26] To stave off mounting criticism of the M267, the National Directorate released a "Manifesto to the People of Cuba" that framed the failed strike as a temporary setback akin to that of the 1956 *Granma* voyage and Castro's July 1953 attack on the Moncada barracks. The manifesto exaggerated the extent of the movement's successes, the strike's duration, and the scope of its reach in a province-by-province account of the three-day strike, from its inception to the final retreat in Oriente. The manifesto exulted, "From Mantua [in Pinar del Río] to Baracoa [in Oriente], workers and employers carried out a great strike movement, with the cooperation of *hacendados* and of our rural Militias and Patrols who valiantly and with precision attacked the tyranny's repressive forces."[27]

Pérez appeared to be gearing up for another strike action in the cities and the countryside; the manifesto categorically stated that "the 26th of July Movement ratifies its strategy of general strike supported by armed action."[28] Unlike the manifestos released in the prior month, Cuban workers were conspicuously absent from the latest exhortation, a tacit recognition that the movement had failed to mobilize Cuban workers—once declared the linchpin of a successful uprising—to overthrow the dictator. Instead, it appeared that Latour's new action plan had some support in Havana, because the manifesto announced that rather than popular mobilization, the movement's "tactic of immediate struggle will be to increase action," political assassination, and economic sabotage in order to keep the militia at the center of the movement's strategy for the time being.[29]

The strike's failure left Taras Domitro completely dejected. He feared that the movement would never overcome the "indolence" of the Cuban people, who were "terrorized" by the regime, not ready to rise up against the dictator.[30] Describing how the strike's failure had affected him, he wrote Latour,

I just spoke with Deborah [Espín] and told her she should have called anyone else but me, since I just came from a meeting that simply destroyed me. I left with my morale lower than that of the soldiers who are fighting against Fidel. My responsibility within the movement obliged me to make certain decisions for the strike that would bring a true beginning to the final stage, and even now I believe that even if at first the government has the advantage over us, only with daring and a massive hard-hitting fight can we save the movement from the ridicule in which it is about to fall, and even more, save the revolution to bring to our nation the freedoms that have cost so many lives.[31]

Before receiving instructions from Latour, who at the time was still in the hills outside of Santiago, Domitro attempted to resurrect the movement from utter disgrace by arranging for Frank Fiorini to fly two more shipments from Miami, with hopefully enough weapons for a second strike by the end of April or early May. He focused on sending as much equipment as possible to Fidel's guerrillas and Latour's militia columns: rifles and ammunition were carried in small quantities to Oriente by young women able to slip through increasingly tight security between Havana and Santiago.[32]

As police cracked down on the movement's safe houses, activists, and sympathizers, Domitro's self-doubt and pessimism deepened, creating a near split personality. This state of mind meant that he had the energy to oversee weapons deliveries to Oriente and prepare the country for another strike on the same day that he wrote Latour, exhausted, pleading to resign his post.[33] By the time Latour's "Eight Point Plan" had reached him at the end of April, police repression and surveillance had shut down all of his land, sea, and air supply operations.[34] On May 3, just as the National Directorate was gathering in the Sierra Maestra to debate the end of the militia-centered insurrection strategy, police raided Domitro's Havana apartment, confiscating his address book and some weapons, and arresting him four days later.[35] As a result of his arrest and that of another weapons runner, police confiscated seven machine guns, 130 pistols, 86 revolvers, 40 grenades, three cars, thousands of rounds of bullets, and equipment to manufacture explosives. The movement's militants in the capital fell into "defeatism and apathy." To make matters worse, the revolutionaries later came to believe that the other arrested courier had confessed to police the names of militants and the locations where Domitro had stockpiled weapons.[36] The movement, he wrote, was "bordering on chaos."[37]

Numerous conflicts within the National Directorate were surfacing between the "civilian" organizers and their comrades in the militia, as well as between the militias in the underground and the rebel army captains in the mountains. Preparing for the inevitable encounter with all of them, Marcelo Fernández addressed the crisis of "skepticism and despondency" within the 26th of July. In a stinging critique of the militarization of the strike that he sent to Fidel Castro, he called on the movement's militants to focus seriously on mobilizing labor.

> In an absurd and inconceivable manner our Movement allowed itself to be swept along by a putschist impetus and two days before the strike forgot about the great battle of those who had been called its vanguard. The work of labor organizing, carried out over nine months, was subordinated to a putsch, developed five days before [the strike]. Armed action failed and this failure was shared by our labor organization, which was not even tested. Our military resources, useful only to deploy sporadic labor support actions against police repression, had been lamentably overestimated to the point of making [the armed actions] the vanguard of the struggle. A costly mistake.[38]

While Latour believed that more "armed action" would "force the fearful and conservative to join the insurrection or be erased by revolutionary action," Fernández attributed the strike's failure to "the existence of an erroneous mentality . . . that the role of workers should be circumscribed to staying in their homes, without actively participating in the strike movement."[39] Despite the emphasis on armed action over popular and worker mobilization, Fernández nevertheless concluded that these obstacles did "not demonstrate that the strategy of general strike is incorrect. It only proves that [the strike] was convened without sufficient resources and organization. We all allowed ourselves to become enthused by the popular climate, forgetting the importance of necessary objective factors."[40] Like his comrades, Fernández instructed M267 militants to intensify action in cities and the countryside, to purge their cells of "confused and embittered" activists, to "regard the General Strike as the final strategy of our struggle," and unlike Pérez or Latour, to "decide that it is fundamental for workers to become the vanguard of the struggle."[41] Elsewhere in Cuba, however, there was deep skepticism about whether the Cuban working class could be counted on to deliver the island from years of dictatorship.

Measured against the rest of the country, the strike in Las Villas province was relatively well organized. Urban commandos held some towns and damaged local industry, while the 26th of July's guerrilla column in the region successfully attacked a military barracks in Quemado de Güines and shut down the central highway. The movement's Las Villas coordinator, Enrique Oltuski, warned the National Directorate before the strike that his province was ill-prepared for anything on the scale the movement was planning, particularly given the lack of arms and of any labor organization by the National Workers Front (FON). Despite the comparative success of his province on April 9, Oltuski issued his own frank analysis of why the strike failed and what the movement should do to recover from the "severe criticism of the vision, capacity, and effort of our national leaders" circulating in the public after the strike. He wrote on the eve of a *sierra-llano* meeting, "Our men fall day after day in the countryside and in the cities. For us, they are Marcelo Salado, Enrique Hart, Pepe Prieto, but for the population they are anonymous men. Citizens are suffering in the face of the increase in gambling and prostitution, the violation of their liberties. So they sympathize with the movement, help it economically, at times giving it shelter in their homes. But from there to risking their security and lives is a long stretch."[42]

Oltuski believed that the movement had to find a way for more of the general population to experience directly the oppressive weight of the Batista dictatorship, so that citizens "feel the lack of work as a result of the shutdown of business and industry; employers go virtually bankrupt from the steep decline of their revenues; large national and foreign industries find themselves without markets for their products; the drop in tourism makes the large hotels impossible to keep up; sugar production is reduced to a minimum yield; and train and highway traffic is interrupted in order to damage gas companies and commerce in general." Only when a sense of chaos and danger "reaches every Cuban's economic, moral and personal security . . . will the people be ready to hurl themselves into the streets." He identified five factors behind the strike's failure: the movement's inability to accurately measure public support, poor organization, an "almost complete absence" of weapons, the militia's decision not to concentrate greater forces in Havana, and the "inadequacy and weakness" of the movement's attempt to mobilize the Cuban working class, which in his analysis had become essentially apolitical.[43]

Without experienced leaders with roots in the working masses, Oltuski lamented that the movement had pinned its highest hopes on a "particular and difficult class," which was paradoxically "the most class-conscious of our social strata and the least independent in terms of leadership."

> Many years of communist sermons and official penetration have made its leaders respond to interests that are not exactly those of the well being of this class. And the most painful is that these machiavellian leaders can always count on support from administrative corruption, and in the end, on the tyranny's brute force. Years of experience have left these leaders well versed in the use of every weapon, and their control at this moment over the acephalous, rudderless, and prostituted working masses is undeniable. Recent events prove this to be the case . . . With its new leadership, a product of im-

provisation (it's easier to improvise a coordinator than a labor leader) [the movement] sought to neutralize the impact of thirty devilish years. With no more resources than the pages of its own idealism, the movement tried to conquer a class that measures its triumphs in salary increases . . . In six months it was impossible [for the movement] to create and consolidate in its thousands of details a labor organization superior to that developed over thirty years of deliberate bad faith. Mathematically impossible. Don't even put forward the argument that the form of convening the strike was a factor in its failure. Had there existed any labor apparatus, any form at all of notice would have been fine.[44]

Oltuski believed it was naive and dangerous for the movement to place any faith in volunteerism—the idea that workers, on their own accord or with a little help from sabotage to their workplace—would join the insurrection. He proposed what appeared to be a synthesis of Latour's and Espín's views: that the revolutionaries sustain a massive intensification of sabotage and armed actions over an extended period in order to "give our young labor leaders needed experience and roots while we remain in the insurrectionist opposition."[45]

Oltuski also touched on the ongoing dispute over whether Havana or Santiago should be the focus of the underground strategy. He was horrified at the movement's failure to concentrate its forces in Havana, Cuba's "dorsal spine in economic and political terms." He too proposed more political assassinations, targeting especially Batista and Eusebio Mujal, arguing, like others in the Revolutionary Directorate, that cutting off the "brain would make the rest of the body crumble." In the rest of the country, the movement should take aim at the "rest of the body, but in Havana we must aim the decisive blow at the head." Yet more political and economic sabotage did not imply curtailing the guerrilla activity. In fact, he argued for expanding guerrilla columns in Pinar del Río and Las Villas, and specifically proposed that the National Directorate send Juan Almeida or Raúl Castro to oversee the expansion. Putting his finger on what others in the National Directorate had been unwilling or unable to perceive or articulate, Oltuski stated that the 26th of July Movement should forgo a general strike as "the goal of the struggle." Instead, a national strike would have to occur as a response to "major military action," as a "means, not an end."[46]

13 | Picking Up the Pieces

APRIL–MAY 1958

> I am the leader of this Movement and I have to as-
> sume the historic responsibility for the stupidities
> of others, and I'm just a shit who can't make a de-
> cision about anything. With the pretext of [avoid-
> ing] caudillismo, everyone is doing whatever he
> pleases. I'm not stupid enough not to realize this,
> nor am I a man prone to visions or ghosts. I am
> not going to give up my critical spirit and intu-
> ition about things, which has helped me so much
> to understand situations, especially now when I
> have more responsibilities than ever before in my
> life. I don't think a chasm will erupt in the Move-
> ment, nor would that be good for the revolution,
> but from now on I am going to take care of our
> own problems.
>
> Fidel Castro to Celia Sánchez, April 16, 1958

FIDEL CASTRO BITTERLY REPROACHED
himself for allowing the underground to take the lead in developing
strategy and for agreeing that the militia would play a major role in the
insurrection. Like Oltuski, he agreed that "it doesn't make sense even to
talk about general strikes." From then on, he wrote, "a strike or the paral-
ysis of the country . . . will be a consequence of revolutionary military
campaign."[1] In the very short run, Castro believed that the army would
exploit the movement's defeat by staging a massive show of force against
rebel columns. He thus quickly sent a personal envoy, Ricardo Lorie Vals,
to Miami to jump-start weapons deliveries and instructed Latour's man,
"Bebo" Hidalgo, to cooperate by sending weapons for the militias while
Lorie procured them for the guerrillas. According to the FBI, which kept
tabs on the revolutionaries' activities in Miami, Mexico, and Venezuela,
Lorie and Hidalgo later developed plans to airdrop material directly to
Castro.[2]

Shortly after the strike failure, Marcelo Fernández traveled to the Sierra
Maestra to talk with Castro and set the stage for a joint *sierra-llano*
meeting in early May. By then Vilma Espín had fled Santiago for Raúl
Castro's encampment in the Sierra Cristal and reported on the state of
the movement and the conflict with Latour. The strike's failure, wrote
Raúl, meant that

a new structuring of our National Directorate is imposing itself after a profound analysis of reality, based on the errors committed—the last being the failure of the strike that they wanted to decree with a fixed time and day, and the worst of all being their desire to subordinate it to isolated actions, yielding instances in which in many sectors the workers didn't even know they had given the order to strike, since [the National Directorate] wanted to make it a secret to surprise the army. Who are the guilty ones? Judge [this affair] as incompetent, in the same way you should analyze all of their previous mistakes. Let's talk for once with revolutionary sincerity!! Much blood has been spilled, much will continue to spill and more than what has already spilled for us to still not have sufficient merit to solve our amateur problems!![3]

Raúl's frustration and intolerance was based not only on differences of tactics and strategy. In fact, since March when he opened the Second Front, his column had relied in part upon supplies from sources under the control of M267 activists in Guantánamo. After the strike these supply lines shriveled. Raúl attributed this unwelcome development not to a lack of resources, police repression, or competing demands within the underground, but to "sterile disputes between groups and factions." He chastised the Guantánamo organizers for doing "awful damage" and for standing in stark contrast to the "unity" that the guerrillas in the Sierra Cristal had guarded from the bickering and divisive urban underground. At a minimum he wanted the entire Guantánamo underground to decide collectively whether "the organization in the cities" could follow suit—that is, overcome their internal bickering and support his front. He clearly felt that he and his column held the moral high ground, warning that should the underground fail to give its full support to his supply operation, "it won't be the first time that we have to survive on our own efforts . . . even though new sacrifices will be necessary, and even though the war lasts longer, and even though more blood will be spilled."[4]

With government troops already gathering near the base camp of one of his companies, Raúl remained at the ready in the Sierra Cristal rather than making the 160 kilometer trek from his base near Mayarí Arriba to participate in person at what was to be called the Mompié meeting. Instead, he weighed in with his brother by outlining how the *sierra* and *llano* should address the profound differences that then distinguished the two factions within the 26th of July Movement.

Sitting down together, all of us, face to face and without prejudice of any nature, nor fear of wounding sensitivities to bluntly lay out the thinking of each one of us about everyone else . . . we will begin to clarify so many issues that have reached us via rumors, which owing to the existing antipathy of both parts are warmly welcomed by one side or the other. Also, sincere con-

fessions of mistakes, even of those that we are not willing to accept for whatever motive, will come to light . . . The presence of bad faith with certain
ends means this is the best solution. I have been proposing a meeting in the
Sierra with every member of the Directorate for a long time and with all sincerity I believe that if we had gone forward with it already we would have
overcome the "divorce" that has done so much damage in the past and in
the present, and, if we don't settle it once and for all, will do much more
damage in the future.[5]

On May 3, 1958, eleven members of the 26th of July Movement met
for two days of "exhaustive and often violent discussion" in the Sierra
Maestra at the home of the Mompié family. Fidel Castro, Che Guevara,
Faustino Pérez, René Ramos Latour, Vilma Espín, Celia Sánchez, Marcelo
Fernández, Antonio "Nico" Torres, Haydée Santamaría, David Salvador,
Luis Buch, and Enzo Infante attended the meeting.[6]

Che later reported that the marathon "was tense, since [the meeting]
had to judge the actions of the *llano* comrades, who in practice had run
the affairs of the 26th of July Movement up to that moment."[7] And judge
it they did. According to his own report, Guevara echoed his earlier criticisms and those of the PSP by attacking David Salvador for attempting a
"sectarian strike, in which the other revolutionary movements would
be" subordinate to the 26th of July. He blamed Faustino Pérez for believing that the militia could seize the capital despite the overwhelming superiority of Batista's police presence. He also faulted René Ramos Latour
for organizing the militias in the *llano* as "parallel troops" to the *sierra*
guerrilla "without the training or the combat morale, and without having gone through the rigorous process of selection in the war."[8] The differences between the rebel army forces and the militia were not just a
matter of semantics. The forces under the command of the rebel army,
which by April 1958 included columns under the command of Fidel Castro, Che Guevara, Raúl Castro, Juan Almeida, and Camilo Cienfuegos
in the Sierra Maestra, northeastern Oriente (the Sierra Cristal), and the
Oriente/Santiago region of the Sierra Maestra, staged hit-and-run actions
against symbols of the Cuban military such as barracks, outposts, and
later government troops concentrated largely in the mountains. The militias, on the other hand, were theoretically to be based in towns and
cities and were to target not only physical and human symbols of the
Batista regime but also economic targets such as highways, utilities, and
sugar mills.

Fidel Castro emerged from the meeting with complete control over all
affairs of the 26th of July Movement. Under a new unified command, he
became general secretary of the movement and commander in chief of

the rebel army. Neither Havana nor Santiago would any longer have any strategic priority. Instead, the Sierra Maestra became the new headquarters for the entire movement. The underground struggle was relegated to the background, Latour's "parallel" militia remained in little more than name, and guerrilla warfare became the movement's only military strategy. "The line of the *sierra* would be followed," wrote Guevara, "that of direct armed struggle, extending it to other regions and in that way taking control of the country. We did away with various naive illusions about attempted revolutionary general strikes when the situation had not matured sufficiently to bring about such an explosion, and without having laid the necessary groundwork for an event of that magnitude."[9]

The National Directorate dissolved, and in its place, Fidel created a "national executive" in the Sierra Maestra. Marcelo Fernández would head a "delegation" of the national executive to be based in Santiago under Castro's direct orders. That group included, for labor, Nico Torres, who was a railroad worker from Guantánamo and had organized partial work stoppages during the 1956 action in Oriente coinciding with the *Granma* landing, as well as, for "propaganda," Arnold Rodríguez, who had worked on the Fangio kidnapping."[10] To oversee the supply of weapons to the Sierra Maestra and rebuild bridges with the exiled Cuban opposition, Fidel sent Haydée Santamaría to Miami just days after the Mompié meeting. Luis Buch was sent to Venezuela with a similar portfolio but not before he and Guevara had developed a Morse code system for communicating between Caracas and the Sierra Maestra. After clearing up their affairs in the cities, David Salvador, Faustino Pérez, and René Ramos Latour would henceforth remain in the Sierra Maestra, while Fidel appointed a major from his own ranks, Delio Gomez Ochoa, to replace Latour and gradually merge the militias into existing or newly created rebel columns. Ochoa and Latour left the Sierra Maestra and headed west for Havana and Pinar del Río, where they began to dissolve the militias, leaving a great deal of bitterness in their wake.[11]

What would become of Latour's militia, the "revolutionary armies" he believed would thrust the country into chaos and popular revolt? In Castro's view, the militias and the guerrillas in rural areas would become less and less distinguishable over the course of the upcoming military campaign, which the rebel army planned to conduct westward across the island from Oriente. "It tends to happen," he wrote "Bebo" Hidalgo in Miami, "that when we open a new front the best people from every area join us, then the tasks of sabotage and attrition are generally carried out by rebel patrols. For example, Bayamo: fifteen days don't go by without combat in the street by patrols that penetrate" from the mountains and then return, "enjoying a degree of security afterward that is not possible in the underground of a small city." For the large cities, especially Havana, Castro took a very different view from Latour, who insisted that the militias significantly increase attacks on industry, transportation, and utilities without reprieve. Castro, on the other hand, felt that the militias should for the time being retreat and retrain, planning for "systematic, continual, and progressive" sabotage in the long term—a diplomatic way of suggesting that the urban militia disappear until the culmination of the rebel army's military campaign. Latour himself died on July 31, 1958, while heading a rebel column in one of the last battles of the summer offensive.[12]

For Guevara, these changes did no more than "register a reality: the political predominance of the *sierra* people, a consequence of their correct point of view and their accurate interpretation of events," and clearly, a consequence not only of the *sierra*'s point of view, but also of the very concrete fact that the strike, the responsibility of the *llano,* had failed.[13] Che Guevara, Raúl Castro, Juan Almeida, and Fidel Castro, the "*sierra* people," would finally exercise the political and military hegemony previously held by the urban underground. In essence, Guevara argued, since it was the *sierra,* and more specifically he and Raúl, that had objected to the April strike and predicted its failure, its alternative—guerrilla war—would take center stage in the insurrection. According to Guevara, the decisions made at Mompié did more than eliminate "some practical decision-making problems" that until then had "prevented Fidel from actually exercising the authority he had earned."[14] By merging the militias with the guerrillas and converting the general strike into only the popular culmination of a military campaign, the decisions made at Mompié eliminated the two pillars of the National Directorate's strategy that had occupied much of the movement's political, human, and material capital since the *Granma* voyage from Mexico in November 1956.

The shift in tactics was also pragmatic. Immediately after the strike, Batista had again suspended constitutional guarantees and declared a state of emergency. The regime had issued a decree ordering prison and fines for perpetrators of sabotage, and for "using any means of publicity or propagation [to] spread false rumors or false or tendentious news which may damage national dignity, alter public peace, tranquillity or confidence, or tend to undermine powers of the State, the economy, public finances, the credit of the nation or Government, banking credit, or value of currency or bonds."[15] Virtually all of the M267's safe houses and meeting places in Havana had been exposed after the strike. The chief of police, Pilar García, had publicly stated in the manhunt for political activists that he wanted neither prisoners nor wounded. The movement lost seven of its Havana-based militia captains to prison, torture, or political assassination. In a report to Fidel after Mompié, Marcelo Fernández described the fate of two "comrades from propaganda" who had been arrested and held in Havana's twelfth precinct. When an M267 attorney went to the police station to inquire about their status, the lawyer himself was beaten and tortured to death and the two activists also murdered. The security forces' efforts to eliminate the underground in Santiago and Havana were so intensive that carrying out a sabotage campaign in the cities, where the regime's repressive apparatus was most concentrated, was no longer viable. Even in Santiago, where the 26th of July had a stronger base of support and more longtime activists, repression and a profound crisis of morale had paralyzed the underground and forced many conspirators to cease their work or to flee abroad or to the comparative safety of nearby rebel columns.[16]

Marcelo Fernández, the only National Directorate member to retain anything close to the role he had performed before the strike, reported the Mompié changes to the 26th of July's provincial coordinators and section chiefs. He explained the merger under Fidel's command of the militia and the rebel army and instructed the underground to send food, medicine, equipment, arms, and money to Castro's troops. Highway and rail traffic was to be restored, workers of all stripes were to be met with outstretched hands, and, if the National Student Front (FEN) agreed, schools should reopen at once.

Before the strike, Fernández often dedicated as many as fifteen pages of his organizational memoranda to describing the work of each section chief of the urban underground: finances, labor, sabotage, propaganda, exile, students, and civic resistance in each province. After Mompié, however, his instructions for the underground occupied only two sentences, a somewhat exhausted call to maintain discipline and adapt to the movement's new focus on armed struggle. If a strike of the magnitude the underground had once imagined were to ever take place, he explained, it would occur only because the rebel army's imminent clash with Batista's soldiers "will provoke the necessary conditions for a future strike movement that perhaps will be produced spontaneously without the need for a specific convening."[17] Once the vanguard, the urban underground had finally been relegated to the revolution's rearguard.

14 | Unity: "Like a Magic Word"

MAY 1958

> I ask myself whether in the end we are serving the
> people, who know and understand the good from
> the bad and will know how to tell the difference
> when it matters between who gave everything of
> themselves and who did not, and who will know
> how to distinguish who is responsible for this en-
> tire tragedy.
>
> Taras Domitro to René Ramos Latour, April 10, 1958

THE MOMPIÉ MEETING HAD FORCED THE
llano members of the National Directorate to acknowledge that the 26th
of July had neither the political tools, the material resources, nor the strategic vision to effectively dominate and mobilize the anti-Batista opposition among labor, students, or white-collar professionals in Cuban society. Once the strategy of a violence-induced general strike had proven
unsuccessful, the Castro brothers, Che Guevara, and Juan Almeida were
free to make the case that success by the rebel army in direct confrontation with the Cuban military was the key to building enough popular
support to unseat the Batista regime. As the *sierra* commanders prepared
for a massive confrontation with the army's 28,000 troops, a skeleton
staff of the National Directorate's underground leadership, Marcelo
Fernández and the new labor coordinator, Nico Torres, made their way to
Santiago and Havana to face the recriminations and repair the damage
that followed the strike.[1]

By this time, the climate in Havana was tense and dangerous. The Popular Socialist Party (PSP) published several scathing attacks blaming the
strike's failure on the 26th of July's militarized approach and refusal to
pursue a broad-based unity among all opposition groups. Although the
government blamed the strike on an alleged unity agreement between
the M267 and the PSP, the party retorted that "had such unity existed,
the current Cuban situation would be another story and surely the
batistiano tyranny would by now be but a bad memory of the past."[2] Eager to distance itself from the 26th of July, the PSP quickly issued a statement denying government claims that the M267, the Communists, and
former President Carlos Prío had jointly masterminded the strike. The

PSP also alerted other Communist parties in Latin America of the fiasco, condemning the M267 for "using armed action to intimidate the working class and remove it from the workplace . . . and rejecting the possibility of carrying out economic strikes before the general strike . . . in the last days of March and the beginning of April." Moreover, the PSP took credit for the isolated instances of success and blamed "leaders of other organizations" for disappearing after calling the strike.[3]

Like Guevara, the PSP attributed a political crisis within the 26th of July to "elements of the right" within the movement, whom the party accused of "working in accord with the North American Embassy and subject to them" and consequently working "against a united front and against mass struggle." There is no evidence whatsoever that either Faustino Pérez, Marcelo Fernández, or David Salvador had anything to do with the American embassy in the months prior to the strike. Still, the PSP believed or erroneously promoted the idea that the movement's reluctance to work arm and arm derived from members' allegiance to the American embassy, which was responsible for making them refuse "to form a united front that would include communists, the basis for the pre-strike struggle against unity." As a result, the PSP argued, the 26th of July was suffering a severe crisis of confidence and legitimacy, particularly among members of the petite bourgeoisie and working class, who once had "blind confidence" in the movement's military victories but had come to realize that "the 26th of July alone will not be able to overthrow Batista."[4]

In his own manifesto after the strike, Faure Chomón of the Student Revolutionary Directorate (DRE) also seized upon the 26th of July's defeat to demand greater opposition integration along the lines of his pre-strike negotiations with Faustino Pérez, as well as "full leadership in strategy, propaganda and organization" in a "unity commission" composed of the DRE, the 26th of July, and any other "insurrectional movement with a proletarian base."[5] Invoking the nation and flag as the great Cuban unifiers, Chomón's statement identified "boastful sectarianism" as "Batista's best ally," a message he later described as consistent with the movement's own conclusions at Mompié and one that numerous opposition figures and many within the movement's own ranks would repeat in the weeks and months following the strike failure.[6]

Before the Mompié gathering and after a steady stream of letters indicating as much, Fidel Castro knew that under the pretext of unity the opposition would attempt to capitalize on the movement's weakness by pushing for a return to a coalition akin to the Cuban Liberation Junta. Following discussions with Marcelo Fernández, Castro took a step both

to placate and undercut the opposition's clamor for unity, and also to satisfy the rebel army's relentless need for weapons. He instructed Mario
Llerena and Raúl Chibás, who were in Miami at the time, to ask Judge
Urrutia, the movement's favored candidate for provisional president, to
come immediately to the Sierra Maestra and establish a provisional government, which would be followed by a request "to friendly Latin American countries to grant us the status of belligerency." If Urrutia agreed and
the international community recognized the provisional government,
the opposition organizations would face, wrote Fernández, "a dilemma:
either they support this Government, and even name delegates or representatives to it (thus we will have achieved unity) or they reject it, which
would show them up."[7] Establishing a provisional government at a moment of tactical weakness would place the 26th of July in a position of
strategic strength vis-à-vis the opposition, Castro wrote, so that "little by
little we will cultivate the support of other groups, after which we will
have achieved unity in the ideal and combative manner . . . But we can't
advocate [unity] too soon, because we would be at the mercy of eternal
disagreements. We must attain unity over the course of events."[8] With a
provisional government in the Sierra Maestra and success on the battlefield, opposition unity would follow—with the 26th of July as the hegemonic force in the anti-Batista struggle.

Success on the battlefield would have to win support not only from the
movement's adversaries in the opposition but also from grassroots supporters and top officials of the 26th of July. Some believed that the movement could not possibly defeat the dictator without a united opposition front and criticized its leaders for having deluded themselves into
attempting a national uprising without the help of other opposition
groups. Others were convinced that the sources of disunity were the opposition groups themselves, who, upset with the movement's ascen-
dancy, withheld weapons before the strike. Though the OA did contribute some twenty-five machine guns to the militia in Las Villas on the eve
of the strike, Enrique Oltuski, the movement's coordinator there wanted
the M267 to make a public and "final summons to the OA and the DRE
for *unity of action*," to force these groups to show their cards and contribute materially to the M267. Were they to reject such an entreaty,
"the people will know why there is no unity and our position will have
emerged strengthened in everyone's eyes."[9]

Indeed, despite the catastrophe, the movement held firm to its refusal
to become but one group among others fighting the dictator. Marcelo
Fernández wrote the provincial coordinators and section chiefs who had
been on the front lines of the strike that on the matter of unity the 26th

of July would continue supporting the "thesis that all revolutionary organizations should coordinate efforts, without having to form a single organization with egalitarian representation like the Liberation Junta, as it would be unjust for our Movement to be reduced to a simple seventh vote, to one seventh of the Revolution."[10] That is, the other opposition groups should still concede that owing to its superior strength of men, arms, resource, and national prominence, the 26th of July was to be regarded as the first among unequals. It proved enormously difficult for the movement to maintain this stance, even within its own front organizations. Labor, student, and civic resistance leaders in Havana accused the 26th of July of gambling with their lives during the strike and demanded a massive purge of the National Directorate's members directly involved in the April events. How was it possible, they asked, to send "believers" off to battle without first telling them that the movement had no defenses?[11]

The Civic Resistance Movement, created as a front organization for white-collar professionals and the middle class, formally broke with the 26th of July to form an independent organization that mirrored the National Directorate's own structure, though without an action and sabotage unit. Under the direction of a Havana engineer, Manuel Ray, the Civic Resistance appealed to the M267 to seek unity by joining a coalition made up of all opposition groups. Marcelo Fernández understood that Civic Resistance members resented the movement for considering them merely a source for money and safe houses. He recognized that they had often toyed with whether to function independently or remain affiliated with the 26th of July. But Fernández made his disagreement with the open break clear and warned that since many Civic Resistance members had embarked on their revolutionary activities as 26th of July militants, and only later joined Civic Resistance under M267 orders, the 26th of July would continue to expect their loyalty if any internecine dispute arose. Though Ray vowed to support "the 26th of July's heroic efforts to give back to Cuba her freedom and sovereignty under the inspiring leadership of Fidel Castro," in the climate of chaos and dissension at that moment, the break from the M267 was a blow to the movement's hegemonic pretenses, if not to its vastly depleted war chest.[12]

In the same month, the executive council of the National Workers Front (FON) met to reorganize and develop a new alliance strategy. After two days of "intense debate," the FON agreed to "banish the militarized mentality" from its labor cadre, develop true "mass struggle," and "build a unified labor organization."[13] Prior to the strike, the 26th of July's labor work had been carried out as a conspiracy, wrote Fernández. "In meetings we talked about buying pistols and dynamite to conduct sabotage, we underestimated [the importance of] propaganda, and we objected to fomenting partial strikes . . . We created an end-game mentality in which everything was subject to the final moment."[14] Thereafter, instead of organizing workplace labor committees as microcosms of the 26th of July's cell structure, the FON's members would recruit workers to join clandestine cells to focus exclusively on recruiting more workers and promoting the agenda of labor, rather than that of the 26th of July.[15]

One member of the FON's national board, Octavio Louit Venzant Bejerano, a railroad comrade of Nico Torres and a M267 labor organizer since 1956, later blamed the movement's gun runner Frank Fiorini as the one "most guilty" for the militarization of the strike.[16] Fiorini "made us believe that the military actions they had planned for April 9 were of such an order of magnitude that there was no need to even inform our labor chiefs about the strike; however, what Fiorini promised did not take place," Bejerano indicated.[17] Back in Havana after his fruitless arms forays to Miami, Fiorini, as mentioned earlier, had apparently insisted on keeping the FON organizers in the dark—arguing that the element of surprise was crucial.[18]

With the pistols finally purged, Nico Torres and Fernández convened meetings of labor organizers linked to the Auténticos, the Ortodoxos, the DRE, the Catholic Church, the PSP, dissident union leaders, and the Federation of University Students (FEU). The talks faced many obstacles, ranging from a dispute over the very name of the new labor front to pressure from the American embassy to exclude the Communists. According to Fernández's report to Castro, the American labor attaché had warned that the United States would find Communist participation unacceptable in a coalition of labor groups opposing Batista. Fernández wrote Fidel that he believed the embassy's meddling could destabilize the creation of a unified labor organization and that those individuals who were participating in the labor talks while also talking to the Americans were "acting in bad faith . . . they talk of unity, but they're afraid of the 26th, of the Communists, and of the Embassy. And fear makes a bad advisor."[19]

After meeting on and off for one month, Nico Torres predicted that, excluding the dissident faction of the CTC, the group would agree upon a joint statement of principles and participate in an inclusive labor coalition to be called the United National Workers Front (FONU). The new unified workers organization would also include the Communist Party, which had overcome its earlier antipathy for the 26th of July because uniting against the regime's imminent "campaign of extermination" of the rebel army was "in the interest of all us who oppose tyranny and want peace and democracy for our country."[20] Not surprisingly, because of its particular concept of unity—as hegemony, not consensus—the 26th of July insisted that only the labor sections of each organization sign the final joint statement creating the FONU. The other groups insisted that all of the member organizations sign the joint statement to leverage a broad-based unity coalition, but the M267 desperately wished to avoid this outcome until it had become palpably stronger—militarily and politically—than the other opposition groups. Perhaps because of this dynamic, the FONU did not formally coalesce and become active until November 1958.[21]

The 26th of July's problems with labor and white-collar professionals were of a different nature and more difficult compared to the predicament that followed for Cuban students, organized by the National Student Front (FEN). By mid-March 1958, the FEN's efforts to organize high school and university students to boycott classes, occupy school buildings, and hold street protests "had been a complete success . . . covering every school without exception, including the private schools," according to Ricardo Alarcón, a FEN leader. Indeed, so effective and complete were the school shutdowns and student mobilization that they helped create a climate of popular activism on the eve of the April strike attempt.[22]

In the massive wave of repression after the strike, schools began to reopen; some, like the private schools, did so under pressure from the police. Because of the movement's shift in strategies, the National Directorate also had decided at Mompié that for the time being all schools (with the exception of the public universities) should open again.[23] It was not a cut-and-dried decision for FEN leaders to call off their troops and allow normal school life to resume. Because of police surveillance of the underground, the FEN was unable to gather openly to consider their options. But dozens of student leaders from private and public schools defied the regime and met clandestinely—under the cover of attending a wedding at the Masonic Temple in downtown Havana—just three blocks from one of the police precincts under the command of the notoriously brutal Colonel Esteban Ventura Novo. "We tried to decide what to do and the majority conclusion," after several hours of heated debate, "was that we lacked sufficient forces to try to block the resumption of school" activities, particularly because of the overwhelming show of police brutality. There was not, however, a complete consensus. According to Alarcón, "Some of the revolutionaries from the Catholic University, Villanueva, disagreed "and after the meeting . . . tried to continue the strike and failed."[24] Nearly two months after the strike, college campuses in Havana, Las Villas, and Oriente were still closed, while private universities in the capital and high schools around the country had reopened. Despite the FEN's relative internal cohesion, after the strike its association with the 26th of July had made it suspect among other student organizations, particularly those linked to the DRE, which insisted that "before creating student (or labor) unity, political unity was necessary."[25]

The 26th of July slowly began to restore its credibility with the opposition forces on the island. But abroad the M267 faced several political, financial, and legal hurdles before it could again establish itself as the lead opposition group. Judge Manual Urrutia believed that the failed strike had severely weakened the 26th of July's support in exile and had "unleashed a 'unity' offensive for whom those who act out of good faith are expressing their desperation . . . and the others their desire to obtain advantages through *malas artes*," or a ruse. Indeed, Urrutia explained that many of the opposition figures associated with the Cuban Liberation Junta, including José Miró Cardona of the Havana Bar Association and the Civic Institutions, Auténtico and Prío spokesman Tony Varona, some Ortodoxos, and members of the DRE, had asked Urrutia to tell Castro that they would support the judge as provisional president only if the 26th of July first acceded to a broad-based unity agreement. Urrutia asked Fidel to clarify what the M267 meant by "unity: unity of action, not the *politiquería* unity." He assured Castro that "if the *politiqueros* make such a unity fail, the people will join you . . . more than ever." Urrutia appeared to share the M267 antipathy for coalition politics but cautioned that "we should not just reject plans under way here to achieve it. *Without losing time* we should reach a *fruitful* unity or some indication that good faith is on our side alone."[26]

Indeed, in counseling Fidel to join a unity agreement as the price for establishing a provisional government with Urrutia at its head, a long-time M267 weapons supplier told Castro that "the Movement lost a bit of prestige in Cuban and international public opinion." In Miami, too, it was "on the defensive," as "other organizations and groups capitalized on a state of public opinion favoring unity between resident and exiled Cubans."[27] Castro was in no mood to be sucked into an unwieldy opposition coalition that he did not yet have the political strength to control. But until Castro indicated some disposition to appease the Miami clamor for unity, and was able to take and hold territory as stipulated under international law, Urrutia denied the request to establish a provisional government in the Sierra Maestra.[28] Once Castro could satisfy his political and legal conditions, Urrutia vowed to raise money and send weapons for the rebel army and to sound out friendly Latin American countries on whether they would recognize the 26th of July as having established a legitimate government.[29]

The American government's response to the upheaval in Cuba still factored into the exiled opposition's political calculations, and many registered their views with the State Department in their ongoing dance to covet favor and prepare for a post-Batista government. At one such visit to Washington, José Miró Cardona, one of the many who aspired to higher office in Cuba, told the Office of Middle American Affairs that in his view Batista's "overthrow had to come through a military coup and that afterwards a military junta would have to take over and form a civilian government to rule until elections could be held."[30] In writing to Castro, however, Miró Cardona made no mention of this apparent preference that a coup overthrow Batista. Instead, he explained that through his informal meetings with American academics, professionals, and officials he had identified widespread concern about the consequences of Batista being overthrown by a general strike, in which either labor or the Communists might play a significant role. Moreover, confirming the 26th of July's suspicions that "opposition unity" was but a ploy to neutralize the revolutionaries, Miró Cardona insisted that the Americans felt a formal opposition alliance was the only way to prevent radical groups from dominating the post-Batista political order on the island. Distancing himself from such views, Miró Cardona wrote that "these prejudices, deeply rooted in the American conscience," made it all the more urgent for Castro to agree to a "provisional government supported by all political and revolutionary groups, which would produce a possible (they are careful with their words) change in North American policy with respect to Cuba, and would translate into frank and decisive support of the Latin American countries that rotate around Washington's orbit."[31]

At the same time Tony Varona, one who allegedly supported such a provisional government, told State Department officials that Castro "ought to have learned from the failure of his April offensive that he cannot go it alone and that unity of the revolutionary opposition is the only answer"—adding that Prío had written Castro with a "six-point program . . . for unifying Prío and Castro forces."[32] Miró Cardona also proposed a plan "that would lack all effectiveness if you do not lend your support." First, he proposed that all political and revolutionary opposition groups sign onto the Civic Institutions' March 1958 call for Batista's resignation and support Judge Urrutia as president of a provisional government. The newly unified opposition, "recognizing, obviously, your leadership," should agree on "action plans" and send Castro "arms, men and money."

A final step would be to appoint the members of the provisional government.[33] Miró Cardona—who later became the Kennedy administration's pick for provisional president of the Democratic Revolutionary Front were the 1961 Bay of Pigs invasion to succeed—did not indicate to Castro or publicly that in his view the provisional government could only be installed either as a result of a coup d'état or through the rebel army's efforts.[34]

Consistent with its past decisions, the 26th of July resisted a power-sharing arrangement that would relegate it to becoming only the armed wing of a multimember coalition. The civilian leaders of the movement were equally unprepared to concede that their tactical defeat required concessions during the power struggle then under way within the opposition. "This 'unity' sentiment," Marcelo Fernández wrote Castro, "is extending throughout the country, even among our own militants. We must take a position on it. We are being asked to define it."[35] Like Oltuski, Fernández felt that the opposition groups would demonstrate their true commitment to "unity" only by recognizing a provisional government in the Sierra Maestra. But it had become evident from Miami that there would be no such development unless the 26th of July first joined an opposition coalition.

Until the M267 could "attain unity over the course of events," as Castro had written, the Sierra would remain a battleground rather than the seat of a new government. In order to realize their preferred scenario, the rebels would have to resist the military offensive against them that had just begun. To do so, they needed to acquire arms without paying the political price of losing their independence. For their part, the other opposition groups had to weigh their desire to unseat Batista against their distaste for ceding power to an unruly, ragtag, radical bunch of extremely young men and women who seemed ready to plunge the island into further chaos—and provoke the displeasure of the Americans by possibly tolerating the Communists and exciting the long-dormant Cuban working class.

Though confident that military victory over the Cuban army would strengthen the rebels and the 26th of July politically, Castro understood that his forces were at their "most critical" stage, with "greater problems and fewer resources than ever, with even our own closest contributors waiting for the offensive to see what will happen" before again giving their full economic, material, and political support.[36] Rebel sympathizers and M267 members promised new shipments of weapons from Venezuela and Costa Rica, while Fidel impatiently waited for the movement's star pilot, Pedro Luis Díaz Lanz, to return from Miami with the matériel that Ricardo Lorie and Bebo Hidalgo had been sent to purchase after the strike.[37] Throughout May 1958, government troops arrived in waves in Oriente, landing on the southern and northern coasts of the province. The war had already begun in the Sierra Cristal; starting May 13, Raúl Castro's troops were assaulted for two weeks with air- and ground-based attacks by troops, bombs, and machine guns. "Send ammunition and cartridges of any kind, as a world of *casquitos* is upon us," he wrote.[38] Finally, on May 29, Díaz Lanz returned from Miami with a low-capacity Cessna filled with Italian carbines, one Garand rifle, and thousands of shells.[39] The "current stage" of the insurrection, wrote Fidel, was "urgent, a matter of life and death, in which upon every weapon the survival of the revolution depends."[40]

15 | The Pact of Caracas

MAY–JULY 1958

> How well you did not to come, how sad one feels
> here . . . perhaps with luck I can soon be with you
> . . . From here I can tell you that this is the most
> unpleasant place on earth, so much loneliness,
> though I couldn't be feeling Cuba more than this,
> at times I feel such a desire to be there that I have
> to control myself not to just run away.
>
> Haydée Santamaría to Celia Sánchez, May 20, 1958

HAYDÉE SANTAMARÍA, "YÉYÉ," LEFT THE
Sierra Maestra for Miami with the deaths of her brother Abel and former boyfriend Boris tormenting her soul, the fate of her jailed fiancé Armando Hart unknown, and the success of the rebel army on her shoulders. To succeed in Miami, Santamaría had to summon all of the strengths she had acquired during her thirty-six years—her intelligence, her revolutionary credentials, her expressiveness, her youth, and her charm—to secure weapons for the revolutionaries and to rebuild the movement's credibility within the opposition.

When she first arrived in Miami, Santamaría replaced some of the individuals representing the 26th of July whose squabbles and infighting the *sierra* considered a principal reason why, despite hundreds of thousands of dollars sent from Cuba, so few weapons from abroad had reached the rebels. Luis Buch, who had delivered the bad news of the M267's break from the Cuban Liberation Junta, left Santiago with his new Morse code system to exercise some control over the pro-M267 exiles in Venezuela. Carlos Franqui returned from Miami to Cuba to broadcast the rebel army's shortwave Radio Rebelde from the Sierra Maestra. And José Llanusa replaced Franqui as the Committee in Exile's "chairman of organization," setting up shop in Manhattan while his wife, María Josefa, and infant daughter lived with Haydée in Miami.[1]

From Llanusa's New York base, the former basketball champion succeeded where others had failed, merging three separate 26th of July "patriotic clubs" into one in the hopes of enabling the movement to raise more money and speak with one voice. Llanusa, who had worked closely in the Havana underground with Haydée, was a creative fundraiser—

planning concerts featuring Spanish classical guitarist Pablo Casals, negotiating big-ticket bond sales with financial advisers for Aristotle Onassis, and producing innovative theatrical productions of up-and-coming Cuban playwrights, such as *The Arms Are Made of Steel* by Pablo Armando Fernández.[2] Luis Buch moved with his family to Caracas, where he too began the tedious and unpopular process of merging various 26th of July splinter groups, raising money, lobbying the new interim government for aid, and negotiating the terms for a new unity pact between the 26th of July and the opposition as the battle in Oriente progressed. Santamaría, Llanusa, and Buch were in nearly constant contact by letter, phone, and cable starting in May 1958, and their common cause and clarity of objectives contributed enormously to their successes in exile. Despite their efforts to massage the egos of the movement's adversaries and assuage the anxieties of its supporters, many of the M267's collaborators in New York, Miami, Caracas, or Costa Rica often remained suspicious of one another, complaining to Fidel, Santamaría, and others about the profligate spending habits of one person, the antidemocratic values of the other, or the excessively anti-Communist public comments of the next.[3]

With her own revolutionary history dating to the July 1953 assault on the Moncada barracks, Santamaría wholeheartedly shared the conviction of Fidel Castro and her fiancé Armando Hart that the 26th of July Movement's commitment to political independence set it apart from all of the other opposition groups then fighting against Batista, including the Ortodoxos-históricos. As Fidel's spokesperson in Miami, she was immediately confronted by the entire exile community's "clamor for unity" and warned Fidel to expect significant problems in raising money without acceding to some form of united effort.[4] For instance, José Miró Cardona told Santamaría, and wrote Fidel, that he had already persuaded former president Carlos Prío to support the rebel army. The *quid pro quo* from Prío and the entire exiled opposition was implicit: equal participation in decision-making during wartime and power-sharing in the post-Batista government.[5] But this arrangement flew in the face of Santamaría's core political instincts of breaking from the *politiquería* of the past. She immediately scheduled a meeting with Prío to undo the damage Miró Cardona had begun, lest a formal alliance with Prío and company taint the purity of her revolution before the movement had recovered its political and military strength.

At the same time, Santamaría's fiancée Armando Hart wrote from prison to warn her against any discussions of pacts like the Cuban Liberation Junta with "Carlos Prío or any zone of his moral comparison, not for ideological but for strategic reasons."[6] The 26th of July, he wrote, must "maintain political equidistance in any government or unity formula" and "oppose the thesis of political coalition," which "the Príos and CIA" are advocating. To circumvent both, Hart insisted that Santamaría avoid involving Prío in the movement's immediate plans. Instead, he counseled developing a flexible alliance with "conservative sectors, with the Church, with the [Civic] Institutions, with the Directorio, [and] with Barquín's group," keeping them "on our side without letting them believe that we've capitulated our position." Indeed, Hart felt so strongly about avoiding Carlos Prío that he counseled Santamaría to consider someone other than Judge Urrutia (whom Prío also supported) as provisional president, while reserving the possibility of running the Santiago judge as "the 26th's candidate in the first elections."

Hart further cautioned that any strategic or political "intransigence" not express itself as ideological, since "we have not proposed anything more ideologically radical" than suggested by the July 1957 Sierra Manifesto and the December 1957 letter by Fidel to the Liberation Junta. Both of these documents set forth a moderate program for modernizing the country, eliminating graft and corruption, establishing civilian control over the military, and giving voice to Cuba's dispossessed. Until the movement could undertake a "deeper indoctrination of its militants," Hart believed the political moment in Cuba was ripe only for a broad-based core agreement that reflected "the true representative forces of society."[7]

But Santamaría pursued a slightly different approach, enticing Prío with the prospect of a role in Cuba's future for the remote possibility that he arm the rebels in the present. Though one year earlier Léster Rodríguez had also pleaded with the former president and student leader for weapons, he had made the mistake of agreeing in exchange to a join a coalition that consigned the 26th of July to equal status with six other opposition groups. Now, though the M267 had been strengthened in Oriente and was stronger than the other opposition groups, it faced a pressing need to overcome discord within its own ranks at home and abroad, apathy and fear in the population, rival guerrilla fronts in Las Villas province, and a military offensive in the Sierra Maestra, for which the rebel army remained severely underequipped. Recounting her high-stakes gamble for the movement's material survival and political independence, Santamaría told Fidel,

I saw Prío, I'm going to tell you everything we talked about. When I saw him I can't deny that I felt like screaming, when I saw him I thought about Abel who went [to Moncada] with just a shotgun to Enrique [Hart] who died in an explosion, about every one of you, in your desperation to get one rifle, it was just terrible, so much so that after shaking his hand I said to him doctor I am here to talk to the boy from the 1930s, with him I can reach an understanding, if you are ready to behave as [you did] then, we can talk; if I have to speak with the Prío of today we will not be able to reach an agreement. I said this to him almost without being aware of it; when I heard what I'd said I thought everything would end right there, but it was just the opposite, he answered that he was ready to talk as I wished. I told him about how for five years I've been watching comrades fall each day, and not only did I tell him about those whom I love so much, but about those who haven't died, about those I've seen screaming for a rifle, that he could fix this [problem], that in the name of those whom he saw die in the struggle against Machado, in the name of those whom I have seen die, in the name of Cuban women who can't hold on any longer, for Cuba. I got down on my knees in front of him so that he would place a rifle in the hands of those that were fighting for freedom and for our Country. He told me that I should show him the way, that he is ready to prove to us that he loves Cuba as much as I do. I told him the way is to send a plane [to you], that if he wanted he could go too, or send someone he trusts completely, that I will go in the plane to guarantee the success of the trip; he has a plane that carries four thousand pounds and the same quantity of equipment, so we agreed that in a few days we'd make the trip, and I told him that in the Sierra we will talk about true unity. I did this to make him commit himself further. He asked me not to tell anyone else about the operation, that it would be a secret between the two of us, since it doesn't in any way damage Ricardo [Lorie's] operation and he already has the money . . . I agreed, and I'm sure that if he does go through with what he told me I more than anyone else am the one to make it happen. It was hard for him to have a woman talk to him like this; he saw my desperation. I told him something else too, let's talk about pacts [in the Sierra], if he doesn't come through with the weapons he knows he will never be able to speak of pacts. I think you can convince him of whatever you think is best—I can tell you he even has bombers. I think I've performed well and I have high hopes that his plane will reach you. If he has misled me as he has so many times before, we lose nothing; quite the contrary we will be able to say so when they start talking about pacts that they were invited to [the Sierra.]"

Playing on Prío's revolutionary past as one of the student leaders who overturned the Machado regime in 1933, rather than his more recent tenure in politics in the '40s and early '50s, and on his vulnerability to the desperate entreaties of a woman, Santamaría opened the door for Prío to "talk about true unity" directly with Fidel in the Sierra Maestra—a veiled reference to the former president's own political future, while apparently enhancing the prospects for getting weapons to the rebels.[8]

Like so many other movement leaders, while Santamaría succeeded in forcing others to snap out of their own "delirium of leadership" and focus instead on defending the rebels, she privately felt plagued by self-doubt and fear. "Only seeing that I am capable of sending you something allows me to continue in these worlds, being away from Cuba, far from everyone. It is worse than jail; I feel strange even knowing that no one is following me, that I can roam freely through the streets," she wrote Castro. She craved affirmation from him that her strategy with Prío was correct.[9] Fidel assured her that "you clearly justify all of the hopes that were placed in you" and reminded her that "everything should be under your control" regarding fueling the military campaign.[10]

Prío strung Santamaría along for over a month of more meetings with further tantalizing notes and messages. By her last meeting with him at the end of June, Santamaría wrote Fidel that "the P" had finally come through with a concrete offer to airdrop one hundred Springfield rifles and 40,000 rounds of bullets, without making the trip to the Sierra Maestra himself. She was sanguine about the offer. If "the P's" offer fell through, she knew that the 26th of July would be able to benefit politically by using the former president's caprice to demonstrate which of the two anti-Batista figures—Prío or Castro—truly supported "unity," and which merely paid lip service to the vaunted goal at the other's expense.

All the while, pressure mounted from opposition politicians in Miami who were eager to know whether the 26th of July would finally capitulate and agree to participate in a coalition. How, implored José Miró Cardona, had Fidel responded to the proposal that a negotiated "unity" agreement precede the establishment of a provisional government? Could Fidel be persuaded to join a pact, asked Lincoln Rodón of the Independent Democratic Party, if Prío put up not only weapons but also one million dollars? Despite her earlier self-doubts, Santamaría did well in this environment; she raised money from wealthy Cubans such as José M. "Pepín" Bosch y Lamarque, president of the Santiago-based Bacardi Rum Company, and became a self-described *"politiquera* with everyone. I tell them how often you think of them, how much you love them, the faith you have in them—I've taken on the task of bringing everyone together around you, later you'll know who will follow or not." "Later" clearly referred to the period after Batista's departure from power, when both Santamaría and her fiancé seemed to assume that the 26th of July would somehow hold power. That unstated objective, after all, stood at the center of this "unity" dance, one that depended almost entirely on the rebels' success on the battlefront. By telling everyone, including

Carlos Prío and José Miró Cardona, that the only way to discuss "unity" was directly with Fidel, and hoping the rebels could resist Batista's offensive, Santamaría delayed compromising the 26th of July's independence until the movement was strong enough to broker an agreement on its own terms.[11]

After the collapse of the Pérez Jimenez dictatorship of Venezuela in January 1958, Caracas became a hotbed for revolutionary activities, hosting exiles from the 26th of July and the Student Revolutionary Directorate, as well as Justo Carrillo, leader of the Agrupación Montecristi, a group of Cuban elites with allies among reformist military officials, and the Puros, reform-minded military officers associated with Ramón Barquín, the imprisoned leader of a 1956 attempted coup.[12] Luis Buch's assignment was to take control of the disparate and often clashing M267 "support committees" in the country, raise money, solicit weapons for the rebel army from the new government, and install the new Morse-code system for "Dos Indios Verdes," or "2IV," the shortwave communication channel between Caracas and the Sierra Maestra.[13]

With communications up and running and over $100,000 in the movement's coffers, Buch, like Santamaría in Miami, focused primarily on reaching out cautiously to the other opposition groups in Caracas.[14] But this would be no easy task even for the most confident of political animals. Having already been the bearer of bad news—when he delivered the letter to Miami withdrawing the 26th of July from the Pact of Miami—Buch was extremely nervous about being thrown back to the lions. This time, he was to ask for money and weapons while keeping potential donors at bay until the movement was ready to reach a formal agreement. Given the stakes, Buch hesitated to trust his own judgment on brokering a "unity" agreement and sought guidance repeatedly from an impatient and otherwise occupied Castro. Indeed, his correspondence suggests that Buch suffered from a self-doubt that plagued many of those who counted themselves as intimate collaborators of the commander in chief, but who operated outside of the Sierra Maestra and under the cloud of uncertainty cast by the still fresh failure of the general strike. "Don't forget," he wrote, "that I am alone here and many times I need direction and especially critiques that always help one to improve and better interpret our organization's thinking."[15] In the middle of the summer offensive, Buch wrote Hart that Fidel "indicated the policies to follow so that I would not make a mistake, as I created nothing, but rather only put in practice his instructions."[16] But Buch had only a general idea of Fidel's wishes. He had to rely on his own judgment to build on Santamaría's work in Miami and knit together an opposition alliance satisfactory to the rebel army without overcommitting the 26th of July.

Buch faced one of the first affronts to his authority when Carlos Prío's former prime minister and point man, Tony Varona, arrived in Caracas in early July. Without Buch's knowledge, Varona had arranged to communicate directly with Fidel on the movement's shortwave connection, which had been ostensibly under Buch's control.[17] Buch found out about it after the fact, and felt this insubordination had exposed his and the movement's "inability and lack of coordination," and had diminished his own importance to the negotiations then under way. "If the 2IV people stick their hands in this unity business they're going to create a huge problem, I don't regard any of them as integrated with the 26th of July Movement's thinking . . . They see politicians as something great and they submit themselves to them unconditionally." He warned that the *sierra* was running a security risk by allowing individuals who were not fully "integrated" into the movement to use its codes. Despite Buch's reservations, Varona and Fidel had actually discussed the terms of agreement for "unity of all revolutionary and political forces fighting against Batista," and Fidel suddenly agreed to send Caracas a document that spelled out these terms.[18]

Why the sudden turn of events? Fidel believed that Prío was indeed about to come through with the airdrops he had promised Santamaría. On July 10, 1958, Santamaría wrote Fidel, "Carlos promised me that he'll drop [materiél] to you every week, with or without unity. I cornered him a bit about that promise and he told me that only a bastard would mislead me. Let me tell you that this hasn't changed my mind about him." Acknowledging that Prío "wants to ingratiate himself" to Fidel, Santamaría also reported that the "P" had also contributed $18,000 toward the purchase of an airplane for Gustavo Arcos to fly weapons in from Costa Rica.[19] Her three months in Miami acting as a *politiquera* had begun to pay off for the movement in political terms as well. She wrote Castro that "no one talks about anything other than this celebrated *unity* . . . It's pretty dangerous, but since it's a reality I have no alternative but to talk about it also. I'm telling you it's dangerous to the point that until three days ago everyone was talking about Fidel, today it's unity, the press too. I'll tell you, I've been able to talk with each organization, and now I see that I didn't lose any time by maintaining good relations with all of them, they've each told me that you will be the one to set forth the points [of agreement]."[20]

Santamaría's assurance that material aid for the rebels was on its way and that the movement would set the terms for a unity agreement, as well as some early tactical success on the battlefield, quickly brought out the pragmatist in Fidel Castro. He dropped his insistence that a provisional government formed in the Sierra Maestra precede his participation in an opposition unity pact. Indeed, the war on the ground was beginning to turn a corner, especially once Raúl Castro had made the risky move in early July of kidnapping forty-two American and Canadian employees of the Moa Bay Mining Company, thereby forcing the air force to stop bombing his area of operations.[21] Broadcast by Radio Rebelde, and the rumor mill, and widely reported from Miami to Caracas, the rebels' military successes quickly strengthened Fidel's ability to dictate the terms of an alliance with the opposition. Santamaría predicted that the battleground victories would guarantee the 26th of July "the strongest vote of all . . . in the junta," referring to the agreement Buch was negotiating in Caracas.[22]

As a result of Castro's shortwave communication with Tony Varona, Miró Cardona and other exile figures immediately flew to Caracas. There, a leery and somewhat befuddled Buch represented the 26th of July in heated and intensive negotiations with representatives from the Ortodoxos, the Auténticos, the Organización Auténtica, the DRE, the Civic Institutions, the Federation of University Students (FEU), the Montecristi Group, Barquín's Puros, and others. Careful to avoid the mistakes of past joint agreements, Fidel Castro had Carlos Franqui and Faustino Pérez draft the text of a core agreement rather than wait for something to come out of negotiations in Caracas. On July 19, Franqui and Pérez transmitted the "Unity Manifesto of the Sierra Maestra" over Radio Rebelde.[23] Culminating months of maneuvering, the next day at the El Conde Hotel in the Venezuelan capital the members of the newly christened Civic Revolutionary Front (FCR) endorsed the text, which, known as the Pact of Caracas, appeared finally to satisfy both the 26th of July's desire for political independence and the opposition's wish for unity.[24]

16 | Hasta La Victoria!

JULY 1958–JANUARY 1959

> In a practical sense unity really hasn't yielded
> what we'd hoped . . . the only advantage it's had is
> for those figures who are always finding some-
> thing wrong in order not to support things,
> they've had no choice but to change, but not
> because of unity itself but rather because of the
> Rebel Army's push, which they see bringing closer
> the hour of triumph . . . [they] now say that it was
> unity that was lacking before and that way they
> make it seem that they've always had positive
> feelings for the Revolution. You know those sorts.
>
> Luis Buch to Armando Hart, September 26, 1958

THE PACT OF CARACAS WAS SOMEWHAT broader than its ill-fated predecessor, the Pact of Miami, but somewhat less substantial and lighter on policy prescriptions than either the Sierra Manifesto or Fidel Castro's 1953 speech "History Will Absolve Me," which was the most explicit on social policy. The new agreement carried the endorsement of the three organizations that then had guerrilla forces deployed on the island: Fidel Castro for the 26th of July Movement, Carlos Prío Socarrás for the Organización Auténtica (OA), and Enrique Rodríguez Loeches for the Student Revolutionary Directorate (DRE). The two major opposition political parties were represented by Manuel Bisbé for the Ortodoxos and Manuel Antonio de Varona for the Auténticos, while Lincoln Rodón signed the pact for the minor Independent Demo-cratic Party. Angel María Santos Buch signed the accord on behalf of the Civic Resistance Movement, and David Salvador, Angel Cofiño, Pascasio Linares, Lauro Blanco, and José M. Aguilera endorsed the agreement for Unidad Obrera, Workers Unity. José Puente and Omar Fernández for the Federation of University Students (FEU) also gave university student sup-port to the Civic Revolutionary Front (FCR). Among the many presiden-tial aspirants signing the Pact of Caracas were Justo Carrillo Hernández for the Montecristi Group, and José Miró Cardona, president of the Havana Bar Association. As the new secretary general of the FCR, Miró Cardona signed the pact on his own accord, without the backing of the Civic Institutions, which were notably absent. Back in Miami, the FCR met frequently. Among its first order of business, the FCR members, with the exception of the DRE, officially endorsed the 26th of July's candidate, Judge Manuel Urrutia Lleó, as provisional president of the republic.[1]

By the end of July 1958, forces under the command of Fidel Castro, Raúl Castro, Che Guevara, Camilo Cienfuegos, and Juan Almeida had beat back the Cuban military's summer offensive against the rebels, winning thirty battles—among them the battles of Las Mercedes, El Jigue, Las Vegas, and Santo Domingo.[2] Breaking through the prevailing gag order on the Cuban press, Radio Rebelde broadcast news of rebel victories to Cubans and abroad. News also spread throughout the internationally based Cuban exile community of everything from blow-by-blow battle accounts fresh from the front to rumors of coups d'état in the capital.

Castro's rebel army expelled the remnants of Batista's forces from the Sierra Maestra in the first half of August. By their own count, the rebels suffered twenty-five deaths with forty-eight wounded. Despite their overwhelming air and ground forces, government troops fared far worse, with 231 dead and 422 prisoners, whom Castro turned over to the International Red Cross. The ten-week clash yielded more weapons and equipment for the rebels than any "committee in exile" had ever been able to send from abroad: over five hundred pieces of equipment, including two tanks, three bazookas, eight mortars, one cannon, one anti-aircraft machine gun, over one hundred machine guns, more than 100,000 bullets, clothing, camping equipment, medicines, and boots. "At this time," Marcelo Fernández reported to movement militants, "the only soldiers from the tyranny who remain in the Sierra Maestra are the 231 cadavers the enemy left behind."[3]

The rebel army's military successes had strengthened Fidel and the 26th of July Movement politically; they could now ease up on their initial demand of forming a provisional government in the Sierra Maestra prior to reaching a broad-based unity agreement. At the same time, so anxious was the opposition to support, benefit from, co-opt, or ride the coattails of a winning ticket that they settled for vaguely stated language in the Pact of Caracas that committed the 26th of July to very little. The new unity agreement called on all civic, political, and revolutionary forces to join together in a broad-based civic-revolutionary coalition similar to that which the Sierra Manifesto had attempted to produce. It asked for massive material reinforcement of all of the guerrilla fronts then fighting against Batista. And it mandated coordinated efforts, but not a joint command, of all civic, revolutionary, and political sectors of Cuban society.[4]

Indeed, from the vantage point of the 26th of July, the Pact of Caracas was significantly and deliberately more general than the Pact of Miami. First, the new accord adopted a "common strategy" of armed insurrection to defeat Batista, "culminating in a great general strike on the civilian front." Second, after Batista's fall, "a brief provisional government" was to guide the nation "to a normal state of affairs" and "establish full constitutional and democratic rights." Third, the Caracas pact referred to a "minimum government program" to punish "those guilty of crimes" and to guarantee "workers rights, fulfillment of international agreements, public order, peace, freedom, as well as the economic, social and political progress of the Cuban people." Fourth, the pact called upon the United States to halt military and other forms of assistance to Batista and emphasized the "national sovereignty and the nonmilitary, republican tradition of Cuba," calling upon "workers, students, professionals, businessmen, sugar plantation owners, farmers and Cubans of all religions, ideologies, and races to join this movement of liberation" and "subscribe to this declaration of unity."

Concluding with an escape clause of sorts, the statement of unity was little more than an exhortation. It noted that, "later, as soon as practicable, we will hold a meeting of each and every representative delegate to discuss and approve the bases of our pledge."[5] That is, until the entire membership of the FCR could actually meet directly with Fidel Castro, presumably in the Sierra Maestra, the 26th of July regarded the statement as "only a declaration of purpose that does not contain any platform on which to structure an organic form of unity."[6] Indeed, unlike the Pact of Miami, which had secret documents laying out a new command structure for the insurrection and a step-by-step process for appointing a provisional government, the Pact of Caracas contained not a single concrete component that spelled out how the anti-Batista forces would actually coordinate efforts on the ground.

The prospect for a future meeting to nail down such "organic structures" and the absence of any formal coordinating mechanism meant that subsequent activities of the FCR in the United States and elsewhere lacked credibility, with Caracas pact signatories unsure of how long their newly formed coalition would hold. José Miró Cardona, the FCR secretary general, was especially aware of the bind in which Castro had placed the opposition. Because Fidel had put off until the future still another meeting "to discuss and approve" the unity accords, Miró Cardona wrote to the leader that he, Miró Cardona, could not fully represent the FCR or speak on behalf of the 26th of July in his frequent contacts with the United States government, during which he reported on the course of the war, the conduct of the rebels, and the opposition's plans for a post-Batista government.[7]

Miró Cardona was correct in his assessment of his standing. Just as Fidel Castro, Armando Hart, and the core leadership of the 26th of July did not want Felipe Pazos to represent formally and officially the 26th of July at the Department of State or anywhere else in 1957, they did not want Miró Cardona to do so one year later. Still, especially after the kidnapping episode involving American citizens earlier that month, Fidel understood that a prominent figure like Miró Cardona, well connected to the American political class, could provide a bridge to Washington that the rebels needed then and for the future. Indeed, Che Guevara later wrote that the members of the Caracas pact, such as Miró Cardona, "represented our aspirations for international recognition." The movement had to give them adequate endorsement to function as a liaison with the governments of the United States, Great Britain, and Latin America, as well as with the International Red Cross, the Organization of American States, and the United Nations, while keeping them sufficiently off balance to prevent what Santamaría called the "delirium of leadership." It was essential that the movement maintain its political, strategic, and operational independence.[8]

In fact, like the Cuban Liberation Junta, shortly after the Pact of Caracas was signed the FCR created commissions for public relations, fundraising, and international relations, as well as a "Supreme Council," all over the objections of the 26th of July leadership in Cuba. The M267 had instructed its members to interpret the new declarations of unity as a green light only to conduct joint military and sabotage operations—the very areas to which the National Directorate had limited its definition of unity since the *Granma* had landed eighteen months earlier. Marcelo Fernández ordered M267 members not to create or join any "deliberative bodies (such as patriotic juntas, unity committees, etcetera)," since any such unified political forces would be subject to the outcome of the deferred Sierra Maestra meeting alluded to in the new agreement. Likewise, Fernández wrote Haydeé Santamaría to put a damper on the new FCR bureaucratic mechanisms proliferating in Miami.[9]

Though they had paved the way for the new unity agreement, Santamaría and her colleagues in exile understood the limits and possibilities of such a bargain. José Llanusa, who had met repeatedly with the FCR during the second stage of meetings in Miami, concluded early in the process that unity could be a double-edged sword for the 26th of July. The Caracas pact had begun to generate offers of significant financial and political support for the rebels, but Llanusa avoided accepting favors in exchange for future services, counseling one colleague in Havana to make no "serious commitments . . . though this does not mean that you should not take advantage of everyone that can be of use to you." Throughout the remaining months of the insurrection, Llanusa, Buch, and Santamaría repeatedly wrote to one another, to Armando Hart, and to Fidel about the problems they encountered when they perceived that members of the DRE, the Ortodoxo Party, and the Puros—as well as Prío, Varona, Miró Cardona, and others—were attempting to take advantage of the 26th of July's success in destabilizing Batista. Llanusa and Santamaría suspected that the DRE, which also had its eyes on power and had already opposed the selection of Urrutia as provisional president, would continue to block anything that the M267 favored. Though Llanusa believed that the Caracas pact may have been useful to "demonstrate to the people that we didn't want the revolution to be our possession," many of the pact's member organizations were, in his view, merely interlopers with limited revolutionary pedigrees.[10]

In Cuba, the success of the rebel army began to transform the consciousness of even the *llano*'s most ardent advocates of an urban-based strategy. After the summer offensive, as Che Guevara and Camilo Cienfuegos moved their forces west into the central plains of the island, Faustino Pérez, writing from the Sierra, described to his old labor comrades in the capital his own metamorphosis, hoping to involve them again in an urban strike to support the rebel army:

> The Movement has always maintained the strategy of armed insurrection and general strike as the correct one in the struggle against the tyranny. Substantively we haven't changed our criteria. But on the 9th of April we suffered a harsh reverse whose negative consequences we have had to pay. It was evident that faith in our methods of struggle suffered in public opinion and among our own militants and even among some leaders. An analysis of the cause of the failure was imposed, and a revision of tactics. The same strategy no longer gave me confidence, though I still thought it was the right one. I thought it wasn't the right time to keep agitating right away for the same slogans in the face of the failure. It was necessary to recover from the blow, raise the specter of struggle with revitalizing events, and that was only possible at the time through the rebel army. We now agree that it is crucial to move beyond the impasse with the other fronts and that's where you have had most of your drive and success. The rebel army has grown considerably; the last campaign has increased its glory and multiplied its strength. Now it is advancing in an invasion force toward the other provinces. Its immediate action will contribute considerably to maturing conditions there. Then work

in the cities will be prioritized, pressure will grow, and the revolutionary climate will heat up again, in workplaces, among every group and corner, as the growing wave will culminate in unified action, complementing the decisive forces, responding to one objective only: The Revolutionary Army (made fundamentally of peasants and workers) and the working class as the vanguard of all the people, in massive rebellion.[11]

And although Miró Cardona, Prío, Varona, or Carrillo may have seen the FCR as their ticket to political relevance in a post-Batista era, long before the dictator's flight, the 26th of July had come to regard the coalition as less and less vital to the revolution's success. Indeed, after several months of focusing almost entirely on their confrontation with the army, the *sierra* again turned to the politics of the end game, summoning Marcelo Fernandéz and Enrique Oltuski for a meeting to prepare the 26th of July's base in the cities to take control of the local, provincial, and national symbols of state power. At the same time, Faustino Pérez explained to Armando Hart, who was by then jailed with many of the Puros at the Isle of Pines, the fleeting relevance of the opposition pact:

> After the failed strike, the clamor for unity took on very large proportions and we were continually accosted. Because of that and after gaining some time and making some faith-revitalizing hits [against Batista] we accepted signing and publicizing a document that called for and accepted unity in principle. Until now there's been nothing more concrete than the fact of Urrutia having been proclaimed president by everyone but the Directorio. Everything else depends upon a meeting of delegates here in the Sierra. In any case we don't believe the Civic Revolutionary Front has any other possibilities other than carrying out its role of propaganda, stimulating and "morally" supporting the struggle in the country, and supporting the provisional government.[12]

Indeed, the closest thing to a meeting of the FCR, such as the pact had stipulated, took place on December 7, 1958, when Luis Buch, Judge Manuel Urrutia, his wife and son, rebel army commander and opposition journalist Luis Orlando Rodríguez, and two others boarded a C-46 cargo plane in Caracas and flew to the Sierra Maestra with seven tons of weapons that Buch, in one of his proudest moments, had acquired as a donation from Venezuela's interim president, Admiral Wolfgang Larrazabal.[13]

By then, Batista's command of the armed forces had all but dissolved. Demoralized army detachments deployed to the provinces of Oriente, Camagüey, and Las Villas had begun to lay down their arms, stay in their barracks, or join the swelling ranks of the rebels. In November, Batista had staged long-delayed presidential elections, running his prime minister, Andrés Rivero Agüero, against the Ortodoxo attorney Carlos Marqúez Sterling. With Rivero Agüero declared the winner, the elections were widely regarded as fraudulent. As a result, widespread popular opposition to Batista intensified and support increased for the revolutionaries, who had become a symbol of deliverance from nearly a generation of corrupt politics. Rumors of coup conspiracies flew among the military's own ranks, Puros at the Isle of Pines, and officers cooling their heels in exile. On December 9, the United States sent a special envoy, William Pawley, a Republican party funder from Florida, to persuade Batista to return to his home in Daytona Beach, Florida, and leave power to a provisional government consisting of Colonel Ramón Barquín, the jailed leader of the Puros; Major Enrique Borbonnet, a Puro sympathetic to the 26th of July; General Martín Díaz Tamayo, a former Batista ally recently arrested for plotting against him; and José Pepín Bosch, of Bacardi Rum. Batista flatly refused the American proposal as well as an initiative by the Papal Nuncio to broker a settlement.[14]

By the fall of 1958, the 26th of July's objectives had clearly evolved from remaining a "revolutionary instrument," as Armando Hart had imagined one year earlier, to entirely reinventing Cuba from the seat of power. Well aware that a military junta or any form of provisional government not under their control might thwart their objectives, the rebel army sent out its own feelers to smoke out the intentions of many of these conspirators. Indeed, Castro himself met with General Eulogio Cantillo, sent by the army's high command. Cantillo at first indicated that he would surrender his troops in Oriente and support the insurrection, but he reversed his stance only days later.[15]

Meanwhile, with the Pawley mission hitting a dead end, the CIA explored potential alternatives that might keep Castro from power: Justo Carrillo of the Montecristi Group, for example, had begun talks with the CIA in November 1958 about springing Colonel Barquín from jail and establishing with him a new governing junta; and Carlos Prío, Tony Varona, and José Miró Cardona—signatories like Carrillo to the Pact of Caracas—obtained last-minute CIA backing for various schemes designed to prevent a 26th of July victory.[16]

Within weeks of Urrutia's arrival in the Sierra Maestra, on New Year's Eve, 1958, Batista fled the country to the Dominican Republic. Batista left the country in the hands of General Eulogio Cantillo, who rather than join the insurrection, agreed instead to lead a junta and sought but failed to persuade the ranking Supreme Court justice, Judge Carlos Piedra, to step in as provisional president.[17] With Batista gone, General Cantillo sent a plane to the Isle of Pines to fetch Colonel Barquín, who returned to Havana, followed shortly by Armando Hart, Borbonnet, and others. Barquín, who had served as Cuba's military attaché in Washington in the first part of the decade, promptly arrested Cantillo and, sending for Justo Carrillo in Miami, briefly considered putting together a mixed civilian-military junta of his own.[18]

The revolutionaries had prepared for this moment. Their recent success in demoralizing the armed forces, and their progress over the twenty-five-month insurgency in exposing and exacerbating the utterly shallow sources of institutional and popular support for the regime, had finally created the political conditions for a general strike—really a national mobilization—of the sort that the National Directorate had hoped to spark in April of 1958. That fall, following talks in the Sierra Maestra with Castro, the coordinators in the *llano* had begun sending instructions throughout the country for movement activists to prepare to take control of the seats of local and provincial government, police stations, and workplaces until the leadership of the rebel army could arrive in Havana to take formal control of the state apparatus. When news spread of Batista's flight on New Year's Eve, throngs of exuberant, incredulous, and relieved residents of Havana poured into the streets, thrusting the capital into complete upheaval, with 26th of July flags and banners cropping up at every corner and television and radio broadcasts reporting the news. The M267 militia, the United National Workers Front (FONU), some mixed DRE-M267 groups, the DRE, and the PSP, the mass media, and massive worker walkouts kept Havana in a euphoric but tense state of popular mobilization.

Barquín soon sensed the difficulty he faced in putting together a new government. By the second of January, M267 commander Camilo Cienfuegos and his forces were arriving at Camp Colombia, headquarters of the Cuban joint chiefs of staff. And Che Guevara established a base at the Spanish fort and prison, La Cabaña. With the masses in the streets, the rebel army in Havana, and Castro calling for a general strike and warning publicly against the threat of a military junta, it quickly became clear where real power lay, and Barquín resigned on January 3.[19]

Hart flew to Santiago. There the 26th of July took complete control of the city without firing a shot, declared it Cuba's provisional capital, established a new provincial government, and, at a ceremony held at the University of Oriente, swore in Judge Manuel Urrutia Lleó as provisional president. After dining with the American consul and his wife in the Oriente capital, Fidel Castro, Celia Sánchez, and a vast coterie of 26th of July rebels initiated their victory march across the island. They stopped along the way for speech after speech, meeting with M267 underground collaborators. As the front cover of one of the first post-Batista editions of *Bohemia* declared, Castro had become the "national hero."[20]

Along the way, local 26th of July coordinators had begun—sometimes easily, sometimes with more difficulty—to establish in provinces and municipalities provisional governments composed mainly of the movement's civilian underground activists. While the 26th of July was certainly the revolutionary force with the largest popular following on the island, more important, over the two-year insurgency it had established the largest territorial presence and most extensive track record in direct military conflict with the Cuban armed forces. Castro's immediate deployment to Havana of Camilo Cienfuegos and Che Guevara, as well as his own trek across the island, were meant to prevent a military junta from taking power. In addition, these moves were intended to establish M267 control over the country and over rival insurgent forces, many of which maintained competing guerrilla fronts in the province of Las Villas (located in the middle of the island between Oriente, the rebel army's stronghold, and Havana). In 1958, under Faure Chomón Mediavilla's command, the DRE had established a guerrilla front in the Escambray mountains of Las Villas and briefly taken the presidential palace, police precincts, and other posts in and around Havana after Batista's flight. Eloy Gutierrez Menoyo, originally an ally of the OA and of the DRE who also commanded a rebel stronghold on the southern coast outside of Cienfuegos, had also sent teams to Havana.

Though Che Guevara had been kept out of the loop during the national strike attempt in April 1958, and, as some would argue, was still relegated to second fiddle with his appointment to take La Cabaña rather than Camp Colombia, during the second half of 1958 he played a central role in establishing M267 hegemony in Las Villas, a crucial step toward taking power in the capital.[21] And there, because of what many in Cuba to this day refer to as the *real* general strike, revolutionary forces and their sympathizers in the media and throughout society prevented widespread chaos during the five days between Barquín's resignation and Fidel Castro's arrival in Havana on January 8, 1959.[22]

By the time Castro arrived, the movement had already drawn up the roster of individuals to form and install the first revolutionary cabinet under Article 40 of the 1940 constitution. Luis Buch, who became minister secretary of the presidency and the cabinet, and Armando Hart, who was to become the minister of education, flew back to Havana with Urrutia to start work.[23] As was the 26th of July's long-standing intention, the new cabinet was not a "gobierno de concentración," a coalition government of the type that Hart had feared one year earlier. The president of the Havana Bar Association and secretary general of the FCR, José Miró Cardona, became prime minister, with his flirtations days earlier with the CIA unknown but perhaps suspected by the revolutionaries. Fidel Castro Ruz was named commander in chief of the armed forces. Roberto Agramonte, Sr., former Ortodoxo presidential candidate and envoy to the Red Cross in Geneva in the last months of the insurrection, became foreign minister. Luis Orlando Rodríguez, once an Auténtico, then an Ortodoxo, founder of Radio Rebelde and editor of Che Guevara's guerrilla press, became minister of the interior. Angel Fernández Rodríguez, an Oriente district attorney who, like Urrutia, sympathized with the M267, became minister of justice. Manuel Ray, an engineer by profession and secretary general of the Civic Resistance Movement, became minister of public works. Humberto Sori Marín, a lawyer whom Armando Hart and the National Directorate had tried to expel from the movement in 1957, became minister of agriculture. Enrique Oltuski, the M267 coordinator in Las Villas, became minister of communication. Faustino Pérez, chairman of the movement's National Strike Committee, became minister for recovery of misappropriated funds. And Osvaldo Dorticós, former mayor of the city of Cienfuegos, a Civic Resistance Movement activist, Communist Party member, and co-conspirator of Oltuski's, became minister for drafting and studying revolutionary laws.[24] The United States formally recognized the new provisional government on January 5, 1959.

By January of 1959 the M267 had finally acquired the political strength to select alone the first revolutionary cabinet—either from its own ranks, from those who had closely collaborated with the movement, or from Cuba's professional and financial elite. Not one member of the first cabinet came from rival opposition groups. The exceptions, Dorticós of the PSP, and Agramonte and Luis Orlando Rodríguez of the Ortodoxos-históricos, had collaborated closely with the 26th of July for years.

The *llano* had surely lost the battle over revolutionary strategy. But it had unquestionably won the far more important war against *politiquería* and for a new political culture—only vaguely defined at the time—that would soon bear little resemblance to the climate of corruption and opportunism that had forged the young revolutionaries' desire for profound change. With the top civilian leadership of the 26th of July heavily represented in the first cabinet, the *llano* and *sierra*—really the entire 26th of July Movement—were again poised to face off against many of the very same forces they had confronted during the insurrection: Cuba's professional elites, political parties, *clases económicas,* bourgeoisie, organized labor, other revolutionary forces, Communists, the U.S. government, and a new generation of increasingly bitter exiles. Many of these battles, most political, some military, endured well into the 1960s and, in the case of those with the U.S. government and portions of the exile community, continue today.

Transitions Then and Now

ONE NEED ONLY SPEND A COUPLE OF days flipping through the Florida and Cuban press to see that, in many ways, *Inside the Cuban Revolution* is still a living story. I am writing this epilogue just weeks after President Fidel Castro fainted from heatstroke at an outdoor speech during the summer of 2001. Such a rare public sign of his mortality prompted speculation over what will happen in Havana, Miami, and Washington after the Cuban leader's inevitable demise. Will his disappearance from the Cuban political stage prompt a transition from authoritarian rule to market democracy? Or has a transition already begun? Indeed, perhaps the emergence of a mixed economy since the end of the Cold War might already be characterized as a transformation with substantial social, and eventually profound political, implications. Or perhaps it would be more accurate to talk about succession, since in virtually every sphere of Cuba's official political, economic, and social life a second and even now third postrevolutionary generation is taking the reins of leadership.

If *fidelismo* continues into the next generation, and quite possibly beyond, will the United States be able to overcome more than forty years of enmity and develop a set of post-Castro policies? How will the various forces within the Cuban exile community respond as Cuba evolves to a post-Castro era? And how will changes in Cuba and within the diaspora affect the long-standing mutual dependence between hardline exiles and American administrations? Already, a community that for years sought to embroil American policymakers in the drive to unseat Fidel Castro is evolving from an exiled opposition force to a foreign aid lobby. Cuban Americans now petition Congress for millions of dollars—not to support a military campaign but instead to create and fund an opposition in Miami and, more importantly, on the island.

This story also sheds some light on how, having once been part of the opposition on the island or in exile, the founding revolutionary generation in power today handles its own opposition in Cuba, in exile, and in the U.S. government. Either through direct experience, or because they have absorbed the lessons of history, Cuban leaders on the island today are now thoroughly equipped to anticipate and avert the attempts by both the hardline Cuban exile community and the U.S. government, as in the 1950s and subsequently, to shape the next era—whether that time arrives through transition, succession, or a hybrid of the two. Indeed, a striking continuity exists between the survival strategies of the Castro forces in the 1950s and those adopted by the Cuban government since the end of the Cold War. These strategies provide useful guideposts for interpreting and even predicting Cuban policy at home, toward the diaspora, and toward the United States now and for years to come.

Inside the Cuban Revolution illustrates six resources contributing to survival and success in the pre-1959 era. The first: alliances at home. The urban underground of the 26th of July cultivated tactical alliances in the 1950s with groups ranging from Cuba's white-collar professional class to the military, the Catholic and Protestant churches, labor, and eventually the Communist Party. Since the Castro group was but one of many forces working against Batista, it depended at crucial moments on alliances, or at least cultivating the impression of desiring alliances, with key individuals. Many of these individuals, in part because of their thwarted sense of ownership over the anti-Batista struggle, became adversaries, indeed enemies, after 1959.

The second resource for the revolutionaries was a diverse supply network. At the beginning of the insurgency, the 26th of July depended almost entirely on the deposed former president, Carlos Prío Socarrás, for weapons and money. But as the insurgency picked up speed and the National Directorate had to balance the competing demands of fighting Batista and becoming the preeminent opposition force, it became politically expedient and militarily necessary to diversify the movement's supply lines and bring in weapons from as many different sources as possible. By early 1958, weapons began to arrive from Costa Rica, Mexico, Venezuela, and the United States.

Cultivating sympathy in the international community was another element of the movement's strategy. Because of members' strong alliances with civil society, mainstream opposition figures, and political parties, the 26th of July expertly raised the profile of their cause against Batista's brutality with the United Nations, the International Committee of the Red Cross, and other foreign governments.

Closely related to that strategy was the movement's astute use of the press. During brief reprieves from government censorship, the 26th of July used the mass media in Cuba, the United States, and elsewhere so effectively that decades after its triumph some Eisenhower administration officials still blamed Herbert Matthews and the *New York Times* for the Castro revolution. And even with press censorship and a state of emergency throughout most of the insurgency, the rebels, who had many friends and co-conspirators in prominent Cuban public relations firms, effectively promoted their cause through the underground press, radio, and even subliminal advertising in commercial magazines.

A fifth component of the rebels' success was the Cuban diaspora living in the United States. In the 1950s, Cubans lived, worked, and studied in New York, Chicago, Tampa, Miami, Bridgeport, Los Angeles, Houston, New Orleans, and elsewhere. Many of them actively raised money for the rebels, organized cultural events, went to Cuba themselves, sent back money, tried to ship weapons there, and angled for a role in a post-Batista political settlement. They regularly violated American neutrality laws, faced indictments by the Justice Department, underwent surveillance by the FBI, consulted with members of Congress and their staffs, and opened themselves up to be led on or cajoled by the State Department (or engaged by the CIA). Toward the end of the insurgency when the moderate, nonviolent opposition had essentially collapsed, many prominent Cuban political and civic leaders regarded Fidel Castro and his revolutionary movement as their return ticket to national politics. The Castro forces spent a great deal of time trying to prevent the various exile groups—who, to be sure, also had substantial ties to the island—from ever merging into any kind of a formal political coalition that might take over the lead role in the war effort (and by implication, the postrevolutionary settlement). Keeping the exiled opposition off balance by dividing it, co-opting it, and exposing its vulnerabilities became crucial to the movement's political success as the rebel army gained territorial and operational strength.

The sixth element of the revolutionaries' strategy relates to how they took advantage of Cuba's geographic proximity to and long-standing economic and political ties to U.S. government and society. Cuban exiles fighting in the anti-Batista struggle overstayed their visas to build political coalitions with exiles in Miami and around the country—and of course, to doggedly and mostly unsuccessfully pursue all manner of weapons deals for the insurgency. Members of the Cuban opposition, in particular of the 26th of July, actively lobbied Congress and the State Department and were a significant factor in the State Department's decision to cut off the supply of weapons to Batista. Aware that a transition was underfoot in Cuba, there was, in fact, a debate in the late 1950s in the State Department about whether to withdraw support from Batista; continue supporting him and move forcefully against the revolutionaries operating from U.S. turf; mediate a transition between Batista and the opposition and explicitly exclude the other radicals, including the Communist Party; or orchestrate a coup. Still, the United States remained largely oblivious to the breadth and depth of the opposition to the dictator, which partially helps explain why it so grossly underestimated the degree of popular support for Castro after he took power.

Playing with what appears to be a weak deck of cards over forty years later, the Cuban regime survives now, almost fifteen years after the collapse of its longtime Soviet benefactor, by managing essentially the same six elements: a domestic political coalition that includes a broad set of new interests; a mixed economy with substantially diversified trade and investment partners; international sympathy for its victimization by American economic sanctions; a sophisticated use of the mass media as a way of exposing a split between moderates and hard-liners in the Cuban American community (the Elian González episode offers a recent example); and the Cuban diaspora, which through legal migration to the United States grows by over twenty thousand each year, sending as much as one billion dollars annually back to Cuba and slowly but perceptibly changing the demographics of South Florida.

Finally, how does the United States, which in word and deed still appears genetically disposed to the demise of the current regime, contribute to its survival? Since the tightening of the embargo in the 1990s, economic sanctions have served as a buffer, permitting Cuba to diversify its trade and investment partners slowly and to integrate cautiously into the global economy without the destabilizing effect that a sudden end of the embargo might cause. Still, the Cuban government has been enormously effective in making its case directly and indirectly against the embargo in the halls of Congress and throughout American society, while at the same time mirroring the controls the U.S. government places on Cuban citizens by controlling contact with Cuba, not by tourists from this country, but by other Americans, whom the Bush White House, some in Congress, and the hard-line exile community now regard as potential agents of subversion. The demographics and political geography of bilateral relations mean that though the United States is the great power imposing a unilateral embargo against a small island, Cuba, too, can pursue its own policy toward the United States, focusing, as the revolutionaries did almost fifty years ago, on those interests and regions whose support might help realize the long-term objective of developing an equitable political, economic, and diplomatic relationship.

I was recently asked why the Cuban government released the documents of the insurgency to me for this book. Of course, the answer relates to the aging and retirement of the first generation of revolutionaries and the judgment that their history should be preserved. But the explanation runs deeper than mere stenography. For decades, the regime operated with a limited concept of its principal constituents: without excessive generalization, these boiled down to peasants, workers, and the armed forces. There were obvious ideological and geopolitical explanations for this emphasis. But Cuba's evolution into a mixed economy has expanded and diversified the domestic interests whose support the regime now needs for continued legitimacy.

Indeed, the international, economic, and generational changes underfoot since the collapse of the socialist bloc have produced a far more varied set of domestic constituencies on the island and in the diaspora. While the government has pointedly not created a multiparty democracy, it has expanded the tent to include Catholics, Protestants, Santeros, and Jews; consolidated control over the military; opened sectors of the economy to capitalism; allowed greater space for intellectuals and artists; decentralized and devolved decision making over resources in many cases to local and provincial party authorities; revived long-dormant ties with the diaspora; and mounted a major campaign to energize the youngest generation on the island to have a stake in the revolution.

Who knows if a master plan connects the release of these documents to these relatively new dynamics? Still, a reinterpretation of the myths of the Cuban insurrection—a story that suggests that the revolution was not made by guerrillas, peasants, and workers alone—may demonstrate to the newly surfacing constituencies that they, too, have a connection to the early history of the Cuban revolution.

About the Research

I conducted the research for this book, originally my dissertation, between 1994 and 1997 in archives located in the United States and Cuba. The government records I consulted in the United States are housed at the Dwight D. Eisenhower Library in Abilene, Kansas, and the National Archives in College Park, Maryland. Portions of the State Department's Record Group 59 are also available on microfilm in the government records department at Georgetown University Library. The on-the-ground reporting from the Havana embassy and the Santiago consulate provides a surprisingly unique documentary record of this period, particularly because Cuban government censorship during most of the period that this book covers prevented the local press from freely reporting political developments and antiregime activities.

I also submitted Freedom of Information Act (FOIA) requests to the Central Intelligence Agency, which I petitioned for intelligence reports and other material related to the 1950s insurgency in Cuba. All of these requests were denied. Thanks to the efforts of the National Security Archive in Washington, D.C., the CIA declassified some historical documents on Cuba that included assessments of the strength of the 26th of July Movement in 1957 and 1958 and the lack of influence of the Communist Party on the Castro forces. I hope that scholars will soon benefit from further declassifications of material from the pre-1959 period, as we have from the material that has been declassified now by both governments about the Bay of Pigs, Operation Mongoose, and the Cuban Missile Crisis.

The heart and soul of this book, however, derives not from American holdings but from material I was fortunate to obtain from Cuban archives. In the last ten years, more and more scholars, many American, have been able to carry out research in Cuban archives across the island. Few of us, however, have had access to archives dealing with the period of the Cuban revolution. The primary adviser for my dissertation, Professor Piero Gleijeses of Johns Hopkins University School of Advanced International Studies (SAIS), recently published the definitive history of Cuban and American policy in Africa from 1959 to 1976, based on archival research from around the world, but notably, too, from several government, party, and military archives in Cuba.

Inspired by his tenacity, creativity, and intellectual honesty, I took on a far more modest endeavor: to use Cuban documents to write a history of the American response to the revolutionary insurrection. Two developments stopped me in my tracks: the CIA denied my FOIA requests, and in 1994, the diplomatic historian Professor Thomas G. Paterson of the University of Connecticut published *Contesting Castro: The United States and the Triumph of the Cuban Revolution,* a superb account of the American response to the insurgency. This book represents my attempt to pick up the pieces from something of a false start.

Because I am the first scholar to ever have access to the complete set of documents discussed in this book, I want to explain a bit of background. Fortunately, during graduate school I worked as the editor of a small Johns Hopkins publication that covered the debates in Washington on Cuba policy, following the ups and downs of the generally poor bilateral relationship. In the early 1990s, before the American government began to characterize American scholars of Cuba and our publications as part of a scheme to subvert Cuba with ideas, *CubaINFO* circulated to a limited audience on the island. Thus, by the time I was able to meet with the keeper of the keys to Cuba's revolutionary archives, Pedro Alvarez Tabío, about the possibility of access to documents on the insurgency, I had developed a bit of goodwill among scholars and officials who follow the bilateral dynamic. And in early 1995, I received word that I would be welcome to begin research.

The vast majority of the primary source documents on which this book is based are housed in the Cuban Council of State's Office of Historic Affairs (OAH) in Havana, Cuba. The archive, also known as the Fondo de Celia (named for Celia Sánchez Manduley, who began collecting the documents held therein even before January 1, 1959), serves as the presidential library of President Fidel Castro Ruz. When I first began research there, the holding, located in a 1950s-style former bank in the Vedado section of Havana, contained only material covering "la lucha contra la tiranía"—the struggle against the tyranny—from March 10, 1952, the date General Fulgencio Batista Zaldívar overthrew President Carlos Prío Socarrás, through January 1, 1959, when the Cuban revolution triumphed.

The OAH holdings include letters, operational plans, and internal memoranda of the military and civilian leaders of the 26th of July during the anti-Batista insurrection, among them Fidel Castro, Raúl Castro, Che Guevara, Juan Almeida, Frank País, Armando Hart, Ricardo Alarcón, Celia Sánchez, Haydée Santamaría, Enrique Oltuski, Marcelo Fernández, Pedro Miret, René Ramous Latour, Gustavo Arcos, Léster Rodríguez, José Llanusa, Luis Buch, and Vilma Espín. Most of the material is organized by author. Some other documents are grouped by category, such as "Exile" and "Underground." During four research trips to Havana between 1995 and 1997, I was able to take home photocopies of nearly one thousand pages of documents, each bearing the official stamp of the Council of State Office of Historic Affairs.

My experience working at this archive was tremendously fruitful. The director of the OAH, Pedro Alvarez Tabío, and his encyclopedically minded deputy, Elsa Montero Maldonado, were unfailingly gracious in their assistance, even though my requests for material must have seemed haphazard. Because for most historical figures whose documents are at the OAH there was no publicly available cataloguing system that I could first consult, I had to articulate the question I was trying to answer, then, if a staff member knew of possible related documents, binders full of material would be carted out to me from the refrigerated bank vault that houses the papers. I worked in a cubicle with my laptop computer for weeks in this fashion. As new questions arose from the documents themselves, I asked for more material. In almost every case, when I asked for something new, the document or documents in question appeared within hours or sometimes a day or two. I say this because there were exceptions that merit some explanation.

All of the documents in this closed archive remain officially unavailable to the public. As a result of the collaboration between the University of Havana and the National Security Archives, the Cuban government has recently embarked on an official declassification of documents pertaining to the Bay of Pigs invasion (or Playa Girón), Operation Mongoose, and the Cuban Missile Crisis. In light of the trend toward declassification, I think it is only a matter of time until more scholars are able to carry out research as I did in the OAH archive. And importantly, by the time I finished my research, the archive began to receive collections covering developments after 1959. For example, it now contains the documents from Vice President Carlos Rafael Rodríguez, who died in 1996. A Communist Party member since the 1930s, Rodríguez was an economist, theoretician, and historian. His documents dealing with the Cuban-Soviet relationship in the 1960s, for example, when he served as a high-level liaison between the Kremlin and the Cuban government, will be enormously important to historians writing about Cuban foreign and economic policy in the 1960s. Alvarez Tabío, a distinguished historian of the revolutionary insurrection himself, has been intimately involved in the release and declassifications of the pre- and post-1959 periods, and deserves enormous credit for understanding the value of primary-source research.

Still, it is clear that there is some material from the 26th of July Movement in the 1950s that will remain beyond the reach of researchers. In my own experience, there were two sets of documents that I was unable to get my hands on, despite repeated requests during my various visits to Cuba. The first is a set of correspondence between Fidel Castro and Carlos Prío that took place during the insurrection. I learned about their exchange of letters from other documents that were released to me. When I asked for the material, I learned that it is not even housed at the OAH, but perhaps, I inferred, in a more personal collection. Though I pushed for the correspondence, I failed to persuade. The second is material that should have been located in the Celia Sánchez collection. At a crucial point in November 1957, Sánchez, who was speaking for Castro, wrote a letter attacking Armando Hart for his handling of several developments in the underground and in the exile community. While I was able to read Hart's response to the letter, I was never able to see the Sánchez letter itself, nor was it present in the binders containing her documents, which I was able to inspect myself. Finally, Celia Sánchez took notes at a crucial meeting of the 26th of July in May of 1958, when the entire underground organization was essentially demobilized by the rebel army. There are very few accounts of this meeting. The most well known is by Che Guevara, and the other is a very brief reference to the meeting by Luis Buch, in which he reports that Sánchez took notes.[1] Her notes to this important meeting appeared not to be in the archive, nor did the archive staff seem to have any idea where any of the missing material from her collection might be located. One can speculate that given the sensitive nature of the material, Sánchez herself may have decided not to include it in the official holdings of the 26th of July Movement, which during the early 1960s was undergoing significant political and ideological growing pains both internally and in relation to the other radical opposition groups on the island. This explanation, however, is somewhat belied by the presence in the archive and in the papers released to me of material that might be thought equally sensitive for similar reasons.

The reader will find, too, that there are some documents from the OAH that are reprinted either in part or in whole in a collection of documents from the Cuban revolution edited by Carlos Franqui and published in Spanish in 1976 and in English in 1980.[2] Franqui worked with the urban underground in Havana, editing *Revolución,* until his arrest in the crackdown that followed the March 1957 DRE-OA assault on the presidential palace. After his release from jail, he worked with the 26th of July's Committee in Exile, first in Costa Rica in 1957 and then, in 1958, in Miami. After returning to the Sierra Maestra later that year, he worked for the rebel army's shortwave radio station, Radio Rebelde. After January 1959 he returned to being the editor of *Revolución.* When he left the paper in the mid-1960s, he went to work at the Fondo de Celia and worked directly with Celia Sánchez at the archive. Franqui left Cuba for good in 1968.

Before his departure, Franqui took photographs of many of the documents that were then in the Fondo. Because of my extensive access to the OAH collections, I had the opportunity to compare many of the original documents with the versions published in the 1976 and 1980 collections and with those housed in Princeton University Library's Carlos Franqui Collection, which contains the photostatic copies of the material that Franqui photographed. I found in many cases that the published versions of the documents did not agree with the originals in the OAH: the published documents omit substantively significant portions of the text in the original documents, but without the standard use of ellipses to indicate where text has been left out. In other cases, the published version of the documents is misdated. I have indicated throughout the book when a document I cite from the OAH archive appears in some form in the Franqui collections and when there are notable discrepancies. While the Council of State has given me photocopies of nearly one thousand pages of documents, many more than those published in the Franqui editions, it is also true that I do not have a copy nor did I see the original of every document published in the Franqui edition. Thus, at times, I cite the documents therein without being able to refer to the original.

Finally, Franqui's collections focus on the correspondence of Fidel Castro and other guerrilla commanders in the *sierra,* leaving out virtually all of the material pertaining to the other members of the 26th of July, particularly those in the urban underground. This imbalance in the published documentary record has contributed to the emphasis in the secondary literature on the guerrilla war as opposed to the urban struggle and Fidel Castro's role in the insurgency. To be sure, it may be that when Franqui left Cuba, the OAH did not contain as much material on the urban underground as it did when I conducted my research there.

Let me comment, too, on other documents one might have hoped to form part of this story. When I found that the OAH archive contains only the documents of the 26th of July Movement, I attempted to gather material also from the DRE and PSP, the Communist Party. I was unsuccessful in obtaining documents from the DRE. Though I did, after two years of entreaties, have the opportunity to interview Faure Chomón Mediavilla, who led the DRE after the March 1957 assassination of José Antonio Echeverría, I was unsuccessful in persuading him to share with me any documentation of his organization from that period, nor is such documentation housed and catalogued in Cuba. In the case of the PSP, Manuel López Díaz, the director of the Institute of Cuban History (ICH) in Havana, was kind enough to permit me to examine the documents of the PSP from the 1950s, which have greatly enhanced the story of this period in Cuban history. While I was conducting this research, the staff of the institute was attempting to recover (and find the money to pay to retrieve) many more documents of the PSP that were still being held in archives of the former Soviet Union. One of the documents cited herein from the PSP collection remained classified during my research, but the ICH permitted me to type the entire document into my computer rather than keep a photocopy as I did in all other cases.

Finally, the interviews I conducted were, in the end, both incredibly satisfying and deeply frustrating. I spent many hours interviewing the individuals listed herein. At no time did any government official attend these interviews, other than those subjects who themselves are or were government officials then. In some cases I interviewed them on more than one occasion. The color, personality, and perspective one can develop from meeting someone is hard to capture from printed documents alone. And, in many cases, the interviews provided hard information that simply does not appear in the written word. But I conducted them at the same time I was working in the archives, and so, not having fully digested the documents at the time, I did not always know the key questions to ask in time to ask them of the right person. As a result, some of my questions remain unanswered.

Finally, the reader will note a glaring absence in the manner of interviews. One of the book's central premises is that for the first sixteen months of the insurgency after his landing from Mexico in December 1956, Fidel Castro had very little to do with the urban struggle. During the research and writing of the manuscript, I chose not to request an interview from President Castro, feeling that interviewing individuals from the National Directorate—the leadership of the 26th of July's urban underground—was a priority, that it was unlikely he would grant the interview, and that I did not have a long list of questions that I needed him to answer. During the summer of 2000, however, in the course of my work on U.S.-Cuba policy at the Council on Foreign Relations, I had the opportunity to meet with President Castro. He mentioned in an offhand remark that few scholars who write about Cuban history bother to interview him. I took this as my cue and told him that I had written a book about Cuba and interviewed dozens of people, but not him. He asked if I would like to interview him, and of course I replied affirmatively because, having had some time to digest my findings, I indeed had developed a long list of questions that I wished to pose. Once I told him that the book was about the urban insurgency, he said (confirming my hypothesis), "Well, I didn't have anything to do with that. You should talk to Hart and Oltuski," two of the urban underground leaders whom I had already interviewed. Nevertheless, we agreed in principle to do the interview. On two subsequent occasions in 2001, once with the Council on Foreign Relations and then while I was in Havana to speak at a conference commemorating the fortieth anniversary of the Bay of Pigs invasion, President Castro and I spoke about sitting down to talk about this early period in the Cuban revolution. The encounter has yet to take place because I suspect he is too busy orchestrating the transition to the post-Castro era to reflect on the pre-Castro period. But I hope this book will raise enough questions to prompt him to schedule an interview.

Notes

INTRODUCTION

1. See "About the Research" for discussion of Cuban archives and my research there.
2. The Cuban government published the diaries in Ernesto "Che" Guevara, *Pasajes de la Guerra Revolucionaria* (Havana: Ediciones Unión, 1963). The diaries were later published in English as *Reminiscences of the Cuban Revolutionary War* (New York: Monthly Review Press, 1967). The entire *Verde Olivo* series as well as several other articles and letters are published in a new English edition edited by Mary-Alice Waters: Ernesto Che Guevara, *Episodes of the Cuban Revolutionary War, 1956–1958* (New York: Pathfinder Press, 1996). In addition, see John Gerassi, ed., *Venceremos! The Speeches and writings of Ernesto Che Guevara* (New York: Macmillan, 1968), which includes *Cuba—Exception or Vanguard?, Guerrilla Warfare: A Method,* and *We Are Practical Revolutionaries,* as well as "Guerrilla Warfare: A Method," originally published in *Verde Olivo,* April 9, 1961, and October 8, 1960, and *Cuba Socialista* 3, no. 25 (September 1963), respectively. Jon Lee Anderson, author of *Che Guevara: A Revolutionary Life* (New York: Grove Press, 1997), obtained the unedited *Diario de un Combatiente* from Guevara's widow, Aleida March. Between January and June 1997, in thirteen supplements to the Cuban government newspaper *Granma,* Pedro Alvarez Tabío published annotated selections of the unedited Guevara diaries. Alvarez Tabío is the director of the Cuban Council of State Office of Historic Affairs. Following a series of interviews with Fidel Castro, the French journalist Regis Debray summarized Guevara's writings and Castro's views on revolutionary theory and guerrilla struggle in *Revolution in the Revolution?* (New York: Monthly Review Press, 1967).
3. Examples of the literature are Carlos Franqui, *Cuba: El Libro de los Doce* (Mexico City: Serie Popular Era, 1966); K. S. Karol, *Guerrillas in Power: The Course of the Cuban Revolution* (New York: Hill & Wang, 1970); Rolando Bonachea and Nelson Valdés, *Revolutionary Struggle, 1947–1958,* vol. 1 of *The Selected Works of Fidel Castro* (Cambridge, Mass.: MIT Press, 1972); Ramón Bonachea and Marta San Martín, *The Cuban Insurrection, 1952–1959* (New Brunswick, N.J.: Transaction, 1974); Carlos Franqui, *Diario de la Revolución Cubana* (Paris: R.

Torres, 1976); Carlos Franqui, *Diary of the Cuban Revolution* (New York: Viking Press, 1980); Tad Szulc, *Fidel: A Critical Portrait* (New York: William Morrow, 1986); Robert Quirk, *Fidel Castro* (New York: Norton, 1993); Thomas Paterson, *Contesting Castro: The United States and the Triumph of the Cuban Revolution* (New York: Oxford University Press, 1994); Jon Lee Anderson, *Che Guevara: A Revolutionary Life* (New York: Grove Press, 1997); and Jorge G. Castañeda, *Compañero: The Life and Death of Che Guevara* (New York: Alfred A. Knopf, 1997).

4. Ricardo Alarcón de Quesada, interview by author, Havana, Cuba, July 3, 1997.

5. For a recent discussion of the political, social, and economic conditions of the pre-1959 period in Cuba, including numerous comments on the similarities and differences between the 1930s and the 1950s, see Jorge Ibarra, *Prologue to Revolution: Cuba 1898–1958* (Boulder, Colo.: Lynne Reinner, 1998).

6. Louis M. Pérez, Jr., in Leslie Bethell, ed., *Cuba: A Short History* (Cambridge: Cambridge University Press, 1993), pp. 57–93.

7. See Hugh Thomas, *Cuba: In Pursuit of Freedom* (New York: Harper and Row, 1971), pp. 609–616, for a discussion of which opposition forces supported and participated in the Welles mediation and which, because of their antipathy toward American interventionism, did not.

8. For a treatment of the cultural ties between the United States and Cuba, see Louis A. Pérez, Jr., *On Becoming Cuban: Identity, Nationality, and Culture* (Chapel Hill: University of North Carolina Press, 1999).

9. Ibarra, *Prologue to Revolution*, p. 29.

10. Ibid., p. 168.

11. Thomas, *Cuba*, p. 801; Armando Hart Dávalos, *Aldabonazo* (Havana: Editorial Letras Cubanas, 1997), pp. 37–40.

12. Guevara, *Episodes of the Cuban Revolutionary War*, p 12.

13. For a fascinating look at the Cuban opposition in the mid-1950s and the SAR's attempt to negotiate a peaceful return to democracy in Cuba, see Marifeli Pérez-Stable, *The Cuban Revolution: Origins, Course, and Legacy* (New York: Oxford University Press, 1993). In addition, the best discussion I know of the period between the early 1930s and the mid-1950s is found on pp. 41–60 of that book.

14. See Louis Pérez, *Cuba and the United States: Ties of Singular Intimacy* (Athens: University of Georgia Press, 1990), for a discussion of the effect on Cuban politics of the American interventions starting in 1898.

15. Bonachea and San Martín, *The Cuban Insurrection*, p. 214.

16. Szulc, *Fidel*, p. 543.

17. Quirk, *Fidel Castro*, p. 167.

18. Paterson, *Contesting Castro*, pp. 139–149.

19. Anderson, *Che Guevara*, p. 318.

20. Castañeda, *Compañero*, p. 114. Two additional treatments offer an alternative view: Robert Taber, *M-26, Biography of a Revolution* (New York: Lyle Stuart, 1961) and Rolando Bonachea and Valdés in their introduction to *Revolutionary Struggle*. Taber writes that the Civic Resistance Movement, a 26th of

July front organization that Taber uses to indicate the urban underground, pressed for the strike to avoid a prolonged military confrontation and that Fidel reluctantly gave his consent. Bonachea and Valdés concur, noting that Faustino Pérez convinced Fidel that the time was ripe for the strike.

21. Thomas, *Cuba,* p. 982.
22. The article has been reproduced in many volumes, most recently in the revised and expanded edition of Guevara, *Episodes of the Cuban Revolutionary War.*
23. Dolores Nieves and Alina Feijóo, eds., *Semillas de Fuego: Compilación Sobre la Lucha Clandestina en la Capital,* vol. 1 (Havana: Editorial de Ciencias Sociales, 1988); and vol. 2, 1990.
24. See Bonachea and Valdés, *Revolutionary Struggle,* pp. 108–109; Bonachea and San Martín, *The Cuban Insurrection,* pp. 222–223; and Paterson, *Contesting Castro,* pp. 143–149, 173. The two recent exceptions are Anderson's *Che Guevara* and Castañeda's *Compañero.*
25. Manuel Piñeiro Losada, interview by author, Havana, Cuba, July 8, 1997.

1. "TACTICS IN POLITICS AND TACTICS IN REVOLUTION ARE NOT THE SAME"

1. Robert Taber, *M-26, Biography of a Revolution* (New York: Lyle Stuart, 1961), p. 160; U.S. Department of State, Joint Weeka Report no. 20, May 15, 1957, RG 59, 737.00 (W)/5–1557, p. 3, Depart of State Records, National Archives, Washington, D.C. (hereafter DSR, NA).
2. For background on País, see Ramón Bonachea and Marta San Martín, *The Cuban Insurrection: 1952–1959* (New Brunswick, N.J.: Transaction, 1974).
3. See Herbert Matthews's article in the *New York Times,* February 24, 1957, p. 1.
4. Fidel Castro, "Appeal to the Cuban People," in Carlos Franqui, ed., *Diary of the Cuban Revolution* (New York: Viking, 1980), pp. 139–140; Tad Szulc, *Fidel: A Critical Portrait* (New York: William Morrow, 1986), p. 406; Jon Lee Anderson, *Che Guevara: A Revolutionary Life* (New York: Grove, 1997), p. 235; Armando Hart Dávalos, *Aldabonazo* (Havana: Editorial Letras Cubanas, 1997); Enrique Oltuski, *Gente del Llano* (Havana: Imagen Contemporanea, 2000); Frank País to Alberto Bayo, May 15, 1957, País Collection, Cuban Council of State Office of Historic Affairs, Havana, Cuba (hereafter OAH).
5. Frank País to 26th of July Comrades, May 15, 1957, País Collection, OAH.
6. U.S. Department of State, Joint Weeka Report no. 20, May 15, 1957, RG 59, 737.00 (W)/5-1957, DSR, NA.
7. Frank País to 26th of July Leaders, May 17, 1957, País Collection, OAH.
8. Ibid.
9. Frank País to Pedro Miret, May 23, 1957, País Collection, OAH; Marcelo Fernández to National Directorate, January 4, 1958, Fernández Collection, OAH.
10. Frank País to 26th of July Leaders, May 17, 1957, País Collection, OAH; Fidel Castro to "El Informante" [Frank País], May 31, 1957, Fidel Castro Ruz Collection, OAH.
11. Frank País to 26th of July Leaders, May 17, 1957, País Collection, OAH.

12. País to the Provincial Directorates of Las Villas and Havana, May 26, 1957, País Collection, OAH.

13. País to Provincial Directorates of Santiago de Cuba, Havana, Matanzas, and Pinar del Río, May 26, 1957, País Collection, OAH.

14. País to 26th of July Leaders, May 17, 1957, País Collection, OAH. For further analysis of País's perspective on how to engage Cuban workers in the insurgency, see Gladys Marel García-Pérez, *Insurrection and Revolution: Armed Struggle in Cuba* (Boulder, Colo.: Lynne Rienner, 1998), pp. 84–87.

15. See, for example, Barry Carr, "Identity, Class, and Nation: Black Immigrant Workers, Cuban Communism, and Sugar Insurgency, 1925–1934," *Hispanic American Historical Review* (Feb. 1998).

16. "Secret" Memorandum for Members, Operations Coordinating Board, Subject: Latin American Progress Report (NSC 5613/1), Contributions on Labor, Whitman File, Dwight D. Eisenhower Library, Abilene, Kansas.

17. Lionel Martin, *The Early Fidel: Roots of Castro's Communism* (Secaucus, N.J.: Lyle Stuart, 1978), pp. 185–188; Lucas Morán Arce, *La Revolución Cubana: Una Version Rebelde* (Ponce, P.R.: Universidad Católica, 1980), p. 52; Frank País to 26th of July Leaders, May 17, 1957, País Collection, OAH.

18. Faustino Pérez and Armando Hart to René Ramos Latour, August 3, 1957, Hart Collection, OAH; Oral History, Faustino Pérez, April 1980, OAH.

19. For detailed descriptions of the plans for the assault, see the three-part series published in March 1959 in *Bohemia* by Faure Chomón Mediavilla, as well as Ramón Bonachea and Marta San Martín, *The Cuban Insurrection: 1952–1959* (New Brunswick, N.J.: Transaction, 1974).

20. U.S. Department of State, Joint Weeka Report no. 12, March 20, 1957, RG 59, 737.00 (W)/3–2057, DSR, NA.

21. Jon Lee Anderson, *Che Guevara: A Revolutionary Life* (New York: Grove, 1997), p. 257; Taber, *M-26*, p. 148; Mario Llerena, *The Unsuspected Revolution: The Birth and Rise of Castroism* (Ithaca, N.Y.: Cornell University Press, 1978), p. 108.

22. Comandante Manuel Piñeiro Losada, interview by author, Havana, Cuba, July 9, 1997. See also Morán Arce, *La Revolución Cubana*, p. 94.

23. Frank País to Alberto Bayo, May 15, 1957, País Collection, OAH; Frank País to Pedro Miret, May 23, 1957, País Collection, OAH; Bonachea and San Martín, *The Cuban Insurrection*, pp. 83–84.

24. Frank País to Alberto Bayo, May 15, 1957, País Collection, OAH.

25. Ibid.

26. Frank País to All M-267 Chiefs, June 6, 1957, País Collection, OAH; Bonachea and San Martín, *The Cuban Insurrection*, p. 134; Rolando E. Bonachea and Nelson P. Valdés, eds., *Revolutionary Struggle, 1947–1958*, vol. 1 of *The Selected Works of Fidel Castro* (Cambridge, Mass.: MIT Press, 1972), p. 97.

27. Frank País to Pedro Miret, May 23, 1957, País Collection, OAH; Taber, *M-26*, pp. 142–144.

28. Frank País to Pedro Miret, May 23, 1957, País Collection, OAH; Frank País to All M-267 Chiefs, June 6, 1957, País Collection, OAH.

29. País wrote Pedro Miret, a close comrade of Castro's and veteran of the July

1953 attack on Moncada, to drop his plans to send a second landing force from Mexico and focus instead on sending money, weapons, ammunition, and fighters to the island. The new plan País suggested was for Léster Rodríguez to go to Mexico and Miami to raise more money and procure weapons, with which Miret or Gustavo Arcos would return to Cuba to take charge of a new front. See Frank País to Pedro Miret, May 23, 1957, País Collection, OAH. Fidel Castro to "El Informante" [Frank País], May 31, 1957, Fidel Castro Ruz Collection, OAH; Léster Rodríguez, interview by author, Havana, Cuba, November 14, 1995.

30. U.S. Department of State, Joint Weeka Report no. 16, April 17, 1957, 737.00 (W)/4–1757, DSR, NA; Herbert Matthews Papers, Columbia University Rare Book and Manuscript Library, box 2; *Times of Havana,* June 3, 1957, p. 4.

31. For a flavor of the debate, see Cuba's leading weekly magazine, *Bohemia,* from April 15, 1957, through July 31, 1957, when Batista again suspended guarantees and assigned censors to all newspaper offices. Corruption under the Prío administration was widely assumed and also reported by Ruby Hart Phillips, the *New York Times* correspondent in Havana. See, for example, her *Cuba: Island of Paradox* (New York: McDowell, Obolensky, 1959).

32. See Hugh Thomas, *Cuba: The Pursuit of Freedom* (New York: Harper and Row, 1971), pp. 789–876; Jaime Suchlicki, *Cuba: From Columbus to Castro* (McLean, Va.: Brassey's [U.S.], Inc., 1990), pp. 130–131.

33. Marifeli Pérez-Stable, "Reflections on Political Possibilities: Cuba's Peaceful Transition That Wasn't, 1954–1956," Occasional Paper Series no. 1, Cuban Research Institute, Florida International University, September 1998, p. 27.

34. Ibid.

35. Chibás's successor as president of the party, Pelayo Cuervo, was assassinated by Batista's police on the evening of March 13, 1957, hours after the DRE attacked the presidential palace. Days later, his own successor, Emilio Ochoa, went into exile in Miami, returning in May 1957 after Batista had restored constitutional guarantees. Agramonte, who succeeded Chibás as presidential candidate for the 1952 elections, went into exile in July 1957 after police stormed his house.

36. Pérez-Stable, "Reflections on Political Possibilities," pp. 20–27.

37. Charles D. Ameringer, "The Auténtico Party and the Political Opposition in Cuba, 1952–57," *Hispanic American Historical Review* 65 (1985): 327–351.

38. "Open Letter from Dr. Carlos Prío Socarrás to President Fulgencio Batista," *Diario las Americas,* June 11, 1957, p. 7.

39. The Frente Cívico de Mujeres Martianas was a politically heterogeneous group of women who facilitated anti-Batista underground activities. It was founded by Carmen Castro Porta, who had also fought in the student underground against the Machado dictatorship in the 1930s. See Carmen Castro Porta, *La Lección del Maestro: El Frente Cívico de Mujeres* Martianas (Havana: Editora Política, 1989).

40. Faustino Pérez to Haydée Santamaría, June 29, 1957, Pérez Collection, OAH; Carlos Franqui Collection, 1952–1981, "Documents of the Cuban Revolution," Manuscripts Division, Rare Books and Special Collections Depart-

ment, Princeton University Library, Princeton, N.J., found in microfilm at Georgetown University.

41. Ibid.

42. Manuel Antonio "Tony" de Varona quoted in "En Cuba," *Bohemia* 49, no. 28 (July 14, 1957): 70.

43. Prío and Castro still danced a tango—that is, alternately engaged and avoided each other—throughout the anti-Batista struggle, communicating through letters and intermediaries. Despite my requests, the Office of Historic Affairs in Havana was unable to identify the location of the complete set of Prío-Castro correspondence. Nor was I able to obtain such material from Prío's collection at the University of Miami. I did find many references to correspondence between Prío and Castro, in Frank País to Pedro Miret, June 18, 1957, País Collection, OAH; René Ramos Latour to Fidel Castro, November 20, 1957, Latour Collection, OAH, Havana, Cuba; Celia Sánchez to Fidel Castro, July 16, 1957, Sánchez Collection, OAH; Carlos Piad to Herbert Matthews, July 5, 1957, Herbert Matthews Papers, Columbia University Rare Book and Manuscript Library, box 1.

44. See, for example, National Committee of the Popular Socialist Party to the 26th of July Movement, a private letter dated February 28, 1957 and released publicly on June 10, 1957, Cuban Institute of History, Havana, Cuba.

45. "Proclamation by the Popular Socialist Party: What Is to Be Done in the Face of the Situation," June 29, 1957. The papers of the PSP are contained in record group 1 at the Cuban Institute of History, Havana, Cuba. *Webster's Third New International Dictionary* defines "putsch" as "a secretly plotted and suddenly executed attempt to overthrow a government or governing body. Syn. Rebellion."

46. See U.S. Department of State, Joint Weeka Report nos. 23–31, June 5, 1957–July 31, 1957, RG 59, 737.00 (W)/6–557, DSR, NA.

47. Jorge I. Domínguez, *Cuba: Order and Revolution* (Cambridge, Mass.: The Belknap Press of Harvard University Press, 1979), pp. 122–123.

48. Herbert Matthews Papers, Columbia University Rare Book and Manuscript Library, box 2, Statements and Reports, June 1957.

49. Ibid.

50. U.S. Department of State, Joint Weeka Report no. 25, June 19, 1957, RG 59, 737.00 (W)/6–1957, DSR, NA.

51. U.S. Department of State, Joint Weeka Report no. 29, July 17, 1957, RG 59, 737.00 (W)/7–1757, DSR, NA.

52. Phillips, *Cuba: Island of Paradox*, pp. 319–323.

53. Frank País to Fidel Castro, July 5, 1957, País Collection, OAH; Franqui, *Diary*, p. 196.

54. By now, País had completed the recruitment, arming, and training of some forty men for a second front in Oriente. The commander of the new column was René Ramos Latour ("Daniel"), a longtime activist in the province who had once worked as an accountant at the American-run mine at Moa Bay. Latour led the new guerrilla fighters to the mountain area of Miranda, near the town of San Luis. But, somewhat humiliated, País wrote Fidel that local

peasants were responsible for a *chivatazo* (major leak) to the army, which ambushed the group before they had even reached their base of operations. The fighters filtered back into Santiago, where País set them up in safe houses. The rebels managed to hide some twenty-five weapons and to salvage a truckload of food, boots, uniforms, and knapsacks, but they lost a significant investment of time and resources. Frank País to Fidel Castro, July 5, 1957, País Collection, OAH; Franqui, *Diary,* p. 196.

55. Celia Sánchez to Fidel Castro, July 7, 1957, Sánchez Collection, OAH; Frank País to Fidel Castro, July 5, 1957, in Franqui, *Diary,* p. 196. Taber, *M-26,* pp. 157–158.

56. Max Lesnik Menendez, "Cuba Pierde Sin Solución Nacional Pero Batista Perderá También," *Bohemia,* 49, no. 29 (July 21, 1957): 48.

57. Francisco Ichaso, "Cabalgata Política: La Formula de Una Junta Militar," *Bohemia* 49, no. 28 (July 14, 1957): 67.

58. U.S. Department of State, Joint Weeka Report no. 28, July 10, 1957, RG 59, 737.00 (W)/7–157, DSR, NA.

2. THE SIERRA MANIFESTO

1. Armando Hart, interview by author, Havana, Cuba, July 22, 1996. Based on information from an unnamed intelligence source, Tad Szulc wrote that the CIA began providing funds and some equipment to the 26th of July Movement at this time; see Szulc, *Fidel: A Critical Portrait* (New York: William Morrow, 1986), p. 419. One of the individuals I interviewed in Cuba corroborated this statement by confiding that her New York–based import-export business had shipped communications equipment to the Sierra through the U.S. consulate in Santiago.

2. Statement by Robert Reynolds, Caribbean Desk Officer, Central Intelligence Agency, 1957–1960, at "Bay of Pigs: Forty Years Later," a conference sponsored by the National Security Archives and the University of Havana, March 22–24, 2001, Havana, Cuba.

3. Frank País to Fidel Castro, July 11, 1957, País Collection, OAH, Carlos Franqui Collection, 1952–1981, "Documents of the Cuban Revolution," Manuscripts Division, Rare Books and Special Collections Department, Princeton University Library, Princeton, N.J., found on microfilm at Georgetown University Library, Washington, D.C.

4. Ibid.

5. Frank País to Faustino Pérez and Armando Hart, June 8, 1957, País Collection, OAH; Frank País to Fidel Castro, July 17, 1957, País Collection, OAH; Carlos Franqui Collection, 1952–1981, "Documents of the Cuban Revolution," p. 206.

6. Frank País to Fidel Castro, July 7, 1957, Carlos Franqui Collection, 1952–1981, "Documents of the Cuban Revolution"; Franqui, *Diary of the Cuban Revolution* (New York: Viking, 1980), p. 205.

7. Herbert Matthews Papers, Columbia University Rare Book and Manuscript Library, box 2, June 1957; "Report," *Bohemia* 49, no. 28 (July 14, 1957): 81.

For his first-person account of the anti-Machado student movement in the 1930s, see Justo Carrillo, *Cuba, 1933: Students, Yankees, and Soldiers* (Coral Gables, Fla.: University of Miami North-South Center, 1994).

8. Justo Carrillo to Fidel Castro, June 25, 1957, Carlos Franqui Collection, 1952–1981, "Documents of the Cuban Revolution"; Franqui, *Diary,* p. 210. In Franqui's collection this document is heavily edited and incorrectly dated. The printed date reads July 25, 1957, but the document in the Princeton collection is dated June 25, 1957.

9. U.S. Department of State Joint Weeka Report no. 27, July 2, 1957, RG 59, 737.00 (W)/7–357, DSR, NA.

10. Celia Sánchez to Fidel Castro, July 7, 1957, Sánchez Collection, OAH; Frank País to Pedro Miret, June 18, 1957, País Collection, OAH; Frank País to Celia Sánchez, July 5, 1957, País Collection, OAH; Celia Sánchez to Fidel Castro, July 7, 1957 and Celia Sánchez to Fidel Castro, July 9, 1957, Sánchez Collection, OAH.

11. See Frank País to Celia Sánchez, July 5, 1957, País Collection, OAH; Celia Sánchez to Fidel Castro, July 7, 1957, Sánchez Collection, OAH; Celia Sánchez to Fidel Castro, July 9, 1957, Sánchez Collection, OAH.

12. Celia Sánchez to Fidel Castro, July 9, 1957, Sánchez Collection, OAH.

13. "Raúl Chibás en la Sierra Maestra," *Bohemia* 49, no. 28 (July 14, 1957): 72–73.

14. Fidel Castro to Celia Sánchez, July 5, 1957, in Franqui, *Diario,* p. 190.

15. U.S. Department of State, Joint Weeka Report no. 28, July 10, 1957, RG 59, 737.00 (W)/7–1057, DSR, NA.

16. "Al Pueblo de Cuba," *Bohemia* 49, no. 30 (July 28, 1957); Celia Sánchez to Haydée Santamaría, August 2, 1957, Sánchez Collection, OAH; Fidel Castro to Celia Sánchez, July 12, 1957, Sánchez Collection, OAH; Frank País to Fidel Castro, July 17, 1957, País Collection, OAH.

17. Szulc, *Fidel: A Critical Portrait,* pp. 424–425; Rolando E. Bonachea and Nelson P. Valdés, eds., *Revolutionary Struggle, 1947–1958,* vol. 1 of *The Selected Works of Fidel Castro* (Cambridge, Mass.: MIT Press, 1972), pp. 99–100; Ramón L. Bonachea and Marta San Martín, *The Cuban Insurrection, 1952–1959* (New Brunswick, N.J.: Transaction, 1974), esp. n. 31, p. 377; Jon Lee Anderson, *Che Guevara: A Revolutionary Life* (New York: Grove, 1997); Carlos Franqui Collection, 1952–1981, "Documents of the Cuban Revolution."

18. Bonachea and San Martín, *The Cuban Insurrection,* nn. 29 and 31, p. 376.

19. Frank País to Fidel Castro, July 7, 1957, País Collection, OAH; Carlos Franqui Collection, 1952–1981, "Documents of the Cuban Revolution." The edited version of this letter that appears in the widely cited Franqui volume excises parts of the text indicating Castro was not informed about this *llano* initiative.

20. Frank País to Fidel Castro, July 5, 1957, País Collection, OAH; Carlos Franqui Collection, 1952–1981, "Documents of the Cuban Revolution"; Franqui, *Diary,* p. 197.

21. Frank País to Fidel Castro, July 7, 1957, País Collection, OAH. While this letter appeared in *Verde Olivo,* August 1, 1965, pp. 6–7, and *Pensamiento Crítico*

29 (June 1969): 252–257, both publications excised this portion of the text, as did Franqui, *Diary*, p. 202.

22. *Politiquería* is a blend of *política*, politics, and *porquería*, filth. I have Marta Varela, director of the New York City Human Rights Commission, to thank for this translation.

23. See the English-language translation of the manifesto published in Bonachea and Valdés, *Revolutionary Struggle*, pp. 343–348.

24. Ibid., p. 344.

25. Ibid.

26. Fidel Castro to Frank País, July 21, 1957, Fidel Castro Ruz Collection, OAH. The "deeds" are a reference to a thwarted plan "to liberate a decisive combat" timed to accompany the release of the manifesto. I have taken pains to show the sequence and precise content of this letter because omissions to date have distorted the interpretation of the relationship between *sierra* and *llano*, Castro and País. Two edited and undated portions of this letter appear in Franqui, *Diary*, pp. 193–196. Bonachea and Valdés reproduced a highly edited one-page version of the letter, dealing mainly with Fidel's fears for País's life, as it was printed by *Granma* in 1968 (*Revolutionary Struggle*, pp. 348–349). The authors did not know that this letter actually contained Fidel's response to País's movement plans, writing elsewhere in the collection that "how Castro reacted to País's [July 7, 1957] letter has never been disclosed." See Bonachea and Valdés, *Revolutionary Struggle*, p. 99.

27. U.S. Department of State, Joint Weeka Report no. 29, July 17, 1957, RG 59, 737.00 (W)/7–1757, DSR, NA.

28. U.S. Department of State, Joint Weeka Report no. 31, July 31, 1957, RG 59, 737.00 (W)/7–3157, DSR, NA.

3. "WE HAD TO ACT A BIT DICTATORIALLY"

1. Frank País to the Municipal Leaders of the 26th of July, undated, País Collection, OAH.

2. Frank País to Faustino Pérez and Armando Hart, June 8, 1957, País Collection, OAH.

3. Frank País to Havana, May 26, 1957, País Collection, OAH.

4. Frank País to Matanzas Coordinator, June 18, 1957, País Collection, OAH.

5. Frank País to Camagüey Coordinator, June 19, 1957, País Collection, OAH.

6. Frank País to Las Tunas and Other Oriente Coordinators, June 18, 1957, País Collection, OAH.

7. Frank País to Norma, Sierra, Agitado, and the Others, June 19, 1957, País Collection, OAH.

8. Frank País to Fidel Castro, July 26, 1957, Carlos Franqui Collection, 1952–1981, "Documents of the Cuban Revolution" Manuscripts Division, Rare Books and Special Collections, Princeton University Library, Princeton, N.J., found on microfilm at Georgetown University Library, Washington, D.C.

9. For accounts of infiltration by *chivatos*, gangsters, and other unsavory figures in Oriente and Havana, see Celia Sánchez to Fidel Castro, July 16, 1957, Sánchez Collection, OAH; Frank País to Fidel Castro, July 17, 1957, País Collection, País Collection, OAH; Carlos Franqui Collection, 1952–1981, "Documents of the Cuban Revolution"; and Armando Hart to Fidel Castro, November 1957, Hart Collection, OAH. Between May and July of 1957, País estimated losses of over 13,000 pesos caused by one individual, a *moncadista* named René "El Flaco" Rodríguez. Rodríguez stole money from the National Directorate, wrote bad checks to the movement's suppliers, sold the movement's weapons, lied to the other members of the Directorate, and otherwise exposed the movement to police penetration, thereby creating much bad blood in the sabotage cells and at the national level. See Frank País to Fidel Castro, July 17, 1957; Carlos Franqui Collection, 1952–1981, "Documents of the Cuban Revolution"; Frank País to Fidel Castro, July 20, 1957, País Collection, OAH.

10. Frank País to *Sierra*, Manzanillo, June 18, 1957, País Collection, OAH. I have not been able to establish the identity of this individual. Enrique Oltuski also used the pseudonym Sierra, but he was based in Havana and later Las Villas, not Manzanillo. Enrique Oltuski, interview by author, Marina Hemingway, Havana, Cuba, July 5, 1997.

11. Reporting on the government's June 30 peace rally, the section "En Cuba" of *Bohemia* noted sabotage in the Oriente towns of Manzanillo, Palma Soriano, Bayamo, San Luis, and Guantánamo, making Oriente "an index of the national reality" and converting the rally of peace into the "peace of a cemetery." *Bohemia* 49, no. 28 (July 14, 1957): 49.

12. Daniel Rodríguez, interview by author, Havana, Cuba, July 6, 1997.

13. Frank País to Fidel Castro, July 7, 1957, País Collection, OAH, for the complete letter; Carlos Franqui Collection, 1952–1981, "Documents of the Cuban Revolution" for a partial version; and Franqui, *Diary of the Cuban Revolution* (New York: Viking, 1980), p. 202, for a heavily edited version. Two Cuban publications also published an edited version of the letter: *Verde Olivo*, August 1, 1965, pp. 6–7; and *Pensamiento Crítico*, no. 29 (June 1969): 252–257.

14. Nelson P. Valdés, "The Cuban Rebellion: Internal Organization and Strategy, 1952–1959," Ph.D. diss., The University of New Mexico, 1978, p. 673.

15. Jon Lee Anderson, *Che Guevara: A Revolutionary Life* (New York: Grove, 1997), p. 276.

16. Rolando Bonachea and Nelson Valdés, eds., *Revolutionary Struggle, 1947–1958*, vol. 1 of *The Selected Works of Fidel Castro* (Cambridge, Mass.: MIT Press, 1972), pp. 99–100. Each of the following authors echoed the Bonachea-Valdés interpretation: Ramón Bonachea and Marta San Martín, *The Cuban Insurrection, 1952–1959* (New Brunswick, N.J.: Transaction, 1974), p. 144; Tad Szulc, *Fidel: A Critical Portrait* (New York: William Morrow, 1986), pp. 423–425; Thomas G. Paterson, *Contesting Castro: The United States and the Triumph of the Cuban Revolution* (New York: Oxford University Press, 1994), p. 93; and ibid., pp. 275–276. The exception is Hugh Thomas, *Cuba: The Pursuit of Free-*

dom (New York: Harper & Row, 1971), pp. 953–955. Valdés, in his exhaustive and insightful dissertation, departed from his earlier conclusion, hinting but offering no evidence that País had something to do with the alliance. See Valdés, "The Cuban Rebellion," pp. 641–642.

17. Frank País to Fidel Castro, July 7, 1957, País Collection, OAH. País, Castro, Hart, Marcelo Fernández, and others habitually referred to themselves in the third person when corresponding with one another.

18. Ibid.

19. Ibid.

20. Ibid.

21. Ibid.

22. Ibid.

23. According to the letter, the new number was thirteen. But later correspondence refers to Léster Rodríguez as a member of the National Directorate, which would bring the number to fourteen. See Frank País to Pedro Miret and Gustavo Arcos, July 8, 1957, País Collection, OAH.

24. Fidel Castro to Frank País, July 21, 1957, Fidel Castro Ruz Collection, OAH. Two edited and undated portions of this letter appear in Franqui, *Diary,* pp. 193–196. From the *Granma* landing in December 1956 to July 1957 totaled seven months; see Franqui, *Diary,* pp. 193–194. Franqui's approach to editing the letter leaves the incorrect impression that the phrases "they've done a great job in," "plans for the next months," and "correct strategy" refer not to the urban underground or the general strike but to the expansion and supply of the Sierra front.

25. Fidel Castro to Frank País, July 21, 1957, Fidel Castro Ruz Collection, OAH. After the battle of El Uvero on May 28, 1957, Castro instructed País to use some of the arms seized after the palace attack for the second front.

26. Frank País to Fidel Castro, July 17, 1957, País Collection, OAH; Carlos Franqui Collection, 1952–1981, "Documents of the Cuban Revolution"; Frank País to Fidel Castro, July 20, 1957, País Collection, OAH.

27. Frank País to Fidel Castro, July 26, 1957, País Collection, OAH; Franqui, *Diary,* p. 212; Carlos Franqui Collection, 1952–1981, "Documents of the Cuban Revolution." The published version of this document omits the portion quoted herein, focusing instead on Frank's description of the growing police surveillance of him.

28. U.S. Department of State, Joint Weeka Report no. 24, June 12, 1957, RG 59, 737.00 (W)/6–1257, DSR, NA.

29. René Ramos Latour to Celia Sánchez, August 1, 1957, in Franqui, *Diary,* pp. 218–220; Vilma Espín, undated, in Franqui, *Diary,* pp. 213–214.

4. DEFINING OPPOSITION UNITY ON THE GROUND

1. Juan Marinello and Blas Roca to Fidel Castro and Leaders of the 26th of July, August 1, 1957, Cuban Institute of History, Havana, Cuba, RG 1.

2. U.S. Department of State, Joint Weeka Report no. 32, August 7, 1957, RG 59, 737.00 (W)/6–125, DSR, NA.

3. Frank País to Labor and Civic Resistance Leaders, July 1957, País Collection, OAH.

4. U.S. Department of State, Joint Weeka Report no. 32, August 7, 1957, RG 59, 737.00 (W)6-125, DSR, NA.

5. Celia Sánchez to Haydée Santamaría, July 31 to August 2, 1957, Sánchez Collection, OAH; Armando Hart and Faustino Pérez to René Ramos Latour, August 3, 1957, Hart Collection, OAH.

6. René Ramos Latour to Celia Sánchez, August 1, 1957, in Franqui, *Diary of the Cuban Revolution* (New York: Viking, 1980), pp. 218–220.

7. Enrique Oltuski, interview by author, Marina Hemingway, Havana, Cuba, July 5, 1997; Armando Hart and Faustino Pérez to René Ramos Latour, August 3, 1957, Hart Collection, OAH. Salvador was one of three underground names used by País: the others were David and Cristian.

8. Armando Hart and Faustino Pérez to René Ramos Latour, August 3, 1957, Hart Collection, OAH.

9. Ibid.

10. Enrique Oltuski, interview by author, Marina Hemingway, Havana, Cuba, July 5, 1997; and Enrique Oltuski, *Gente del Llano* (Havana: Imagen Contemporanea, 2000), pp. 108–126.

11. Armando Hart and Faustino Pérez to René Ramos Latour, August 3, 1957, Hart Collection, OAH. For País's discussions with the same unnamed officer, see Frank País to Fidel Castro, July 17 and July 20, 1957, País Collection, OAH, and Franqui, *Diary*, p. 208.

12. Armando Hart and Faustino Pérez to René Ramos Latour, August 3, 1957, Hart Collection, OAH.

13. Ibid.

14. U.S. Department of State, Joint Weeka Report no. 32, August 7, 1957, RG 59, 737.00 (W)6-125, DSR, NA.

15. Ibid.

16. Faustino Pérez to Léster Rodríguez, August 9, 1957, Pérez Collection, OAH.

17. Fidel Castro to Celia Sánchez, August 11, 1957, Fidel Castro Ruz Collection, OAH; Franqui, *Diary*, pp. 220–222.

18. For one of the only first-hand accounts of the Cienfuegos uprising, see Robert Taber, *M-26, Biography of a Revolution* (New York: Lyle Stuart, 1961). For a history of the Cuban military, see Louis A. Pérez, Jr., *Army Politics in Cuba, 1898–1958* (Pittsburgh: University of Pittsburgh Press, 1976).

19. Faustino Pérez to René Ramos Latour, September 9, 1957, Pérez Collection, OAH.

20. Armando Hart, Circular to Provincial Directorates, undated (Fall 1957), Hart Collection, OAH.

21. Carlos Franqui published much of the correspondence between Fidel Castro, René Ramos Latour, Che Guevara, Armando Hart, and Celia Sánchez regarding the *sierra*'s suspicions that the *llano*'s inadequate supply for the *sierra* re-

sulted from both incompetence and sabotage. See Carlos Franqui, *Diario de la Revolución Cubana* (Paris: R. Torres, 1976); and Mario Llerena, *The Unsuspected Revolution: The Birth and Rise of Castroism* (Ithaca, N.Y.: Cornell University Press, 1978), p. 156.

22. René Ramos Latour to Fidel Castro, September 15, 1957, Latour Collection, OAH.

23. Armando Hart to Fidel Castro, October 16, 1957, Hart Collection, OAH. Portions of this document, though not the text cited here, appear in Franqui, *Diario* and Franqui, *Diary*.

24. Armando Hart to Gentlemen Directors of the Combined Civic Institutions, October 1957, Hart Collection, OAH. I was unable to find a copy of the original proposal from the Civic Institutions to which Hart's letter refers. The term "clases economicas" was used in Cuba during the 1930s, 1940s, and 1950s to indicate the opposite of "las clases populares," or the workers and dispossessed. It does not translate directly either to upper class or bourgeoisie, or even more awkwardly, to the "owner class." I have thus left the expression stand in its original Spanish.

25. Armando Hart to 26th of July Militants: Circular to Militants no. 1, October 1957, Hart Collection, OAH.

26. Ibid.

27. Ibid.

28. National Committee of the Popular Socialist Party, "Declaration of the Popular Socialist Party: The Struggle against the Tyranny, the Pact of Miami, and What Is Missing from the Current Situation," October 30, 1957, Institute of Cuban History, Havana, Cuba, RG 1, 1/2.4/11/4/253–258.

29. Armando Hart to 26th of July Militants: Circular to Militants no. 1, October 1957, Hart Collection, OAH.

30. Armando Hart to Léster Rodríguez, Pedro Miret, Gustavo Arcos, and Mario Llerena, October 15, 1957, Hart Collection, OAH.

31. Armando Hart to Gentlemen Directors of the Combined Civic Institutions, October 1957, Hart Collection, OAH.

5. FEAR AND LOATHING IN MIAMI

1. Jorge G. Castañeda, *Compañero: The Life and Death of Che Guevara* (New York: Alfred A. Knopf, 1997), pp. 108–109.

2. Frank País to Fidel Castro, July 11, 1957, País Collection, OAH; Léster Rodríguez, interview by author, Havana, Cuba, November 14, 1995. The 26th of July cell at Guantánamo continued to ferret out ammunition, however; the Americans had failed to explicitly prohibit such smuggling in their arrangement with País.

3. Faustino Pérez to Léster Rodríguez, August 9, 1957, Pérez Collection, OAH.

4. Léster Rodríguez to Frank País, July 28, 1957, Rodríguez Collection, OAH.

5. Mario Llerena to National Directorate, August 30, 1957, Llerena Collection, OAH.

6. Léster Rodríguez to Frank País, July 28, 1957.

7. Ibid.

8. Ibid.

9. Ibid.

10. Faustino Pérez to Léster Rodríguez, August 9, 1957, Pérez Collection, OAH.

11. Léster Rodríguez to National Directorate, August 19, 1957, Rodríguez Collection, OAH. Mujal was of Catalonian descent.

12. Ibid.

13. Léster Rodríguez to René Ramos Latour, September 9, 1957, Rodríguez Collection, OAH.

14. Ibid.

15. Celia Sánchez to Fidel Castro, September 1957, Sánchez Collection, OAH.

16. Léster Rodríguez to René Ramos Latour, September 9, 1957, Rodríguez Collection, OAH.

17. Celia Sánchez to Fidel Castro, September 29, 1957, Sánchez Collection, OAH.

18. Mario Llerena, Léster Rodríguez, Gustavo Arcos, Pedro Miret, and Felipe Pazos to National Directorate, September 28, 1957, Rodríguez Collection, OAH. See also Mario Llerena, *The Unsuspected Revolution: The Birth and Rise of Castroism* (Ithaca, N.Y.: Cornell University Press, 1978). Until now, Llerena's 1960s Spanish-language manuscript in the Cuba collection at the Hoover Institution in Palo Alto, California, followed by its English-language 1978 publication, have provided the only first-hand accounts of Cuban exile politics during the insurrection. To date, Llerena's account and Cuban documents published by Carlos Franqui in 1976 and 1980 have informed all subsequent treatments of this incident, including Hugh Thomas, *Cuba: The Pursuit of Freedom* (New York: Harper and Row, 1971); Ramón Bonachea and Marta San Martín, *The Cuban Insurrection, 1952–1959* (Cambridge, Mass.: MIT Press, 1972); Robert E. Quirk, *Fidel Castro* (New York: Norton, 1993); Thomas G. Paterson, *Contesting Castro: The United States and the Triumph of the Cuban Revolution* (New York: Oxford University Press, 1994); and Jon Lee Anderson, *Che Guevara: A Revolutionary Life* (New York: Grove, 1997). Jorge G. Castañeda, *Compañero: The Life and Death of Che Guevara* (New York: Alfred A. Knopf, 1997), does not include Llerena among his sources.

19. Mario Llerena to Faustino Pérez and Armando Hart, October 5, 1957, Llerena Collection, OAH.

20. Ibid.

21. Ibid. The State Department's William Wieland, then director of the office of Middle American Affairs in the Bureau of Inter-American Affairs, not Secretary Dulles, met with Carlos Prío in Washington in September 1957. A report on the meeting notes that Prío told Wieland an American intermediary, Wallace Rouse, had agreed to arrange a meeting with John Foster Dulles in New York, but the meeting never materialized. The memorandum makes no reference to U.S. mediation in the Cuban conflict, but does report having warned Prío to curtail his support for revolutionary activities. U.S. Department of State, Memorandum of Conversation, Roy Rubottom, Assistant Secretary of State of Inter-American Affairs to "The Acting Secretary," September

21, 1957, RG 59, 737.00/9–2157, DSR, NA. Also see Llerena, *The Unsuspected Revolution*, pp. 132–153.

22. Armando Hart to Léster Rodríguez, Pedro Miret, Gustavo Arcos, and Mario Llerena, October 15, 1957, Hart Collection, OAH. A portion of this document, though not the text quoted here, appears in Llerena, *The Unsuspected Revolution*, p. 136.

23. Mario Llerena to National Directorate, August 30, 1957, Llerena Collection, OAH.

24. For a sense of Betancourt's interaction with American officials, see the records of conversations published in "Cuba," *Foreign Relations of the United States, 1958–1960*, vol. 6 (Washington, D.C.: U.S. Government Printing Office, 1991).

25. Armando Hart to Léster Rodríguez, Pedro Miret, Gustavo Arcos, and Mario Llerena, October 15, 1957, Hart Collection, OAH. Hart routinely referred to the U.S. Department of State as the Ministerio del Estado, the term used in Cuba at the time for the Cuban foreign ministry.

26. "The North American Department of State and the Grave Cuban Political Crisis," October 1957, Hart Collection, OAH.

27. Ibid.

28. Ibid. For the role of U.S. ambassador Sumner Welles in the 1933 U.S. mediation efforts, see Irwin F. Gellman, *Roosevelt and Batista: Good Neighbor Diplomacy in Cuba, 1933–1945* (Albuquerque: University of New Mexico Press, 1973); Jules Benjamin, *The United States and the Origins of the Cuban Revolution: An Empire of Liberty in an Age of National Liberation* (Princeton, N.J.: Princeton University Press, 1990); and Thomas, *Cuba*, p. 997.

29. "The North American Department of State and the Grave Cuban Political Crisis," October 1957, Hart Collection, OAH.

30. Ibid. Hart sent this report to Fidel Castro on November 8, 1957. See Armando Hart to Fidel Castro, November 8, 1957, Hart Collection, OAH.

31. "Constituida la 'Junta de Liberación Cubana'," *Diario Las Americas*, October 18, 1957, p. 1; "Anti-Batista Bloc Organizes in U.S.: Refugee Party Chiefs Meet at Miami to Bring About Provisional Regime," *New York Times*, October 18, 1957, p. 11; "600 Editores Del Hemisferio Asisten a Asamblea de SIP," *Diario Las Americas*, October 17, 1957, p. 1.

32. "Constituida la 'Junta de Liberación Cubana'," *Diario Las Americas*, October 18, 1957, pp. 1, 7.

33. A recent biographer of Che Guevara, Jon Lee Anderson, writes that "apart from the standard calls for Batista's resignation, fair elections, and a return to constitutionality . . . the issue of economic injustice was similarly passed over with a tepid clause promising only to create more jobs and raise living standards" (Anderson, *Che*, p. 293). Franqui's summary of the Pact of Miami gives this impression, but the press coverage of the junta and its public and private documents show that on the matter of domestic policy, the Miami pact closely reflected the tone of the Sierra Manifesto. See Franqui, *Diary*, p. 247.

34. "Constituida la 'Junta de Liberación Cubana'," *Diario Las Americas*, October 18, 1957, pp. 1, 7.

35. Ibid.

36. "Secret Bases: Organization and Powers of the Cuban Liberation Junta," October 12, 1957, José Miró Cardona Collection, OAH.

37. Ibid.

38. "Opposition in Cuba," *New York Times*, October 18, 1957, p. 22. A review of the Latin American press coverage of the liberation junta found brief notices in *La Prensa* of Lima, Peru, *La Nación* of Costa Rica, and *La Prensa* of Nicaragua.

39. Armando Hart to Luis Buch, October 19, 1957, Hart Collection, OAH; U.S. Department of State, Joint Weeka Report no. 38, September 18, 1957, RG 59, 737.00(W)/9–1857, DSR, NA.

40. U.S. Department of State, Memorandum of Conversation, John L. Topping re. Oppositionist Activities in Florida, October 3, 1957, RG 59, 737.00/10–357, DSR, NA; U.S. Department of State Office Memorandum from C. Allan Stewart, Office of Middle American Affairs to Roy Rubottum, Assistant Secretary of State for Inter-American Affairs, October 16, 1957, RG 59, 737.00/10–1657, DSR, NA. Dubois worked in army intelligence during World War II, and went on to become an instructor for Latin American officers attending the command and staff officers course at Fort Leavenworth. According to his son, Jules Dubois, Jr., the senior Dubois "decided to leave the reserves because he was being accused by various military dictators of being an agent for the CIA. He had no love for the Agency and believed that by leaving the reserves that the accusations would cease . . . I recall him telling me that in good conscience he needed to make a clean break." After retiring from military intelligence work in 1952, Dubois, Sr. reported on Latin America for the *Chicago Tribune*. Personal correspondence to author from Jules Dubois Jr., July 10, 2001. For Dubois's perspective on this period, see Jules Dubois, *Fidel Castro: Rebel Liberator or Dictator?* (Indianapolis: Bobbs-Merrill, 1959).

41. U.S. Department of State, Memorandum of Conversation, "Cuban Political Situation," October 17, 1957, RG 59, 373.00/10–1757, DSR, NA.

42. Recent biographers of Che Guevara, reflecting Guevara's own views of the liberation junta, have described it as, for example, "a political manifesto designed to warm Washington's heart" or have suggested that the Pact of Miami "called for U.S. mediation in the civil war." See Anderson, *Che*, p. 293; Castañeda, *Compañero*, p. 108. Castañeda seems to have drawn this conclusion from Franqui, whose 1976 Spanish-language edition of *Diary of the Cuban Revolution* reproduces a short article that Franqui wrote in early October from Costa Rica. Like Mario Llerena, he had heard rumors that Prío, representing other opposition politicians, had met with John Foster Dulles to begin a mediation.

6. TAMING THE *POLITIQUEROS* IN EXILE

1. Armando Hart to Luis Buch, October 19, 1957, Hart Collection, OAH.

2. Luis Buch, *Más Allá de los Codigos* (Havana: Editorial Ciencias Sociales, 1995).

3. Léster Rodríguez, interview by author, Havana, Cuba, November 14, 1995;

Armando Hart to Augustín Navarrete and René Ramos Latour, November 25, 1957, Hart Collection, OAH.

4. Luis Buch to Armando Hart and National Directorate, November 1957, Buch Collection, OAH.

5. Faure Chomón, interview by author, Havana, Cuba, July 10, 1997; Mario Llerena, *The Unsuspected Revolution: The Birth and Rise of Castroism* (Ithaca, N.Y.: Cornell University Press, 1978), p. 156.

6. Léster Rodríguez interview, November 14, 1995.

7. René Ramos Latour to Fidel Castro, November 9, 1957, Latour Collection, OAH. A portion of this letter, in which Latour quotes to Fidel from an October 20, 1957 letter by Felipe Pazos to Faustino Pérez, appears in Carlos Franqui, *Diario de la Revolución Cubana* (Paris: R. Torres, 1976), p. 330, but is misdated as October 9, 1957. An edited version of the letter also appears in the English version; see Franqui, *Diary of the Cuban Revolution* (New York: Viking, 1980), pp. 246–247.

8. Quoted in Raúl Castro to Fidel Castro, November 20, 1957, Raúl Castro Ruz Collection, OAH; Franqui, *Diario*, pp. 335–337; Franqui, *Diary*, pp. 248–250. The Cuban Council of State Office of Historic Affairs did not have the original Pazos letter.

9. Luis Buch to Armando Hart and National Directorate, November 1957, Buch Collection, OAH. In his own account of the period, Dubois underestimates his influence on the Cuban opposition and barely acknowledges the extent of his contact- and information sharing with the Department of State. See Jules Dubois, *Fidel Castro: Rebel Liberator or Dictator?* (Indianapolis: Bobbs-Merrill, 1959). The State Department's decimal files 737.00 for this period document Dubois's role as an interlocutor in the Miami-Havana milieu.

10. Armando Hart to Felipe Pazos and Léster Rodríguez, October 26, 1957, Hart Collection, OAH. Llerena, *The Unsuspected Revolution*, pp. 138–139 contains direct citations of two paragraphs of this five-page single-spaced typewritten letter, but not the text quoted herein. See also "Opposition in Cuba," *New York Times*, October 18, 1957, p. 22.

11. Armando Hart to Felipe Pazos and Léster Rodríguez, October 26, 1957, Hart Collection, OAH.

12. Ibid.

13. Ibid.

14. Ibid.

15. Luis Buch to Armando Hart and National Directorate, November 1957, Buch Collection, OAH.

16. Armando Hart to Felipe Pazos and Léster Rodríguez, October 26, 1957, Hart Collection, OAH.

17. Armando Hart to Carlos Franqui, Léster Rodríguez, and Mario Llerena, October 29, 1957, Hart Collection, OAH.

18. Armando Hart to Carlos Franqui, Mario Llerena, and Léster Rodríguez, November 3, 1957, Hart Collection, OAH. Hart sent to Miami official credentials signed by Fidel Castro that ratified the National Directorate's October 15 designation of Franqui, Llerena, Rodríguez, and Chibás as members of the Com-

mittee in Exile; reproduced in Llerena, *The Unsuspected Revolution*, pp. 139–140.

19. Mario Llerena to Faustino Pérez, November 10, 1957, Llerena Collection, OAH.

20. Armando Hart to Fidel Castro, November 8, 1957, Hart Collection, OAH; Franqui, *Diario*, pp. 327–329. The 1980 Franqui English edition contains a partial version of this document.

21. René Ramos Latour to Fidel Castro, November 9, 1957, Latour Collection, OAH. Franqui excised this portion of the text in both the English and Spanish versions of his published diaries.

22. Celia Sánchez to René Ramos Latour, November 9, 1957, Sánchez Collection, OAH.

23. Luis Buch to Armando Hart and National Directorate, November 1957, Buch Collection, OAH.

24. Léster Rodríguez, interview by author, Havana, Cuba, November 14, 1995.

25. "Contribution to Weeka," American Embassy, November 19, 1957, RG 59, 737.00/9–1957, DSR, NA.

26. Celia Sánchez to René Ramos Latour, November 9, 1957, Sánchez Collection, OAH.

27. Armando Hart to Provincial Directorates and Committee in Exile, November 15, 1957, Hart Collection, OAH.

28. Ibid.

29. Armando Hart to Fidel Castro, November 8, 1957, Hart Collection, OAH. Portions of this letter appear in Franqui, *Diario* and Franqui, *Diary*.

30. Armando Hart, Circular to Militants, no. 2, November 1957, Hart Collection, OAH.

31. Armando Hart to Provincial Militants, October 1957, Hart Collection, OAH.

32. Ibid.

33. To Workers of All Militancies, November 10, 1957, Hart Collection, OAH; and Armando Dávalos Hart, *Aldabonazo* (Havana: Editorial Letras Cubanas, 1997), pp. 271–273.

34. Armando Hart to Provincial Directorates and the Committee in Exile, Organization Circular no. 2, November 15, 1957, Hart Collection, OAH.

7. WITH FRIENDS LIKE THESE, WHO NEEDS ENEMIES?

1. Armando Hart to Provincial Directorates and the Committee in Exile, Organization Circular no. 2, November 15, 1957, Hart Collection, OAH; Armando Hart to the Provincial Chiefs of Organization, November 21, 1957, Hart Collection, OAH.

2. Armando Hart to Fidel Castro, November 22, 1957, Hart Collection, OAH; Armando Hart to Augustín Navarrete and René Ramos Latour, November 25, 1957, Hart Collection, OAH. Portions of Hart's letter to Castro appear in Carlos Franqui, *Diario de la Revolución Cubana* (Paris: R. Torres, 1976), pp. 340–341 and Franqui, *Diary of the Cuban Revolution* (New York: Viking, 1980), pp. 252–253.

3. *Bohemia* 50 (February 2, 1958), supplement: 8; René Viera, "Reloj del Acontecer Cubano," *Diario Las Americas,* January 14, 1958, p. 9.

4. Armando Hart to Mario Llerena, November 19, 1957, Hart Collection, OAH.

5. Armando Hart, "Proposals for the Movement's Delegates to Present at the Liberation Junta," December 1957, Hart Collection, OAH.

6. Ibid.

7. Ibid.

8. René Ramos Latour to Celia Sánchez, December 5, 1957, Latour Collection, OAH; Carlos Franqui Collection, 1952–1981, "Documents of the Cuban Revolution," Manuscripts Division, Rare Books and Special Collections Department, Princeton University Library, Princeton, N.J., found in microfilm at Georgetown University, Washington, D.C.

9. Luis Buch to Armando Hart and Haydée Santamaría, December 11, 1957, Buch Collection, OAH; also in Mario Llerena, *The Unsuspected Revolution: The Birth and Rise of Castroism* (Ithaca, N.Y.: Cornell University Press, 1978), p. 152.

10. Ibid.

11. Armando Hart to Fidel Castro, November 22, 1957, Hart Collection, OAH; Llerena, *The Unsuspected Revolution,* pp. 152–153. On November 8 Hart sent Fidel the Betancourt report on U.S. policy toward Cuba; see Felipe Pazos's October 20, 1957 letter to Faustino Pérez, the junta's secret and published documents, Hart's October 26 letter to Pazos and Rodríguez, his October 29 letter to the Exile Committee, the October 1957 National Directorate "Bulletin to Militants," and Armando Hart to Fidel Castro, November 8, 1957, Hart Collection, OAH. Franqui misdates the November 8 letter as October 8 in *Diario,* p. 327. In the English-language version, he records the date correctly but excises the portion indicating that Hart had kept Fidel fully informed throughout the negotiations with the junta (Franqui, *Diary,* p. 245).

12. Raúl Castro to Fidel Castro, November 20, 1957, Carlos Franqui Collection, 1952–1981, "Documents of the Cuban Revolution"; Franqui, *Diario,* p. 335–337; Franqui, *Diary,* pp. 248–250.

13. Che Guevara to Fidel Castro, December 9, 1957, Carlos Franqui Collection, 1952–1981, "Documents of the Cuban Revolution"; Franqui, *Diario,* p. 355; Franqui, *Diary,* p. 264; Che Guevara to René Ramos Latour, December 14, 1957, in Franqui, *Diario,* p. 361 and Franqui, *Diary,* p. 268; Che Guevara to Fidel Castro, December 15, 1957, Carlos Franqui Collection, 1952–1981, "Documents of the Cuban Revolution," Franqui, *Diario,* p. 363, and Franqui, *Diary,* p. 270; René Ramos Latour to Fidel Castro, December 18, 1957, Carlos Franqui Collection, 1952–1981, "Documents of the Cuban Revolution"; René Ramos Latour to Che Guevara, December 18, 1957, in Franqui, *Diario,* p. 365, and Franqui, *Diary,* p. 272.

14. Quoted from Che's diary in Paco Ignacio Taíbo, II, *Guevara, Also Known as Che* (New York: St. Martin's, 1997), p. 54.

15. Che Guevara to Fidel Castro, December 15, 1957, Carlos Franqui Collection, 1952–1981, "Documents of the Cuban Revolution"; Franqui, *Diario,* pp. 363–364; Franqui, *Diary,* pp. 270–271.

16. U.S. Department of State, Secret Memorandum to Assistant Secretary of State for Inter-American Affairs Roy Rubottom from William Wieland and C. Allan Stewart, "Possible United States Courses of Action in Restoring Normalcy to Cuba," November 21, 1957, RG 59, 737.00/11–2157, DSR, NA. This memorandum is summarized in a footnote in "American Republics," *Foreign Relations of the United States, 1955–1957*, vol. 6 (Washington, D.C.: Government Printing Office, 1991), p. 865.

17. Ibid.

18. U.S. Department of State Secret Memorandum of Conversation, November 13, 1957, RG 59, 737.00/11–1358, DSR, NA.

19. Hugh Thomas, *Cuba: The Pursuit of Freedom* (New York: Harper and Row, 1971), p. 611.

20. Ibid. Historian Thomas Paterson offers the best treatment of U.S. policy during this period in *Contesting Castro: The United States and the Triumph of the Cuban Revolution* (New York: Oxford University Press, 1994). In his discussion of the State Department's November and December 1957 policy review (pp. 109–112), Paterson omits Wieland's suggestion that the United States engage the Cuban Liberation Junta in a mediation with Batista, despite Wieland's own emphasis in the memo that the United States make every effort to avoid seeming to replay the 1933 attempted mediation between Machado and the opposition.

21. Confidential "Official-Informal" letter, William Wieland to C. Allan Stewart, December 3, 1957, RG 59, 737.00/12–357, DSR, NA.

22. U.S. Department of State, William Wieland to Roy Rubottom, "Policy Recommendation for Restoration of Normalcy in Cuba," December 19, 1957, in "American Republics," pp. 870–876.

23. Luis Buch to Armando Hart and Haydée Santamaría, December 11, 1957, Buch Collection, OAH. Alex and Alejandro were Fidel Castro's underground names.

24. Luis Buch to Armando Hart and Haydée Santamaría, December 11, 1957, Buch Collection, OAH; Luis Buch to Armando Hart, November 1957, Buch Collection, OAH; Luis Buch, interview by author, Havana, Cuba, November 5, 1995.

25. Confidential Incoming Telegram, Havana Embassy to Secretary of State, October 18, 1957, RG 737.00/10–1857, DSR, NA.

26. Luis Buch to Armando Hart and Haydée Santamaria, December 11, 1957, Buch Collection, OAH.

27. Faustino Pérez to Armando Hart and Other Comrades, December 9, 1957, Pérez Collection, OAH.

28. Armando Hart to Celia Sánchez, December 6, 1957, Hart Collection, OAH; Franqui, *Diario*, p. 354. I asked for the Sánchez letter to which Hart was replying but it was not in the collection of her documents nor in Hart's collection at the archive.

29. Armando Hart to Celia Sánchez, December 6, 1957; Franqui, *Diario*, p. 354. Castro's 1953 speech "History Will Absolve Me" advanced a more explicit social agenda than the Sierra Manifesto; it outlined policies for agrarian reform,

educational reform, public housing reform, nationalization of electricity and telephone services, and payment of taxes by tax evaders. It also proposed restoration of the 1940 constitution, judicial reform, profit sharing for workers, reform of the sugar industry, and confiscation of property from individuals who had acquired it through fraudulent means. The Sierra Manifesto was far more general, proposing that a "minimum government program will be formed to guarantee the punishment of those who are guilty of crimes, workers' rights, fulfillment of international agreements, public order, peace, freedom, as well as economic, social and political progress of the Cuban people." Rolando E. Bonachaea and Nelson P. Valdés, eds., *Revolutionary Struggle, 1947–1958*, vol. 1 of *The Selected Works of Fidel Castro* (Cambridge, Mass.: MIT Press, 1972), pp. 343–348. For discussion of the difference between the two, see Theodor Draper, *Castroism: Theory and Practice* (New York: Praeger, 1965) and K. S. Karol, *Guerrillas in Power: The Course of the Cuban Revolution* (New York: Hill and Wang, 1970), pp. 161–162.

30. Armando Hart, "Proposal to Comrade Fidel Castro Regarding the Movement's Policies in Relation to the Civic Institutions, and the Designation of a Figure That Could Be the Substitute of the Dictator Batista," December 1957, Hart Collection, OAH.

31. Ibid. In his own account Urrutia indicates no knowledge of the process by which the movement chose him as president. See Manuel Urrutia Lleó, *Fidel Castro and Company, Inc: Communist Tyranny in Cuba* (New York: Praeger, 1964).

32. Felipe Pazos's son Javier had reached Fidel's base after a stint with Che Guevara. While Javier, too, agreed with the decision to break with the junta, he was deeply conflicted about whether he should remain with the guerrillas. He knew Fidel's denunciation of the pact was also an attack on his father and felt that remaining in the mountains would limit his father's ability to respond publicly. Pazos thus left the Sierra Maestra in early January, only to be arrested weeks later. Celia Sánchez to Haydée Santamaría, January 22, 1957, Sánchez Collection, OAH.

33. Fidel Castro to the Members of the Cuban Liberation Junta, December 14, 1957, Fidel Castro Ruz Collection, OAH; Carlos Franqui Collection, 1952–1981, "Documents of the Cuban Revolution"; Bonachea and Valdés, *Revolutionary Struggle*, pp. 351–363. *Diario Las Americas* in Miami published the letter in January 1958 and *Bohemia* in Havana published it in February 1958 during a period free of press censorship.

34. Raúl Castro to Fidel Castro, November 20, 1957, Carlos Franqui Collection, 1952–1981, "Documents of the Cuban Revolution"; Fidel Castro to the Cuban Liberation Junta, in Bonachea and Valdés, *Revolutionary Struggle*, p. 354.

35. Ibid., p. 357. See also Armando Hart to Haydée Santamaría, December 17, 1957, Hart Collection, OAH.

36. Fidel Castro to the Cuban Liberation Junta, in Bonachea and Valdés, *Revolutionary Struggle*, p. 358.

37. Ibid., p. 363.

38. Luis Buch, interview by author, Havana, Cuba, November 5, 1995.

39. Luis Buch to National Directorate, December 29, 1957, Buch Collection, OAH.

40. Luis Buch to National Directorate, December 28, 1957, Buch Collection, OAH.

41. Haydée Santamaría to René Ramos Latour, December 28, 1957, Santamaría Collection, OAH; Luis Buch to National Directorate, December 28, 1957, Buch Collection, OAH.

42. Faure Chomón Mediavilla, interview by author, Havana, Cuba, July 10, 1997; Faure Chomón to Fidel Castro, *Diario Las Americas,* January 9, 1957, p. 4.

43. U.S. Department of Justice, Press Release and Summary of Grand Jury Charges, February 13, 1958, RG 59, 737.00/2–458, DSR, NA; "Prío Indictment," U.S. Department of State, "Secret" Memorandum re. Case of Prío et al., February 4, 1958, RG 59, box 2, 737.00/2–458, DSR, NA. In Miami, police marched the handcuffed former president down the street. Prío's arrest was uniformly condemned by liberal, independent, and conservative editors in Cuba and opposition circles in Miami. Radio pundit and presidential aspirant José Pardo Llada chastised the United States that the "man who slept in Churchill's bed at the White House tonight sleeps in a cell in Miami." U.S. Department of State, Incoming Telegram, Earl E. T. Smith to Secretary of State, February 19, 1958, RG 59, box 2, 737.00/2–1758, DSR, NA.

44. U.S. Department of State, "Official-Informal-Confidential" Letter, Terrence Leonardy to John L. Topping, April 11, 1958, RG 59, box 5, 737.00/4–1158, DSR, NA; Thomas, *Cuba,* p. 986.

45. "Arms Stored Here for Cuba Invasion: Federal Agents Watching Plotters," *Houston Post,* February 17, 1958, p. 1; "Paper Says Cuban Rebels Map Invasion from Houston," *The Times of Havana,* February 17, 1958, p. 16; "Charges Filed on Three in Cuban Group: Firearms Cache Believed Found," *Houston Post,* February 18, 1958, p. 1; "Cuban Arms Might Be U.S. Surplus," *Houston Post,* February 21, 1958, p. 1. A *Houston Post* journalist rifled through the garbage behind the raided Cuban safe house and found a cardboard box that seemed to have contained twenty armor-piercing cartridges from a St. Louis Ordnance plant built during World War II.

46. Léster Rodríguez, interview by author, Havana, Cuba, November 14, 1995; Raúl Castro to Fidel Castro, November 20, 1957, Carlos Franqui Collection, 1951–1981, "Documents of the Cuban Revolution." After 1959, Rodríguez served as military captain for the province of Guantánamo. In the 1970s and 1980s he served as ambassador in the Middle East and Southeast Asia, including Syria and Vietnam. Neither historians nor witnesses to the insurrection acknowledge his eventual success in finally bringing weapons to the island. The most recent example of this omission appears, ironically, in Luis Buch, *Más Allá de los Códigos* (Havana: Editorial de Ciencias Sociales, 1995). Rodríguez died of prostate cancer in 1998. Buch died of old age in 2001.

47. The exception is the first-hand account by Mario Llerena (see his *The Unsuspected Revolution,* p. 140). Until now, his account and official Cuban documents published by Carlos Franqui in 1976 and 1980 have informed all subsequent treatments of this incident, including Thomas, *Cuba;* Ramón

Bonachea and Marta San Martín, *The Cuban Insurrection, 1952–1959* (New Brunswick, N.J.: Transaction, 1974); Robert E. Quirk, *Fidel Castro* (New York: Norton, 1993); Thomas G. Paterson, *Contesting Castro: The United States and the Triumph of the Cuban Revolution* (New York: Oxford University Press, 1994); and Jon Lee Anderson, *Che Guevara: A Revolutionary Life* (New York: Grove Press, 1997).

48. Armando Hart to Haydée Santamaría, December 17, 1957, Hart Collection, OAH.

49. Haydée Santamaría to René Ramos Latour, December 24, 1957, Santamaría Collection, OAH. Santamaría quotes Hart's letter, written from the Sierra Maestra, to Latour. "Pablo" is Alonso "Bebo" Hidalgo, an Oriente activist. I have translated "total war" from the Spanish *guerra general*. The parentheses are Santamaría's.

50. Haydée Santamaría to René Ramos Latour, December 28, 1957, Santamaría Collection, OAH.

51. Ibid.

8. TOTAL WAR?

1. U.S. Department of State, Incoming Telegram, Ambassador Earl E. T. Smith to Secretary of State, January 25, 1958, RG 59, 737.001/1–2558, DSR, NA.

2. "Manifesto to the Nation: The Road That Cuba Needs," January 28, 1958, Institute of Cuban History, Havana, Cuba, RG 1, 1/2.4/11.4.1.1/7–24.

3. René Ramos Latour to Alonso "Bebo" Hidalgo, February 1, 1958, Latour Collection, OAH.

4. Marcelo Fernández, Motion no. 1, Current Structure of the National Directorate, January 26, 1958, Fernández Collection, OAH.

5. René Ramos Latour to Alonso 'Bebo' Hidalgo, February 1, 1958, Latour Collection, OAH.

6. Marcelo Fernández, Motion no. 3, Organization of the National Student Front (FEN), January 26, 1958, Fernández Collection, OAH; Ricardo Alarcón de Quesada, interview by author, Havana, Cuba, July 3, 1997.

7. Marcelo Fernández, Motion no. 3, Organization of the National Student Front, January 26, 1958, Fernández Collection, OAH. For Castro's December 14, 1957 letter to the signatories of the Pact of Miami, see Rolando E. Bonachea and Nelson P. Valdés, eds., *Revolutionary Struggle, 1947–1958*, vol. 1 of *The Selected Works of Fidel Castro* (Cambridge, Mass.: MIT Press, 1972), pp. 351–363.

8. FEN to National Directorate, February 15, 1958, OAH; Herbert Matthews Papers, Cuban Reports, 1952–1960, March 1958, box 2, Columbia University Library Rare Book and Manuscript Library; Ricardo Alarcón de Quesada, interview by author, Havana, Cuba, July 3, 1997. For a first-hand account of student politics in Cuba, see Jaime Suchliki, *University Students and Revolution in Cuba, 1920–1968* (Coral Gables, Fl.: University of Miami Press, 1969).

9. Marcelo Fernández, Motion no. 6, Work Plan for the Month of February, January 26, 1958, Fernández Collection, OAH.

10. Gladys Marel García-Pérez, *Insurrection and Revolution: Armed Struggle in Cuba, 1952–1959* (Boulder, Colo.: Lynne Rienner, 1998), pp. 52–95.

11. Marcelo Fernández, Motion no. 1, Current Structuring of the National Directorate, January 26, 1958, Fernández Collection, OAH.

12. Ibid.

13. Marcelo Fernández, Motion no. 6, Drawing Up a Work Plan for the Month of February, January 26, 1958, Fernández Collection, OAH.

14. René Ramos Latour to Fidel Castro, January 13, 1958, Latour Collection, OAH.

15. Fidel Castro to René Ramos Latour, February 1, 1958, Fidel Castro Ruz Collection, OAH.

16. Fidel Castro to Santiago Leaders, January 13, 1958, in Carlos Franqui, *Diario de la Revolución Cubana* (Paris: R. Torres, 1976), p. 378; Celia Sánchez to René Ramos Latour, February 1, 1958, Sánchez Collection, OAH.

17. René Ramos Latour to Fidel Castro, February 4, 1958, Latour Collection, OAH.

18. Ibid.

19. Ibid.

20. Nydia Sarábia, "René Ramos Latour, Comandante en la Ciudad y en La Sierra," *Bohemia* 55, no. 31 (August 2, 1963): 25–26, 43–44. Latour organized the militia as follows: five men under orders of one corporal made up one squad of six men; three squads under orders of one sergeant composed one platoon of nineteen men; and three platoons under the orders of one lieutenant made up one company of fifty-eight men. In Santiago, Latour created four squads beginning in January of 1958.

21. René Ramos Latour to Fidel Castro Ruz, February 4, 1958, Latour Collection, OAH. Emphasis in original.

22. Ibid.

23. Ibid., p. 7.

24. Ibid.; René Ramos Latour to Pedro Miret and Gustavo Arcos, January 7, 1958, Latour Collection, OAH.

25. René Ramos Latour to Alonso "Bebo" Hidalgo, February 18, 1958, Latour Collection, OAH; René Ramos Latour to Alonso "Bebo" Hidalgo, March 18, 1958, Latour Collection, OAH; José Llanusa to National Directorate, "Report on Trip to Haiti," April 16, 1958, Llanusa Collection, OAH; Mario Villamía to Fidel Castro, May 11, 1958, Exile Collection, OAH.

26. Gustavo Arcos to Faustino Pérez, January 13, 1958, Arcos / Miret Collection, OAH; Fidel Castro to René Ramos Latour, February 1, 1958, Fidel Castro Ruz Collection, OAH.

27. Bebo Hidalgo to René Ramos Latour and National Directorate, January 26, 1958, Exile Collection, OAH; Taras Domitro to René Ramos Latour, January 24, 1958, Domitro Collection, OAH.

28. René Ramos Latour to Alonso "Bebo" Hidalgo, February 1, 1958, Latour Collection, OAH; Bebo Hidalgo to René Ramos Latour and National Directorate, January 26, 1958, Exile Collection, OAH.

29. Taras Domitro to René Ramos Latour, February 11, 1958, Domitro Collec-

tion, OAH. None of the scholarly or popular accounts of this period refer to Domitro's role in the insurrection.

30. Taras Domitro to René Ramos Latour, January 24, 1958, Domitro Collection, OAH.

31. Ibid.

32. Ibid.

33. I have seen only two passing references to the movement's attempt to open a guerrilla front in Pinar del Río: Faustino Pérez in "La Huelga de Abril, un reves que se convirtió en victoria," Dolores Nieves and Alina Feijóo, *Semillas de Fuego*, vol. 1: *Compilación Sobre la Lucha Clandestina en la Capital* (Havana: Editorial de Ciencias Sociales, 1989), pp. 64–68; and Cesar, Coordinator, and Others to Fidel Castro and National Directorate, May 1958, Pinar del Río Collection, OAH.

34. Pedro Miret to Faustino Pérez, January 13, 1958, Arcos / Miret Collection, OAH.

35. Taras Domitro to René Ramos Latour, January–April 1958, Domitro Collection, OAH.

36. Taras Domitro to René Ramos Latour, February 16, 1958, Domitro Collection, OAH.

37. Ibid.; U.S. Department of State Incoming Telegram, Earl E. T. Smith to Secretary of State, February 21, 1958, RG 59, box 2, 737.00/2–1958, DSR, NA.

38. René Ramos Latour to Alonso "Bebo" Hidalgo, February 18, 1958, Latour Collection, OAH.

39. René Ramos Latour to Pedro Miret, February 23, 1958, Latour Collection, OAH.

9. THE GOLDEN AGE OF THE *LLANO*

1. Mirta Rodríguez Calderón, "La Habana Insurreccional," *Granma*, February 3, 1988, p. 3; Dolores Nieves and Alina Feijóo, eds., *Semillas de Fuego*, vol. 1: *Compilación Sobre la Lucha Clandestina en la Capital* (Havana: Editorial de Ciencias Sociales, 1989), p. 35.

2. Arnold Rodríguez, "Como y Por Que Secuestramos a Fangio," *Juventud Rebelde*, February 21, 1988, pp. 8–9; Arnold Rodríguez, "Como y Por Que Secuestramos a Fangio," *Juventud Rebelde*, pt. 2 February 28, 1988, pp. 10–11; Nieves and Feijóo, *Semillas de Fuego*, vol. 1, pp. 40–54; *Houston Post*, February 24, 1958, p. 1; and "En Cuba," *Bohemia* 50, no. 9 (March 2, 1958): 94–95. Fangio returned to Cuba in 1981 as an executive for Mercedes Benz, and met Fidel Castro for the first time. For a biography of Lucero, see Renán Ricardo Rodríguez, *El Héroe del Silencio* (Havana: Editora Política, 1986).

3. U.S. Department of State, Joint Weeka Report no. 9, February 26, 1958, RG 59, box 8, 737.00/2–2658, DSR, NA.

4. Faustino Pérez to Armando Hart, October 9, 1958, Pérez Collection, OAH; U.S. Department of State, Joint Weeka Report no. 9, March 5, 1958, RG 59, 737.00 (W)/3–558, DSR, NA.

5. Mirta Rodríguez Calderon, "Golpes al Espínazo de la Tiranía," *Granma*, March 8, 1988, p. 3; in Nieves and Feijóo, *Semillas de Fuego*, vol. 1, pp. 55–58; U.S. Department of State, Joint Weeka Report no. 9, March 5, 1958, RG 59, 737.00 (W)/3–558, DSR, NA.

6. "Los Ablandará la Huelga de Hambre?" *Bohemia* 50, no. 8 (February 23, 1958): 69.

7. Ernesto Che Guevara, "Evolution of Rebel Army Columns and Fronts, December 1956 to late 1958," in Mary-Alice Waters, ed., *Episodes of the Cuban Revolution, 1956–1958* (New York: Pathfinder Press, 1996), pp. 464–465.

8. Raúl Castro to Fidel Castro, April 17, 1958, Raúl Castro Ruz Collection, OAH. For an account of the early days of Raúl Castro's column in the Sierra Cristal, see "Diario de Campaña," in Edmundo Desnoes, ed., *La Sierra y El Llano* (Havana: Casa de las Americas, 1961).

9. Celia Sánchez to René Ramos Latour, March 1, 1958, Sánchez Collection, OAH.

10. U.S. Department of State, Joint Weeka Report no. 10, March 11, 1958, RG 59, 737.00(W)/3–1158, DSR, NA; "Estudiantes: Huelga Indefinida," *Bohemia* 50, no. 11, (March 16, 1958) supplement, p. 6; Mirta Rodríguez Calderón, "1958: Arde la Huelga en las Aulas," *Granma*, March 30, 1988, p. 3; *Semillas de Fuego*, vol. 1, p. 59.

11. For a detailed description of militant labor activism in the province of Matanzas during the insurgency, see Gladys Marel García-Pérez, *Insurrection and Revolution: Armed Struggle in Cuba, 1952–1959* (Boulder, Colo.: Lynne Rienner, 1998).

12. Enrique Oltuski, interview by author, Marina Hemingway, Havana, Cuba, July 5, 1997.

13. "Rebels Extend Operations to Las Villas Province," *The Times of Havana*, March 10, 1958, p. 2. For an account of the opening of Chomón's Segundo Frente Del Escambray by a DRE member, see Enrique Rodríguez Loeches, *Bajando Del Escambray* (Havana: Editorial Letras Cubanas, 1962).

14. Enrique Oltuski to Marcelo Fernández, February 26, 1958, Oltuski Collection, OAH.

15. U.S. Department of State, Joint Weeka Report no. 9, February 26, 1958, RG 59, box 8, 737.00(W)2–2658, DSR, NA.

16. "Contra Esto y Aquello," *Bohemia* 50, no. 9 (March 2, 1958): 65; "Mujal: El Gran Puntal," *Bohemia* 50, no. 11 (March 16, 1958): 74.

17. Foreign Service Dispatch, American Embassy, Havana to Department of State, re. Important Meeting of the CTC Executive Committee, February 27, 1958, RG 59, 857.062/2–2758, DSR, NA.

18. U.S. Department of State, Joint Weeka Report, no. 11, March 18, 1958, RG 59, 737.00(W)3–1858, DSR, NA.

19. Foreign Service of the United States of America, "Outgoing Telegram," no. 646, Earl E. T. Smith to Secretary of State, April 3, 1958. RG 59, 837.062/4–358, DSR, NA.

20. "De la CTC al Pueblo de Cuba," *Diario de la Marina*, March 30, 1958, p. 3; U.S. Department of State Foreign Service Dispatch, "Cuban Confederation of

Workers Publishes Statement Rejecting General Political Strike; Action Constitutes Support for Government," April 2, 1958, RG 59, 837.062/4–258, DSR, NA.

21. Homar Bigart, "Rebel Chief Offers Batista Plan to End Cuban Revolt," *New York Times,* February 26, 1958, p. 1. In late January, Bigart and Oriente Liberal party congressman Manuel "Nene" Jesús de Léon Ramírez visited Fidel in the Sierra Maestra.

22. "Exhortación del Episcopado," *Bohemia* 50, no. 9 (March 2, 1958): 71; "Exhortación del Episcopado: En Favor de la Paz," February 25, 1958, in *La Voz de la Iglesia en Cuba: 100 Documentos Episcopales* (Mexico City: Obra Nacional de la Buena Prensa, 1995), pp. 40–41; Carlos Franqui, *Diario de la Revolución Cubana* (Paris: R. Torres, 1976), p. 386; "Declarations of the PSP: On the Catholic Episcopate's Proposals Regarding the Political Crisis," March 3, 1958, Institute of Cuban History, Havana, Cuba, RG 1/2.4/11–4.A-1. For a description of how the United States repeatedly missed opportunities to support the moderate opposition in a peaceful solution to the Cuban crisis, see the first-hand account by a former American diplomat posted to the Havana embassy, Wayne S. Smith, *The Closest of Enemies: A Personal and Diplomatic History of the Castro Years* (New York: W. W. Norton, 1987), pp. 20–27.

23. U.S. Department of State Division of Research for American Republics, Special Paper no. A-8–3, "Attitudes of Politically Influential Groups in Cuba toward the June One Elections," March 6, 1958, RG 59, 737.00/3–658, DSR, NA.

24. "Exhortación del Episcopado," *Bohemia* 50, no. 9 (March 2, 1958): 71; Franqui, *Diario,* p. 386. See also "Declarations of the PSP: On the Catholic Episcopate's Proposals Regarding the Political Crisis," March 3, 1958, Institute of Cuban History; Smith, *Closest of Enemies,* pp. 20–27.

25. Marcelo Fernández to Provincial Coordinators, National Section Coordinators, Organization Circular CO-2, March 18, 1958, Fernández Collection, OAH.

26. René Ramos Latour to Alonso 'Bebo' Hidalgo, March 15, 1958, Latour Collection, OAH.

27. Celia Sánchez, diary entry, March 4, 1958, Sánchez Collection, OAH. "Dr. Morán" refers to Lucas Morán Arce, one of the attorneys in Santiago who defended the surviving members of the *Granma* expedition in their May 1957 trial. Morán Arce also authored *La Revolución Cubana (1953–1959): Una Versión Rebelde* (Ponce, P.R.: Universidad Católica, 1980).

28. Marcelo Fernández to Provincial Coordinators, National and Section Chiefs, Organization Circular CO-2, March 18, 1958, Fernández Collection, OAH. Marcelo Fernández to Carlos Franqui and Alonso "Bebo" Hidalgo, March 30, 1958, Fernández Collection, OAH.

29. Secret Memorandum for Director of Central Intelligence, "Report on [excised portion]'s Visit to the Fidel Castro Headquarters in the Sierra Maestra, 12–26 March 1958," April 11, 1958, Central Intelligence Agency Openness Program October 1998 CD-rom release, National Security Archive, Washington, D.C.

30. René Ramos Latour to Alonso "Bebo" Hidalgo, March 15, 1958.

31. Faustino Pérez to Armando Hart, October 3, 1958, Pérez Collection, OAH.

Three individuals who attended this crucial meeting—Marcelo Fernández, Faustino Pérez, and René Ramos Latour—confirmed separately that the National Directorate had used the emergency meeting prompted by Fidel's *New York Times* statements in order to convince Castro that the opportunity was ripe for urban insurrection and general strike. This evidence overturns the standard history, which to date has uniformly assumed that Fidel forced the urban underground to undertake the strike in order to expose the *llano's* weakness and thus exert full control over the direction and radicalization of the anti-Batista war effort. For example, Ramón Bonachea and Marta San Martín provide an overview of the genesis, unfolding, and aftermath of the strike in *The Cuban Insurrection, 1952–1959* (New Brunswick, N. J.: Transaction, 1974), pp. 200–215. They offer two pieces of evidence to support their argument that at this meeting Fidel, or the *sierra*, forced the urban underground to call the strike. First, they write that during the meeting "it was Fidel Castro, not the *llano* . . . who pressed for the idea of the strike," as evidenced in a document drafted by Marcelo Fernández, dated March 18, 1958, entitled "Circular de Organización CO-2." This document is excerpted in the manuscript of Mario Llerena's *The Unsuspected Revolution: The Birth and Rise of Castroism* (Ithaca, N.Y.: Cornell University Press, 1978). I have in my possession the entire document, a six-page account of the March meeting and the movement's work plan for that month, which includes guidelines for setting up strike committees in preparation for the general strike. The document does not state that Fidel insisted on the strike over the *llano's* objections (Marcelo Fernández, Organization Circular CO-2, March 18, 1958, Fernández Collection, OAH). The second piece of evidence the authors cite to demonstrate that the *llano* actually opposed the strike comes from an interview by Cuban journalist Nydia Sarabia with Captain Carlos Chaín, who stated, "When the April strike was organized in the month of May [sic], Daniel [Latour] made observations in general regarding the weaknesses of the Movement across the island, with the exception of Oriente, and he recommended that wherever conditions existed, the Movement in the cities should prepare to move into guerrilla struggle." It may be that Latour confided to Chaín his concerns about the lack of preparation in the cities, but there is no evidence of this in his papers. On the contrary, the new documentation amply demonstrates that before the strike he was one of the staunchest advocates of an urban strategy, precisely because of his faith in the militia's ability to sustain it. See Nydia Sarabia, "René Ramos Latour: Comandante en la Ciudad y en la Sierra," *Bohemia* 55, no. 31 (August 2, 1963): 26–27.

32. Rolando E. Bonachea and Nelson P. Valdés, eds., *Revolutionary Struggle, 1947–1958*, vol. 1 of *The Selected Works of Fidel Castro* (Cambridge, Mass.: MIT Press, 1972), pp. 373–378.

33. U.S. Department of State, Joint Weeka Report no. 11, March 18, 1958, RG 59, 737.00(W)/3–1858, DSR, NA.

34. U.S. Department of State, Joint Weeka Report no. 10, March 11, 1958, RG 59, 737.00(W)3–1158, DSR, NA; Fidel Castro to José Pardo Llada, February 28, 1958, in Franqui, *Diario*, p. 387; Fidel Castro to News Director, CMKC Radio, Santiago de Cuba, March 9, 1958, in Franqui, *Diario*, p. 390.

35. Marcelo Fernández to Fidel Castro, March 20, 1958, Fernández Collection, OAH.
36. U.S. Department of State, Joint Weeka Report no. 10, March 11, 1958, RG 59, 737.00 (W)/3-1158, and no. 11, March 18, 1958, RG 59, 737.00 (W)3-1858, DSR, NA; "Justicia: Denuncias y Acusaciones," *Bohemia* 50, no. 11, supp. (March 16, 1958): 9–10.
37. "Why Our Party Supports the Sierra Maestra," *Carta Semanal,* March 12, 1958, Institute of Cuban History, Havana, Cuba, RG1, 1/1.7/2.28.12/249–256; "Manifesto of the PSP: Let Us Overthrow the Tyranny Directly through Mass Action and General Strike," March 13, 1958, Institute of Cuban History, Havana, Cuba, RG 1, 1/2.4/11.4.A.1/35–44.
38. On suspension of weapons sales see Paterson, *Contesting Castro,* chap. 11, pp. 125–149 and "Cuba," *Foreign Relations of the United States, 1958–1960,* vol. 6 (Washington, D.C.: Government Printing Office, 1991), pp. 1–117.
39. Cuban Reports, 1952–1960, March 1958, Herbert Matthews Papers, box 2, Columbia University Rare Book and Manuscript Library.
40. Franqui, *Diario,* p. 402.
41. U.S. Department of State, Joint Weeka Report no. 12, March 25, 1958, RG 59, 737.00(W)/3–2558, DSR, NA.
42. Department of State, Joint Weeka Report no. 11, March 18, 1958, RG 59, 737.00 (W)/3-1858, DSR, NA; *Carta Semanal,* March 12, 1958, Institute of Cuban History, Havana, Cuba; U.S. Department of State, Joint Weeka Report, no. 12, March 25, 1958, RG 59, 737.00(W)/3–2558, DSR, NA. The Department of State's Joint Weeka reports for this period provide a thorough account of the underground's sabotage campaign, including, for example, explosions at power plants in Havana, at sugar refineries in Oriente and Camagüey, and at an American-owned vegetable packing warehouse in Las Villas. See U.S. Department of State, Joint Weeka Report no. 9, March 5, 1958, RG 59, 737.00(W)/3–558, DSR, NA.
43. Marcelo Fernández to Provincial Coordinators, National Section Coordinators, Organization Circular CO-2, March 18, 1958, Fernández Collection, OAH.
44. Ibid. The document refers to the roving bands of independent guerrillas in and around Baire, Bayamo, Alto Songo, Guantánamo, Maratí, Mayarí, Sagua la Grande, and Baracoa, which the 26th of July had just begun to absorb, and which Raúl Castro and Juan Almeida would eventually incorporate entirely into their new columns in northern and eastern Oriente.
45. Ibid.

10. THE ARMS RACE

1. René Ramos Latour to Juan Almeida Bosque, March 27, 1958, Latour Collection, OAH.
2. René Ramos Latour to Provincial and Municipal Action Chiefs, Chiefs of Companies, Platoons and Squadrons, March 1958, Latour Collection, OAH.
3. Marcelo Fernández, Report to the Executive of the National Directorate, Current State of the Movement, May 31, 1958, Fernández Collection, OAH.

4. René Ramos Latour to Alonso "Bebo" Hidalgo, March 15, 1958, Latour Collection, OAH.

5. René Ramos Latour to Juan Almeida Bosque, March 18, 1958, Latour Collection, OAH.

6. René Ramos Latour to Alonso "Bebo" Hidalgo, March 18, 1958, Latour Collection, OAH; René Ramos Latour to Juan Almeida Bosque, March 18, 1958, Latour Collection, OAH.

7. René Ramos Latour to Alonso "Bebo" Hidalgo, March 18, 1958, Latour Collection, OAH.

8. Celia Sánchez to Faustino Pérez, April 2, 1958, Sánchez Collection, OAH; Luis Buch, *Más Allá de los Códigos* (Havana: Editorial de las Ciencias Políticas, 1995). The precise amount of guns and ammunition that arrived from Costa Rica is something of a mystery. One account based on an interview with Figueres suggests that an enormous quantity reached the rebels. Other accounts suggest a far more modest amount. Indeed, in a 1968 interview, President José Figueres stated that the shipment included 250 machine guns, 250 automatic rifles, one million rounds of ammunition, 225 .60 mm mortars, bazookas, tripod machine guns, dynamite, and hand grenades—"enough weapons," according to his interviewers, "to arm nearly the entire M-26-7 urban underground in Havana." See Ramón Bonachea and Marta San Martín, *The Cuban Insurrection, 1952–1959* (New Brunswick, N.J.: Transaction, 1974), p. 205. But the only Cuban documents and interviews that mention this shipment report a more modest contribution: 50,000 30.06 caliber shells, 30,000 9 millimeter shells, 5,000 50 caliber shells, 10,000 45 caliber shells, two 50 caliber machine guns, forty-six 60 millimeter harquebuses and 50 Mauser rifles with 5,000 bullets. Twelve passengers accompanied the shipment, including Miret, Matos, and Díaz Lanz. See Buch, *Más Allá de los Códigos*, pp. 142–146. A note from Celia Sánchez to Faustino Pérez just after the delivery reported that Miret and Matos had come with "fifty-something weapons and some 100,000 shots." See Celia Sánchez to Faustino Pérez, April 2, 1958, Sánchez Collection, OAH.

9. Taras Domitro to René Ramos Latour, March 27, 1958, Domitro Collection, OAH.

10. Faustino Pérez to Marcelo Fernández [Zoilo] and Other Comrades, March 25, 1958, Pérez Collection, OAH; Marcelo Fernández to Fidel Castro, March 30, 1958, Fernández Collection, OAH; Marcelo Fernández to Che Guevara, March 30, 1958, Fernández Collection, OAH; René Ramos Latour to Fidel Castro, April 1, 1958, Latour Collection, OAH; Faustino Pérez to Armando Hart, October 3, 1958, Pérez Collection, OAH; Gerardo Pérez Puelles, interview by author, Havana, Cuba, November 12, 1995.

11. Herbert Matthews Papers, "Cuban Reports, 1952–1960," box 2, Columbia University Rare Book and Manuscript Library. Matthews regularly briefed the State Department on his Cuban visits. See Memorandum of a Telephone Conversation between the Deputy Director of the Office of Middle American Affairs, C. Allan Stewart, in Washington and Herbert Matthews of the *New York Times* in New York, April 3, 1958, in "Cuba," *Foreign Relations of the United*

States, 1958–1960, vol. 6 (Washington, D.C.: Government Printing Office, 1991), pp. 78–80.

12. Faustino Pérez to Marcelo Fernández [Zoilo] and Other Comrades, March 25, 1958, Pérez Collection, OAH. *Hierros* is slang for arms.

13. Taras Domitro to René Ramos Latour, March 29, 1958, April 1, 1958, Domitro Collection, OAH; Herbert Matthews, March 1958 notes, "Cuban Reports, 1952–1960," box 2, Columbia University Rare Book and Manuscript Library.

14. René Ramos Latour to Juan Almeida Bosque, April 4, 1958, Latour Collection, OAH.

15. René Ramos Latour to Fidel Castro, April 1, 1958, Latour Collection, OAH.

16. Alonso "Bebo" Hidalgo to René Ramos Latour, April 3, 1958, Exile Collection, OAH.

17. Taras Domitro to Fidel Castro, April 5, 1958, Domitro Collection, OAH.

18. In fact, none of the weapons deliveries he attempted on the eve of the general strike was successful. In July 1958, as Raúl Castro held hostage some forty-two Canadian and American employees from the Moa nickel mine in Oriente, Fiorini went to the Sierra Maestra with a proposal for Fidel Castro regarding how to leverage the hostages for weapons. Introducing the matter to Fidel, Marcelo Fernández wrote that Fiorini "has a plan he wants to outline for you. It consists of the following: there is a Florida millionaire by the name of Sam Kay who is a political friend of Nixon. Through a lawyer, Sanford Freed, also from Florida, [Kay] has offered us a sizable amount of money if we release the detained Americans; then, when the 1960 presidential campaign comes, Nixon would be able to make it known that he had 'resolved' the Americans' release. As you can see, this is something close to blackmail; nevertheless, Frank says that instead of money we might propose weapons, and that these men could obtain them. You decide." Marcelo Fernández to Fidel Castro, July 7, 1958, Fernández Collection, OAH. The implications of this vignette are tantalizing. After the revolutionary triumph, Fiorini joined a spate of counterrevolutionary ventures, beginning as early as October 1959 when, according to Howard Hunt, he copiloted flights dropping anti-Castro leaflets over Havana with Pedro Luis Díaz Lanz, his old flying buddy and the recently defected chief of the Cuban air force. According to Warren Hinckle, throughout the 1960s Fiorini worked for the CIA in Operation Mongoose, under the name of Frank Sturgis. Bringing the picture full circle, Sturgis was one of the four burglars hired by the Nixon White House to break into the Democratic National Headquarters at the Watergate in 1972; see E. Howard Hunt, *Give Us This Day: The Inside Story of the CIA and the Bay of Pigs Invasion by One of Its Key Organizers* (New Rochelle, N.Y.: Arlington House, 1973), p. 98. For Sturgis's work with counterrevolutionary groups in Cuba and for his role in the Watergate break-in, see Warren Hinckle and William Turner, *Deadly Secrets: The CIA Mafia War against Castro and the Assassination of J. F. K.* (New York: Thunder's Mouth Press, 1992), pp. 50–55 and 341–364. Jon Lee Anderson quotes Che Guevara's unpublished diary, which notes that "a suspicious gringo with messages from people in Miami and some eccentric plans" arrived at Guevara's base, but that "Fidel received word that the gringo was either FBI or

hired to kill him." Pedro Alvarez Tabío, director of the Office of Historic Affairs, told Anderson that the visitor was probably Frank Fiorini, though there is a one-month discrepancy between Guevara's recording of the visit and Fernández's letter to Fidel explaining Fiorini's intentions. See Jon Lee Anderson, *Che Guevara: A Revolutionary Life* (New York: Grove Press, 1997), p. 326. In any case, the new material suggests that García (also known as Fiorini or Sturgis) might have been working indirectly for Richard Nixon since at least 1958.

19. Raúl Castro's diary entry suggests that he believed the weapons made it to the Sierra Maestra after a crash landing that burned the plane but spared the weapons, and that it was the plane from Costa Rica that the rebels burned after it landed with a damaged wing. Based on the diary entry, Bonachea and Valdés write that this shipment provides "further evidence of how the Sierra Maestra leadership demanded (and always obtained) what Castro, in an August 11, 1957, letter to 'Aly' (Celia Sánchez) characterized as 'The most fitting slogan of the day ought to be "All guns, All bullets and all Resources to the Sierra."'" Bonachea and Valdés, *Revolutionary Struggle*, n. 55, p. 389. The authors did not know that the Fiorini flight never made it to Cuba (Raúl Castro to Fidel Castro, April 17, 1958, Raúl Castro Ruz Collection, OAH.) Portions of this letter are reproduced in Edmundo Desnoes, ed., *La Sierra y El Llano* (Havana: Casa de las Americas, 1961), pp. 223–225. See also René Ramos Latour to Raúl Castro, April 7, 1958, Latour Collection, OAH.

20. Cuban navy patrols were so concentrated along the Pinar del Río coastline that once the *Corojo* left Mexico, Domitro alerted Fidel to expect Suarez to land in Oriente: "You should be on the alert for Suarez's arrival and have some militia ready to make contact with them because under these circumstances once they unload they'll have to convert themselves into guerrillas in order to salvage the equipment." Taras Domitro to Fidel Castro, April 6, 1958, Domitro Collection, OAH.

21. "Exposition by the Provincial Directorate of the 26 of July Movement of Pinar del Río to the National Directorate," May 29, 1958, Underground Collection, OAH.

22. Marcelo Fernández, Report to the Executive of the National Directorate, Current State of the Movement, May 31, 1958, Fernández Collection, OAH.

23. René Ramos Latour to Raúl Castro, April 7, 1958, Latour Collection, OAH.

24. Taras Domitro to René Ramos Latour, April 1, 1958, Domitro Collection, OAH; Marcelo Fernández, Report to the Executive of the National Directorate, Current State of the Movement, May 31, 1958, Fernández Collection, OAH.

25. Taras Domitro to René Ramos Latour, April 4, 1958 and April 5, 1958, Taras Domitro to Fidel Castro, April 6, 1958, and Taras Domitro to René Ramos Latour, April 10, 1958, all in Domitro Collection, OAH.

26. Marcelo Fernández to Fidel Castro, April 6, 1958, Fernández Collection, OAH.

27. Faustino Pérez to Fidel Castro, April 2, 1958, Pérez Collection, OAH.

11. POLITICS AND POPULAR INSURRECTION

1. See Hugh Thomas, *Cuba: The Pursuit of Freedom* (New York: Harper and Row, 1971), pp. 586–715, for the ABC strategy in the 1930s and for the best overview of armed and nonviolent antidictatorial activities in Cuba in the 1930s. Also see Jaime Suchlicki, *Cuba: From Columbus to Castro* (McLean, Va.: Brassey's [U.S.], Inc., 1990), pp. 99–125.

2. Thomas, *Cuba*, p. 871.

3. Gladys Marel García-Peréz, *Insurrection and Revolution: Armed Struggle in Cuba, 1952–1959* (Boulder, Colo.: Lynne Rienner, 1998).

4. Jorge I. Domínguez, *Cuba: Order and Revolution* (Cambridge, Mass.: The Belknap Press of Harvard University Press, 1979), p. 73.

5. Carmelo Mesa-Lago, *The Labor Force, Employment, Unemployment, and Underemployment in Cuba: 1899–1970* (Beverly Hills, Calif.: Sage Publications, 1972), pp. 26–28.

6. Domínguez, *Cuba*, pp. 122–123.

7. Marifeli Pérez-Stable, *The Cuban Revolution: Origins, Course, and Legacy* (New York: Oxford University Press, 1993), pp. 48–60.

8. Havana Propaganda Commission to the Directorate of the 26th of July Revolutionary Movement, May 1958, Marcelo Fernández Collection, OAH; Oral History, Octavio Louit Venzant Bejerano, undated, OAH.

9. U.S. Department of Labor, Bureau of Labor Statistics, *Foreign Labor Information Series: Labor in Cuba* (Washington, D.C.: Government Printing Office, May 1957), pp. 10–11.

10. James O'Connor, *The Origins of Socialism in Cuba* (Ithaca, N.Y.: Cornell University Press, 1970), pp. 179–181.

11. U.S. Department of Labor, Bureau of Labor Statistics, *Foreign Labor Information Series, Labor in Cuba*, pp. 3–6; U.S. Department of Commerce, *Investments in Cuba: Basic Information for United States Businessmen* (Washington, D.C.: Government Printing Office, 1956), p. 169. See Pérez-Stable, *The Cuban Revolution*, pp. 52–60, for a discussion of state-labor relations under Batista.

12. Thomas, *Cuba*, p. 1176.

13. "Cuba: The Socialist Model," in Carmelo Mesa-Lago, *Market, Socialist, and Mixed Economies: Comparative Policy and Performance, Chile, Cuba, and Costa Rica* (Baltimore: Johns Hopkins University Press, 2000), p. 172; Domínguez, *Cuba*, p. 121. The movement's chances of engaging unionized workers were further diminished because CTC strikers would not receive support benefits during any walkout.

14. Pérez-Stable, *The Cuban Revolution*, pp. 52–60; Efrén Córdova, *Castro and the Cuban Labor Movement: Statecraft and Strategy in a Revolutionary Period, 1959–1961* (Lanham, Md.: University Press of America, 1987), pp. 54–55; García-Peréz, *Insurrection and Revolution*.

15. Thomas, *Cuba*, p. 1456; "Secret" NSC Briefing, "Cuba," April 13, 1958, Central Intelligence Agency Openness Program, October 1998 CD-ROM release, The National Security Archive, Washington, D.C.

16. Jaime Suchlicki, *Cuba*, p. 121; Thomas, *Cuba*, p. 733.

17. Pérez-Stable, *The Cuban Revolution*, p. 55.

18. For a discussion of the CIA's efforts to strengthen the BRAC, see Lyman Kirkpatrick, *The Real CIA* (New York: Macmillan, 1968), pp. 156–183.

19. Thomas, *Cuba*, pp. 567–627, 687–708.

20. Oral History, Octavio Louit Venzant Bejerano, undated, OAH.

21. Rolando Bonachea and Nelson P. Valdés, eds., *Revolutionary Struggle, 1947–1958*, vol. 1 of *The Selected Works of Fidel Castro* (Cambridge, Mass.: MIT Press, 1972), p. 376.

22. "Our Opinion of Fidel Castro's Recent Manifesto," *Carta Semanal*, March 24, 1958, supplement, Institute of Cuban History, RG 1, 1/17/2:28.92/289–292. See also Lionel Martin, *The Early Fidel: Roots of Castro's Communism* (Secaucus, N.J.: Lyle Stuart, 1978), pp. 209–215; and Pérez-Stable, *Cuban Revolution*, pp. 43–55.

23. Jon Lee Anderson, *Che Guevara: A Revolutionary Life* (New York: Grove, 1997); and Jorge G. Castañeda, *Compañero: The Life and Death of Che Guevara* (New York: Alfred A. Knopf, 1997).

24. Che Guevara to Fidel Castro, March 1958, Ernesto Guevara Collection, OAH.

25. Thomas, *Cuba*, p. 981; Lionel Martin, *The Early Fidel: Roots of Castro's Communism* (Secaucus, N.J.: Lyle Stuart, Inc.), pp. 211–212.

26. Fidel Castro, "To Cuban Workers from the Sierra Maestra," March 26, 1958, Fidel Castro Ruz Collection, OAH; Fidel Castro to "Padre A," March 30, 1958, Fidel Castro Ruz Collection, OAH.

27. Fidel Castro to "Padre A," March 30, 1958, Fidel Castro Ruz Collection, OAH.

28. Vilma Espín to Celia Sánchez, April 1, 1958, Espín Collection, OAH.

29. Faustino Pérez to Fidel Castro, April 2, 1958, Pérez Collection, OAH.

30. Oral History, Faustino Pérez, 1988, OAH.

31. To Esteemed Friend Alejandro, April 7, 1958, Underground Collection, OAH.

32. Ibid. The signature on the letter is ineligible. See also Urgent Memorandum to Fidel Castro, Chief of the Rebel Forces, and the Entire National Directorate of the 26th of July Movement, April 6, 1958, Institute of Cuban History, Havana, Cuba, RG 1, 1/2.4/11.4.1/47–48.

33. Urgent Memorandum, April 6, 1958, Institute of Cuban History.

34. Ibid. Although one of its agents had penetrated Castro's inner circle in the mountains in March of 1958, the CIA remained unaware of the internal discussions (prompted in part by PSP contacts with Guevara and Castro) regarding how to deal with Cuban labor. In April 1958, the CIA noted, "We have not found much evidence of Communist influence in Castro's movement although there are some communists in his organization." After the two-week stay in the Sierra, the CIA agent "found no evidence of significant Communist penetration." "Secret" NSC Briefing, "Cuba," April 13, 1958.

35. National Committee, PSP, "The Current Situation and the Strike," April 7, 1958, Institute of Cuban History, Havana, Cuba RG 1, 1/2.4/11.4.A.1/49–53.

36. Che Guevara to Camilo Cienfuegos, April 3, 1958, Guevara Collection, OAH; Che Guevara to Camilo Cienfuegos, April 5, 1958, Guevara Collection, OAH;

Vilma Espín to Che Guevara, April 7, 1958, Espín Collection, OAH; Ernesto Guevara to Fidel Castro, April 7, 1958, Guevara Collection, OAH.

37. Che Guevara to Fidel Castro, April 8, 1958, Guevara Collection, OAH.
38. Faustino Pérez to Fidel Castro, April 2, 1958, Pérez Collection, OAH.
39. "Proclamation by the Directorio Revolucionario from the Sierra de Escambray," February 25, 1958, Herbert Matthews Papers, box 2, Columbia University Rare Book and Manuscript Library.
40. Thomas, *Cuba*, p. 979.
41. Faure Chomón Mediavilla, interview by author, Havana, Cuba, July 8, 1997; Oral History, Faustino Pérez, 1998, OAH.
42. Faustino Pérez to Marcelo Fernández [Zoilo] and Others, March 25, 1958, Pérez Collection, OAH; Oral History, Faustino Pérez, 1998, OAH.
43. Faustino Pérez to Fidel Castro, April 2, 1958, Pérez Collection, OAH; U.S. Department of State, Joint Weeka Report no. 13, April 2, 1958, RG 59, 737.00 (W)/4–258, DSR, NA.
44. "Plan for the Organization and Development of the Revolutionary General Strike," copy 8, undated, Fernández Collection, OAH.
45. Ibid.
46. Ibid.
47. René Ramos Latour to Fidel Castro, February 4, 1958, Latour Collection, OAH.
48. René Ramos Latour to Alonso "Bebo" Hidalgo, March 15, 1958, Latour Collection, OAH.
49. "Plan for the Organization and Development of the Revolutionary General Strike," copy 8, undated, Fernández Collection, OAH.
50. Ibid.
51. Ibid.
52. Ibid.
53. Oral History, Octavio Louit Venzant Bejerano, undated, OAH.
54. Oral History, Antonio ("Nico") Torres Cherdebeaux, undated, OAH.
55. Marcelo Fernández to Fidel Castro, March 20, 1958, Fernández Collection, OAH.

12. "BORDERING ON CHAOS"

1. Confidential Incoming Telegram, Department of State, Earl E. T. Smith to Secretary of State, April 9, 1958, RG 59, box 14, 837.0624/4–958, DSR, NA. Taras Domitro to René Ramos Latour, April 10, 1958, Domitro Collection, OAH; Faustino Pérez to Zamora and Others, April 13, 1958, Pérez Collection, OAH; Marcelo Fernández, "Report to the Executive of the National Directorate: Current State of the Movement," May 31, 1958, Fernández Collection, OAH.
2. "Sagua la Grande Escribió su Nombre en La Historia, El Nueve de Abril," *Bohemia* 51, no. 14 (April 5, 1959): 36; Enrique Oltuski to Marcelo Fernández, February 19, 1958, Oltuski Collection, OAH; Captain "Samuel" and Coordinator

"Martinez," Sagua la Grande to Enrique Oltuski, May 10, 1958, Underground Collection, OAH.

3. René Ramos Latour to All Militants of the 26th of July Movement's Action Cadre, undated, Latour Collection, OAH; Taras Domitro to René Ramos Latour, April 10, 1958, Domitro Collection, OAH; "Manifesto to the People of Cuba," April 17, 1958, Underground Collection, OAH.

4. Vilma Espín to René Ramos Latour, April 11, 1958, Espín Collection, OAH.

5. "Secret" NSC Briefing, "Cuba," April 13, 1958, Central Intelligence Agency Openness Program, October 1998 CD-ROM release, National Security Archive, Washington, D.C.; and Foreign Service Despatch, American Embassy, Havana to Department of State, Washington, "The General Strike Attempt of April 9," April 21, 1958, RG 84, 837.062/4–2158, DSR, NA.

6. Vilma Espín to René Ramos Latour, April 11, 1958, Espín Collection, OAH; Marcelo Fernández to René Ramos Latour, Vilma Espín, and "Cervantes," April 10, 1958, Fernández Collection, OAH.

7. Vilma Espín to René Ramos Latour, April 11, 1958, Espín Collection, OAH.

8. René Ramos Latour to Vilma Espín and Comrades of the National Directorate, April 10, 1958, Latour Collection, OAH; René Ramos Latour to Alonso "Bebo" Hidalgo, April 22, 1958, Latour Collection, OAH. Column number nine was named for José "Pepito" Tey, an urban commando who died in the November 1956 Santiago strike.

9. René Ramos Latour to Vilma Espín, April 13, 1958, Latour Collection, OAH.

10. Vilma Espín to René Ramos Latour, April 14, 1958, Espín Collection, OAH; Vilma Espín to Dear Comrade, April 15, 1958, Espín Collection, OAH; Carlos Franqui, *Cuba: El Libro de Los Doce* (Mexico City: Serie Popular Era, 1966), p. 163.

11. René Ramos Latour to Vilma Espín, April 15, 1958, Latour Collection, OAH.

12. Ibid.

13. Ibid.; Secret Memorandum, Roy Rubottom, Assistant Secretary of State for Inter-American Affairs to Secretary of State, "Arms Policy with Respect to Cuba," August 11, 1958, in "Cuba," *Foreign Relations of the United States, 1958–1960*, vol. 6 (Washington, D.C.: Government Printing Office, 1991), p. 192.

14. René Ramos Latour to Vilma Espín, April 16, 1958, Latour Collection, OAH; René Ramos Latour to All Provincial and Municipal Militia Chiefs, April 22, 1958, Latour Collection, OAH.

15. René Ramos Latour to Juan Almeida Bosque, April 16, 1958, Latour Collection, OAH.

16. René Ramos Latour to Alonso "Bebo" Hidalgo, April 22, 1958, Latour Collection, OAH.

17. Ibid.

18. Ibid.

19. See the five-part series by veteran journalist Marta Rojas in *Bohemia* 51, nos. 51–56 (March–May 1959).

20. Raúl Castro to Fidel Castro, April 20, 1958, Raúl Castro Ruz Collection, OAH.

21. Juan Almeida Bosque to Fidel Castro, April 21, 1958, Almeida Collection, OAH.

22. René Ramos Latour to Juan Almeida Bosque, April 15, 1958, Latour Collection, OAH.

23. Juan Almeida Bosque to Fidel Castro, April 21, 1958, Almeida Collection, OAH.

24. Ibid.

25. Raúl Castro to Fidel Castro, April 28, 1958, Raúl Castro Ruz Collection, OAH.

26. Faustino Pérez to Zamora and Other Comrades, April 13, 1958, Pérez Collection, OAH.

27. "Manifesto to the People of Cuba," April 17, 1958, Underground Collection, OAH.

28. Ibid.

29. Ibid.

30. Taras Domitro to René Ramos Latour, April 11, 1958, Domitro Collection, OAH.

31. Taras Domitro to René Ramos Latour, April 10, 1958, Domitro Collection, OAH.

32. Taras Domitro to René Ramos Latour, April 13, 1958, Domitro Collection, OAH; Taras Domitro to Vilma Espín, April 18, 1958, Domitro Collection, OAH.

33. Taras Domitro to René Ramos Latour, April 13, 1958, Domitro Collection, OAH; Taras Domitro to Vilma Espín, April 18, 1958, Domitros Collection, OAH.

34. Taras Domitro to René Ramos Latour, April 28, 1958, Domitro Collection, OAH.

35. Ibid.; Marcelo Fernández, "Report to the Executive of the National Directorate: Current State of the Movement," May 31, 1958, Fernández Collection, OAH.

36. Marcelo Fernández, "Report to the Executive of the National Directorate: Current State of the Movement," May 31, 1958, Fernández Collection, OAH.

37. Taras Domitro to René Ramos Latour, April 29, 1958, Domitro Collection, OAH.

38. Marcelo Fernández to Provincial Coordinators and National Section Chiefs, Organization Circular CO-3, Santiago de Cuba, April 21, 1958, Fernández Collection, OAH.

39. René Ramos Latour to All Provincial and Municipal Militia Chiefs, April 22, 1958, Latour Collection, OAH; ibid.

40. Marcelo Fernández to Provincial Coordinators and National Section Chiefs, Organization Circular CO-3, Santiago de Cuba, April 21, 1958.

41. Ibid.; Havana Propaganda Commission to the Leadership of the 26th of July Revolutionary Movement, undated, Fernández Collection, OAH.

42. Enrique Oltuski to National Directorate, April 30, 1958, Oltuski Collection, OAH.

43. Ibid.

44. Ibid.
45. Ibid.
46. Ibid.

13. PICKING UP THE PIECES

1. Fidel Castro to Mario Llerena and Raúl Chibás, April 25, 1958, Fidel Castro Ruz Collection, OAH; Carlos Franqui, *Diario de la Revolución Cubana* (Paris: R. Torres, 1976), p. 428.
2. Fidel Castro to Alonso "Bebo" Hidalgo, April 25, 1958, Fidel Castro to Ricardo Lorie, April 25, 1958, Fidel Castro to Mario Llerena and Raúl Chibás, April 25, 1958, and Fidel Castro to Celia Sánchez, April 16, 1958, all in Fidel Castro Ruz Collection, OAH. Portions of these documents are contained in Franqui, *Diario.* See also Emery J. Adams, Office of Security to William Wieland, Department of State, Office of Inter-American Affairs, October 22, 1958, RG 59, 737.00/10–2258, DSR, NA.
3. Raúl Castro to Fidel Castro, April 28, 1958, Raúl Castro Ruz Collection, OAH.
4. Raúl Castro to Comrades, May 2, 1958, Raúl Castro Ruz Collection, OAH.
5. Raúl Castro to Fidel Castro, April 28, 1958, Raúl Castro Ruz Collection, OAH.
6. Che Guevara, "A Decisive Meeting," *Verde Olivo,* November 22, 1964; also in Guevara, *Episodes of the Cuban Revolutionary War, 1956–1958,* ed. Mary-Alice Waters (New York: Pathfinder Press, 1996), p. 318; Luis Buch, *Más Allá de los Códigos* (Havana: Editorial de Ciencias Sociales), pp. 142–151.
7. Guevara, *Episodes,* p. 316.
8. Ibid., pp. 317–318.
9. Ibid., pp. 321.
10. Gladys Marel García-Peréz, *Insurrection and Revolution: Armed Struggle in Cuba, 1952–1959* (Boulder, Colo.: Lynne Rienner, 1998), p. 85.
11. Guevara, *Episodes,* pp. 319–321; Buch, *Más Allá de los Códigos,* p. 146; Francisco Pividal Padrón, *El Movimiento 26 de Julio en Venezuela y Quienes Lo Apoyaron* (Michoacan, Mexico: Universidad Michoacana de San Nicolás de Hidalgo, 1996); Pinar del Río Coordinator to Fidel Castro and National Directorate, May 29, 1958, Pinar del Río Collection, OAH.
12. Fidel Castro to Alonso "Bebo" Hidalgo, June 3, 1958, Fidel Castro Ruz Collection, OAH.
13. Guevara, *Episodes,* pp. 321.
14. Ibid.
15. U.S. Department of State, Joint Weeka Report no. 17, April 23, 1958, RG 59, 737.00(W)/4–2358, DSR, NA.
16. Marcelo Fernández, "Report to the Executive of the National Directorate: Current State of the Movement," May 31, 1958, OAH; Vilma Espín to Che Guevara, May 30, 1958, Espín Collection, OAH.
17. Marcelo Fernández, Organization Circular, CO-4 to Provincial Coordinators and National Section Chiefs, May 9, 1958, Fernández Collection, OAH.

14. UNITY: "LIKE A MAGIC WORD"

1. According to a recently declassified CIA memorandum written to Allen Dulles, the Cuban army at the time numbered 28,000 men. This number would be more readily available to the American government than the number of Castro rebels, which the same agent believed totalled some 1,200, "excluding administrative and support personnel." The revolutionaries' own reports, however, include numbers no higher than three hundred at the end of 1957 and could not have tripled three months later. See "Secret" Memorandum for Director of Central Intelligence, "Report on [excised portion]'s Visit to the Fidel Castro Headquarters in the Sierra Maestra, 12–26, March, 1958," April 11, 1958, Central Intelligence Agency Openness Program, October 1998 CD-ROM release, National Security Archive, Washington, D.C.
2. "Declarations of the PSP: The Government's Lies about the Strike and the Situation," April 12, 1958, Institute of Cuban History, Havana, Cuba, RG 1, 1/2.4/11.4.A-1/54–60.
3. Information from "Popular Socialist Party: On the Events of April 9 and Perspectives on the Situation in Cuba," April 1958, Institute of Cuban History, Havana, Cuba, RG 1, 1/2.4/11.4-A.1/65–69. The Institute of Cuban History maintained the "classified" status of this document and would not allow me to keep a photocopy as I had for all others, but it did permit me to type the entire document into my computer.
4. National Committee, PSP, "The 26th of July's Situation," May 1, 1958, Institute of Cuban History, Havana, Cuba, RG 1, 1/2.4/11.4.A.2/1–5.
5. Faure Chomón Mediavilla, "Manifesto of the Directorio Revolucionario in Response to the Events of the 9th of April," April 1958, Herbert Matthews Collection, box 2, Columbia University Rare Book and Manuscript Library.
6. Faure Chomón Mediavilla, interview by author, Havana, Cuba, July 8, 1997.
7. Marcelo Fernández to Fidel Castro, June 5, 1958, Fernández Collection, OAH.
8. Fidel Castro to Mario Llerena and Raúl Chibás, April 25, 1958, in Carlos Franqui, *Diario de la Revolución Cubana* (Paris: R. Torres, 1976), p. 427.
9. Enrique Oltuski to Marcelo Fernández, April 30, 1958, Oltuski Collection, OAH, emphasis in original; Mario Villamía to Fidel Castro, May 22, 1958, Exile Collection, OAH.
10. Marcelo Fernández to Provincial Coordinators and National Section Delegates, Organization Circular, CO-4, May 9, 1958, Fernández Collection, OAH.
11. Jorge Rangel [labor], Ricardo Alarcón [students], Carlos [militia] to Fidel Castro and Delegation of the National Directorate Residing in Havana, undated, Underground Collection, OAH.
12. Civic Resistance Movement Circular, May 22, 1958, Underground Collection, OAH; Marcelo Fernández to Provincial Coordinators and National Section Chiefs, Organization Circular, CO-5, June 23, 1958, Fernández Collection, OAH; Marcelo Fernández, "Report to the Executive of the National Directorate: Current State of the Movement," May 31, 1958, Fernández Collection, OAH.
13. Marcelo Fernández, "Report to the Executive of the National Directorate:

Current State of the Movement," May 31, 1958, Fernández Collection, OAH.

14. Ibid., p. 4.

15. Ibid., p. 12.

16. Gladys Marel García-Pérez, *Insurrection and Revolution: Armed Struggle in Cuba, 1952–1959* (Boulder, Colo.: Lynne Rienner, 1998), p. 84.

17. Oral History, Octavio Louit Venzant Bejerano, OAH.

18. Years after García resurfaced as Frank Sturgis in the Watergate break-in scandal, Comandante Manuel Piñeiro Losada, a founder of Cuban intelligence services after the revolution, indicated that after 1959 the new Cuban government came to believe that even during the insurrection García had been an American agent, with orders to sabotage the prestrike weapons deliveries. Though the underground surname García, unaccompanied by a legal name, appears in State Department papers listing the underground and legal names of Cuban exiles involved in weapons smuggling from the United States in 1958, I have seen no additional evidence linking Fiorini directly to the FBI, which at the time was conducting surveillance against the Cuban exiles and could plausibly have worked with Fiorini to interrupt weapons deliveries to the rebels on the ground. See Manuel Piñeiro Losada, interview by author, Havana, Cuba, June 30, 1997; U.S. Department of State, Memorandum of Conversation, February 4, 1958, RG 59, box 5, 737.00/2–458, DSR, NA; and Oral History, Octavio Louit Venzant Bejerano, OAH. Bejerano singled out Fiorini as the individual "most guilty" for the militarization of the April strike. In January 1959, Fiorini was still involved with the rebels. In an AP wire photo, rifle in hand, he was identified as a Cuban rebel captain, standing on top of what the caption describes as "the covered mass grave of 75 followers of ex-dictator Fulgencio Batista who were executed Monday [January 12, 1959] after being convicted of crimes by a Cuban military tribunal" (*The State*, Colombia, S.C., January 14, 1959, p. 1). I am grateful to Neill Macaulay, who also fought with the rebels, for sharing a photocopy of this photograph with me.

19. Marcelo Fernández to Fidel Castro, June 16, 1958, Fernández Collection, OAH. The Joint Weeka reports issued weekly by the U.S. embassy make no mention of American attempts to control the character of an opposition labor front.

20. *Carta Semanal*, May 28, 1958, Institute of Cuban History, Havana, Cuba, RG 1, 1/17/2:28/13/73–80.

21. Marcelo Fernández to Provincial Coordinators and National Section Chiefs, Organization Circular CO-5, June 23, 1958, Fernández Collection, OAH; Marcelo Fernández to Fidel Castro, June 25, 1958, Fernández Collection, OAH.

22. Ricardo Alarcón de Quesada, correspondence to author, May 17, 2001; Ricardo Alarcón de Quesada, interview by author, Havana, Cuba, July 3, 1997.

23. Marcelo Fernández, "Report to the Executive of the National Directorate: Current State of the Movement," May 31, 1958, Fernández Collection, OAH.

24. Ricardo Alarcón de Quesada, correspondence to author, May 17, 2001.
25. Marcelo Fernández, "Report to the Executive of the National Directorate: Current State of the Movement," May 31, 1958, Fernández Collection, OAH.
26. Manuel Urrutia to Fidel Castro, May 14, 1958, Exile Collection, OAH. Emphasis in original.
27. Mario Villamía to Fidel Castro, May 22, 1958, Exile Collection, OAH.
28. Manuel Urrutia to Fidel Castro, May 14, 1958, Exile Collection, OAH.
29. Ibid.
30. U.S. Department of State, Confidential Memorandum of Conversation, "Cuban Political Developments," May 21, 1958, RG 84, box 4, DSR, NA.
31. Manuel Urrutia to Fidel Castro, May 14, 1958, Exile Collection, OAH; José Miró Cardona to Fidel Castro, May 28, 1958, Exile Collection, OAH.
32. U.S. Department of State, Confidential Memorandum of Conversation, "Cuban Political Developments and Uruguayan Support for Cuban Opposition Resolution Condemning Batista," May 21, 1958, RG 84, box 4, DSR, NA.
33. José Miró Cardona to Fidel Castro, May 28, 1958, Exile Collection, OAH.
34. José Miró Cardona, Speech before the Florida Bar Association, May 15, 1958, Exile Collection, OAH.
35. Marcelo Fernández to Fidel Castro, June 5, 1958, Fernández Collection, OAH.
36. Fidel Castro to Ricardo Lorie, June 2, 1958, Fidel Castro Ruz Collection, OAH.
37. Gustavo Arcos to Faustino Pérez, May 1, 1958, Arcos Collection, OAH; Gustavo Arcos to Alonso Hidalgo, May 21, 1958, Arcos Collection, OAH; Ricardo Lorie to Fidel Castro, May 16, 1958, Lorie Collection, OAH; Fidel Castro to Celia Sánchez, May 6, 1958, Fidel Castro Ruz Collection, OAH, and Franqui, *Diario,* p. 437; Fidel Castro to Celia Sánchez, May 8, 1958, Fidel Castro Ruz Collection, OAH, and Franqui, *Diario,* p. 439; Fidel Castro to Celia Sánchez, May 11, 1958, Fidel Castro Ruz Collection, OAH, and Franqui, *Diario,* p. 438; Fidel Castro to Ricardo Lorie, June 2, 1958, Fidel Castro Ruz Collection, OAH; Fidel Castro to Alonso "Bebo" Hidalgo, June 3, 1958, Fidel Castro Ruz Collection, OAH.
38. Marcelo Fernández to Fidel Castro, June 5, 1958, Fernández Collection, OAH. Fernández reprinted part of Raúl Castro's May 1 letter.
39. Buch, *Más Allá de los Códigos* (Havana: Editorial de Ciencias Sociales, 1995), pp. 154–155; Alonso Hidalgo to Fidel Castro, May 1958, Exile Collection, OAH; Ricardo Lorie to Fidel Castro, May 29, 1958, Exile Collection, OAH.
40. Fidel Castro to Ricardo Lorie, June 2, 1958, Fidel Castro Ruz Collection, OAH.

15. THE PACT OF CARACAS

1. María Joséfa Llanusa, interview by author, Havana, Cuba, June 24, 1997.
2. *Las Armas Son de Hierro* (The arms are made of steel) is a 1957 play by poet and playwright Pablo Armando Fernández, winner in 1996 of Cuba's National Book Award. Pablo Armando Fernández, interviews by author, Havana, Cuba, July, 4, 1995, Washington, D.C., September 29, 1995; José Llanusa, interviews

by author, Havana, Cuba, November 14, 1996, June 26, 1997; José Llanusa to Filiberto Zamora, July 4, 1958, Llanusa Collection, OAH; José Llanusa to Haydée Santamaría, July 26, 1958, Llanusa Collection, OAH; Marcelo Fernández to Fidel Castro, June 5, 1958, Fernández Collection, OAH.

3. Ricardo Lorie to Fidel Castro, May 16, 1958, Lorie Collection, OAH; Gustavo Arcos to Alonso "Bebo" Hidalgo, May 21, 1958, Arcos Collection, OAH; Marcelo Fernández to Fidel Castro, June 5, 1958, Fernández Collection, OAH; Mario Llerena to Fidel Castro and National Directorate, June 10, 1958, Llerena Collection, OAH; Manuel Urrutia to Fidel Castro, June 20, 1958, Exile Collection, OAH; Haydée Santamaría to Fidel Castro, June 19, 1958, Santamaría Collection, OAH. Mario Llerena, *The Unsuspected Revolution: The Birth and Rise of Castroism* (Ithaca, N.Y.: Cornell University Press, 1978).

4. Haydée Santamaría to Fidel Castro, May 20, 1958, Santamaría Collection, OAH.

5. José Miró Cardona to Fidel Castro, May 28, 1958, Miró Cardona Collection, OAH.

6. Armando Hart to "Haydée" May 21, 1958, OAH. In August 1958 Hart was transferred from prison at the Boniato military barracks to the Isle of Pines.

7. Ibid.

8. Haydée Santamaría to Fidel Castro, May 21, 1958, Santamaría Collection, OAH.

9. Ibid.

10. Fidel Castro to Haydée Santamaría, June 1, 1958, in Carlos Franqui, *Diario de la Revolución Cubana* (Paris: R. Torres, 1976), p. 460. I do not have access to the original letter, so I cannot compare the version published by Franqui with the original text.

11. Haydée Santamaría to Fidel Castro, June 19, 1958, Santamaría Collection, OAH. For background on the movement's fundraising in and out of Cuba, see Alfred Padula, "Financing Castro's Revolution, 1956–1958," *Revista/Review Interamericana* 8 (Summer 1978): 234–246.

12. In Pividal Padrón, *El Movimiento 26 de Julio en Venezuela y Quienes lo Apoyaron* (San Nicolás de Hidalgo, Mexico: Universidad Michacana, 1996), pp. 252–253.

13. Luis Buch, *Más Allá de los Códigos* (Havana: Editorial de Ciencias Sociales, 1995).

14. Luis Buch to Armando Hart, August 11, 1958, Buch Collection, OAH.

15. Luis Buch to National Directorate, August 20, 1958, Buch Collection, OAH.

16. Luis Buch to Armando Hart, August 11, 1958, Buch Collection, OAH.

17. In Pividal Padrón, *El Movimiento,* pp. 252–253.

18. Ibid., p. 248; Ramón Bonachea and Marta San Martín, *The Cuban Insurrection, 1952–1959* (New Brunswick, N.J.: Transaction, 1974), p. 238.

19. Haydée Santamaría to Fidel Castro, July 10, 1958, Santamaría Collection, OAH; Bonachea and San Martín, *Cuban Insurrection,* p. 240.

20. Haydée Santamaría to Fidel Castro, July 10, 1958, Santamaría Collection, OAH.

21. For a discussion of Operación Antiaérea, see Thomas G. Paterson, *Contesting Castro: The United States and the Triumph of the Cuban Revolution* (New York: Oxford University Press, 1994), pp. 160–172, and Arleigh Burke, chief of naval operations to Joint Chiefs of Staff, July 10, 1958, "Kidnapping of U.S. Citizens by Cuban Rebels, June–July, 1958," in "Cuba," *Foreign Relations of the United States, 1958–1960* (Washington, D.C.: Government Printing Office, 1991), pp. 117–157. Raúl Castro's collection at the OAH contains several documents related to the kidnapping, though I am not aware of any scholarly Cuban account of this episode.

22. Haydée Santamaría to Fidel Castro, July 10, 1958, Santamaría Collection, OAH.

23. Marcelo Fernández to National Section Delegates, Provincial Coordinators, Municipal Coordinators, Organization Circular, CO-6, August 22, 1958, Fernández Collection, OAH.

24. For the text of the Pact of Caracas, see Rolando E. Bonachea and Nelson P. Valdés, eds., *Revolutionary Struggle, 1947–1958*, vol. 1 of *The Selected Works of Fidel Castro* (Cambridge, Mass.: MIT Press, 1972), pp. 386–389.

16. HASTA LA VICTORIA!

1. For the text of the Pact of Caracas, see Rolando E. Bonachea and Nelson P. Valdés, eds., *Revolutionary Struggle, 1947–1958*, vol. 1 of *The Selected Works of Fidel Castro* (Cambridge, Mass.: MIT Press), pp. 386–389; and Ramón Bonachea and Marta San Martín, *The Cuban Insurrection, 1952–1959* (New Brunswick, N.J.: Transaction, 1974), pp. 238–240. Unidad Obrera preceded FONU, the unified labor front that coalesced in November 1958 out of the Frente Obrero Nacional (FON) following the April 1958 general strike.

2. Jon Lee Anderson, *Che Guevara: A Revolutionary Life* (New York: Grove Press, 1997), pp. 319–336; Bonachea and Valdés, *Revolutionary Struggle*, pp. 108–112; and Carlos Franqui, *Diario de la Revolución Cubana* (Paris: R. Torres, 1976), pp. 500–551.

3. Marcelo Fernández to National Section Delegates, Provincial Coordinators, Municipal Coordinators, Organization Circular CO-6, August 22, 1958, Fernández Collection, OAH.

4. Bonachea and Valdés, *Revolutionary Struggle*, pp. 386–389; Bonachea and San Martín, *The Cuban Insurrection*, pp. 238–240; Luis Buch to Comrades of the National Directorate, August 20, 1958, Buch Collection, OAH; and Marcelo Fernández to National Section Delegates, Provincial Coordinators, Municipal Coordinators, Organization Circular CO-6, August 22, 1958, Fernández Collection, OAH. The full text of the accord also appears in Jules Dubois, *Fidel Castro: Rebel Liberator or Dictator?* (Indianapolis: Bobbs-Merrill, 1959), pp. 280–282.

5. Bonachea and Valdés, *Revolutionary Struggle*, pp. 386–389; Bonachea and San Martín, *Cuban Insurrection*, pp. 238–240.

6. Marcelo Fernández to National Section Delegates, Provincial Coordinators, Municipal Coordinators, Organization Circular, CO-6, August 22, 1958, Fernández Collection, OAH.

7. José Miró Cardona to Fidel Castro, August 1958, José Miró Cardona to Luis Buch, August 2, 1958, José Miró Cardona to Secretary of State John Foster Dulles, July 31, 1958, José Miró Cardona to President Eisenhower, August 22, 1958, and José Miró Cardona to Fidel Castro, September 16, 1958, all in Miró Cardona Collection, OAH.

8. Ernesto Che Guevara, *Episodes of the Cuban Revolutionary War, 1956–58*, ed. Mary-Alice Waters (New York: Pathfinder Press, 1996), p. 322; Haydée Santamaría to Fidel Castro, May 21, 1958, Santamaría Collection, OAH; Thomas, *Cuba: The Pursuit of Freedom* (New York: Harper and Row, 1971), pp. 991–992.

9. Marcelo Fernández to National Section Delegates, Provincial Coordinators, Municipal Coordinators, Organization Circular CO-6, August 22, 1958, Fernández Collection, OAH; Marcelo Fernández to Haydée Santamaría, August 19, 1958, Fernández Collection, OAH.

10. José Llanusa to Delio Gomez Ochoa, September 3, 1958, Llanusa Collection, OAH; José Llanusa to Fidel Castro and the National Directorate, December 6, 1958, Llanusa Collection, OAH; Haydée Santamaría to Fidel Castro, October 8, 1958, Santamaría Collection, OAH; Haydée Santamaría to Luis Buch, October 8, 1958, Santamaría Collection, OAH.

11. Faustino Pérez to Leaders of the Havana Labor Section, September 19, 1958, Pérez Collection, OAH.

12. Faustino Pérez to Armando Hart, October 9, 1958, Pérez Collection, OAH.

13. Luis Buch, interview by author, Havana, Cuba, November 5, 1995; Buch, *Más Allá de los Códigos* (Havana: Editorial de Ciencias Sociales, 1995), pp. 175–176.

14. For the Pawley mission, see Thomas G. Paterson, *Contesting Castro: The United States and the Triumph of the Cuban Revolution* (New York: Oxford University Press, 1994), p. 209, and Armando Hart Dávalos, *Aldabonazo* (Havana: Editorial Letras Cubanas, 1997), p. 192.

15. For blow-by-blow accounts of these events, see John Dorschner and Roberto Fabricio, *The Winds of December: The Cuban Revolution, 1958* (New York: Coward, McCann & Geoghegan, 1980). See also "Cuba," *Foreign Relations of the United States, 1958–1960,* Vol. 6 (Washington, D.C.: Government Printing Office, 1991), pp. 226–228: Paterson, *Contesting Castro,* pp. 216–225; and Tad Szulc, *Fidel* (New York: William Morrow, 1986), pp. 457–459.

16. Paterson, *Contesting Castro,* pp. 217–218. Justo Carrillo was involved with Cuban exiles in the planning of the Bay of Pigs Invasion in 1962 to unseat Fidel Castro from power.

17. "Cuba," *Foreign Relations of the United States, 1958–1960,* p. 336.

18. Paterson, *Contesting Castro,* pp. 229–230; ibid., p. 315.

19. For a first-person account of this period and details on Barquín's brief tenure at Camp Colombia, see Hart, *Aldabonazo,* pp. 189–197.

20. Paterson, *Contesting Castro,* pp. 130–147; *Bohemia* 51, no. 2 (January 11,

1959), front cover. The first four issues of *Bohemia* in 1959 contain hundreds of photographs and reports that had been censored from publication during the insurgency. For a discussion of Fidel Castro's arrival and activities in Las Villas, see Enrique Oltuski, *Gente del Llano* (Havana: Imagen Contemporanea, 2000), pp. 231–254.

21. Jorge G. Castañeda, *Compañero: The Life and Death of Che Guevara* (New York: Alfred A. Knopf, 1997), pp. 140–142.

22. Address by Fidel Castro Ruz at "Bay of Pigs: Forty Years Later," a conference sponsored by the National Security Archives and University of Havana, March 22–24, 2001, Havana, Cuba; Ramón Sanchez Parodi, interview with author, Havana, Cuba, February 22, 1995; Thomas, *Cuba,* p. 1033.

23. "Proclama Revolucionaria de Santiago de Cuba y La Sierra Maestra," undated, reproduced in Hart, *Aldabonazo,* pp. 292–297.

24. Department of State Dispatch from the Embassy in Cuba to the Department of State, January 19, 1959, in "Cuba," *Foreign Relations of the United States, 1958–1960,* pp. 370–372. José Llanusa founded Cuba's national sports program and later became minister of education. And Haydée Santamaría founded and directed one of Latin America's most important cultural institutions, Casa de las Americas. She committed suicide in 1980 just months after Celia Sánchez died of cancer.

ABOUT THE RESEARCH

1. Ernesto "Che" Guevara, *Episodes of the Cuban Revolutionary War, 1956–58,* ed. Mary-Alice Waters (New York: Pathfinder Press, 1996), p. 322; and Luis Buch, *Más Allá de los Códigos* (Havana: Editorial de Ciencias Sociales, 1995), p. 143.

2. Carlos Franqui, *Diario de la Revolución Cubana* (Paris: R. Torres, 1976); and Franqui, *Diary of the Cuban Revolution* (New York: Viking Press, 1980).

Bibliography

UNPUBLISHED PERSONAL PAPERS AND RECORDS

Columbia University Rare Book and Manuscript Library, New York, New York
    Herbert L. Matthews Papers
The George Meany Memorial Archives, Silver Spring, Maryland
    Serafino Romualdi Reports
    Jay Lovestone Papers
    International Affairs, Record Group 1–027, Series 9, Sub-series 2, Cuba, 1949–1960
Princeton University Library Rare Books and Special Collections Department
    Carlos Franqui Collection

PAPERS AND RECORDS AT U.S. ARCHIVES AND PRESIDENTIAL ARCHIVES

Central Intelligence Agency Records, Washington, D.C., Freedom of Information Act
Dwight D. Eisenhower Library, Abilene, Kansas
    Dwight D. Eisenhower Papers, Ann Whitman File
    Gordon Gray Papers
    White House Central Files
    White House Office Records
National Archives of the United States, Archives II, Hyattsville, Maryland
    U.S. Department of State Records, Record Group 59, Record Group 84
        Decimal Files
        Lot Files
Naval Historical Center, Washington Navy Yard, Washington, D.C.
    Chief of Naval Operations / Admiral Burke Files

PUBLISHED U.S. GOVERNMENT DOCUMENTS

"American Republics." In *Foreign Relations of the United States, 1955–1957,* vol. 6. Washington, D.C.: U.S. Government Printing Office, 1991.
"Cuba." In *Foreign Relations of the United States, 1958–1960,* vol. 6. Washington, D.C.: U.S. Government Printing Office, 1991.

PAPERS AND RECORDS AT FOREIGN ARCHIVES

Cuban Council of State Office of Historic Affairs, Havana, Cuba
    Roberto Agramonte, Sr., Collection
    Gustavo Arcos Collection
    Juan Almeida Bosque Collection
    Luis Buch Rodríguez Collection
    Fidel Castro Ruz Collection
    Raúl Castro Ruz Collection
    Vilma Espín Guillois Collection
    Exile Collection
    Marcelo Fernández Font Collection
    Ernesto "Che" Guevara de la Serna Collection
    Armando Hart Dávalos Collection
    Alonso Hidalgo Barrios Collection
    Ricardo Lorie Vals Collection
    José Llanusa Goebel Collection
    Mario Llerena Collection
    Pedro Miret Collection
    José Miró Cardona Collection
    Agustín Navarrete Collection
    Enrique Oltuski Asachi Collection
    Frank País García Collection
    Faustino Pérez Hernández Collection
    Pinar del Río Collection
    René Ramos Latour Collection
    Léster Rodríguez Pérez Collection
    Celia Sánchez Manduley Collection
    Haydée Santamaría Cuadrado Collection
    Taras Terlebauka Domitro Collection
    Underground Collection
    Manuel Urrutia Lleó Collection
Institute of Cuban History, Havana, Cuba
    Record Group 1, Papers of the Popular Socialist Party (PSP)

ORAL HISTORIES

Faustino Pérez Hernández, Office of Historic Affairs, Cuban Council of State, Havana, Cuba
Octavio Louit Venzant Bejerano, Office of Historic Affairs, Cuban Council of State, Havana, Cuba
Antonio "Nico" Torres Cherdebeaux, Office of Historic Affairs, Cuban Council of State, Havana, Cuba

INTERVIEWS CONDUCTED BY JULIA SWEIG

Ricardo Alarcón de Quesada, July 3, 1997, Havana, Cuba
Luis Buch Rodríguez, November 5, 1995, Havana, Cuba

Faure Chomón Mediavilla, July 8, 1997, Havana, Cuba
José María Cuestas, June 20, 1996, Havana, Cuba
Armando Hart Dávalos, July 20, 1996; July 8, 1997, Havana, Cuba
Fabian Escalante, November 8, 1995, Havana, Cuba
Pablo Armando Fernández, numerous occasions, 1995–1997, Havana, Cuba and
    Washington, D.C.
José Llanusa Goebels, numerous occasions, 1995–1997, Havana, Cuba
María Josefa Llanusa, numerous occasions, 1995–1997, Havana, Cuba
Enrique Oltuski Asachi, July 5, 1997, Havana, Cuba
Alberto Pérez Clavillar, July 1, 1997, Havana, Cuba
Gerardo Pérez Püelles, November 20, 1995, Havana, Cuba
Manuel Piñeiro Losada, July 24, 1996; June 30, 1997; July 8, 1997, Havana, Cuba
Daniel Rodríguez, July 4, 1997; July 6, 1997, Havana, Cuba
Natalia (Naty) Revuelta, July 4, 1997, Havana, Cuba
Arnold Rodríguez, July 6, 1997, Havana, Cuba
Léster Rodríguez Pérez, November 14, 1995, Havana, Cuba
Ramon Sánchez Parodi, February 22, 1995, Havana, Cuba
Hugo Yedra, June 30, 1997, Havana, Cuba

CORRESPONDENCE TO JULIA SWEIG

Ricardo Alarcón de Quesada, May 17, 2001
Jules Dubois, Jr., July 10, 2001
Ramon Sánchez Parodi, September 27, 1994; May 30, 1996

NEWSPAPERS AND PERIODICALS

Bohemia
Diario de la Marina
Diario Las Americas
Miami Daily News
The Miami News
La Nación, San José, Costa Rica
New York Times
La Prensa, Lima, Peru
La Prensa, Managua, Nicaragua
Revolución
El Tiempo
The Times of Havana

UNDERGROUND CUBAN PRESS

Buletín de la Junta de Liberación Cubana
Carta Semanal
El Cubano Libre
Resistencia Civica
Revolución
Vanguardia Obrera

MEMOIRS, PARTICIPANT ACCOUNTS, AND DOCUMENTARY COLLECTIONS

Alvarez Tabío, Pedro. *Diario de la Guerra, Diciembre de 1956–Febrero de 1957.* Havana: Oficina de Publicaciones del Consejo de Estado, 1986.

Báez, Luis. *Secretos de Generales.* Havana: Editorial Simar, S. A., 1996.

Batista Zaldívar, Fulgencio. *Cuba Betrayed.* New York: Vantage, 1962.

Bethel, Paul. *The Losers.* New Rochelle, N.Y.: Arlington House, 1969.

Bonachea, Rolando E., and Nelson P. Valdés, eds. *Revolutionary Struggle, 1947–1958,* vol. 1 of *The Selected Works of Fidel Castro.* Cambridge, Mass.: MIT Press, 1972.

Brennan, Ray. *Castro, Cuba, and Justice.* Garden City, N.Y.: Doubleday, 1959.

Buch, Luis. *Más Allá de los Códigos.* Havana: Editorial de Ciencias Sociales, 1995.

Carrillo, Justo. *Cuba, 1933: Students, Yankees, and Soldiers.* Coral Gables, Fla.: University of Miami North-South Center, 1994.

Casuso, Teresa. *Castro and Cuba.* New York: Random House, 1961.

Dubois, Jules. *Fidel Castro: Rebel Liberator or Dictator?* Indianapolis: Bobbs-Merrill, 1959.

Espín, Vilma. *1000 Fotos Cuba.* Havana: Commission of Revolutionary Orientation, Partido Comunista Cubano, 1979.

Franqui, Carlos. *Cuba: El Libro de los Doce.* Mexico City: Serie Popular Era, 1966.

———. *Diario de la Revolución Cubana.* Paris: R. Torres, 1976.

———. *Diary of the Cuban Revolution.* New York: Viking, 1980.

Gerassi, John, ed. *Venceremos! The Speeches and Writings of Ernesto Che Guevara.* New York: Macmillan, 1968.

Guevara, Ernesto "Che." *Episodes of the Cuban Revolutionary War, 1956–58,* ed. Mary-Alice Waters. New York: Pathfinder Press, 1996.

———. *Pasajes de la Guerra Revolucionaria.* Havana: Ediciones Unión, 1963.

———. *Reminiscences of the Cuban Revolutionary War.* New York: Monthly Review Press, 1967.

Guevara, Che, and Raúl Castro. *La Conquista de la Esperanza: Diarios Inéditos de la Guerrilla Cubana, Diciembre 1956–Febrero 1957.* Mexico City: Editorial Joaquín Mortiz, 1995.

Hart Dávalos, Armando. *Aldabonazo.* Havana: Editorial Letras Cubanas, 1997.

Hunt, Howard. *Give Us This Day.* New Rochelle, N.Y.: Arlington House, 1973.

Lazo, Mario. *Dagger in the Heart: American Policy Failures in Cuba.* New York: Funk and Wagnalls, 1968.

Llerena, Mario. *The Unsuspected Revolution: The Birth and Rise of Castroism.* Ithaca, N.Y.: Cornell University Press, 1978.

Lockwood, Lee. *Castro's Cuba, Cuba's Fidel.* New York: Vintage, 1969.

Lopéz-Fresquet, Rufo. *My Fourteen Months with Castro.* Cleveland: World, 1966.

Macaulay, Neill. *A Rebel in Cuba: An American Memoir.* Chicago: Quadrangle, 1970.

Matthews, Herbert L. *The Cuban Story.* New York: George Braziller, 1961.

McManus, Jane, ed. *From the Palm Tree: Voices of the Cuban Revolution.* Secaucus, N.J.: Lyle Stuart, 1983.

Meneses, Enrique. *Fidel Castro.* New York: Taplinger, 1966.

Miranda Pelaez, Georgelina. *Las Pascuas Sangrientas: 1957–1987.* Holguín, Cuba: Combinado de Periódicos General Jose Miró Argenter, 1987.

Morán Arce, Lucás. *La Revolución Cubana, 1953–1959: Una Versión Rebelde.* Ponce, P.R.: Universidad Católica, 1980.

Oltuski, Enrique. *Gente del Llano.* Havana: Imagen Contemporanea, 2000.

Pavón, Luis, ed. *Días de Combate.* Havana: Instituto del Libro, 1970.

Phillips, Ruby Hart. *Cuba: Island of Paradox.* New York: McDowell, Obolensky, 1959.

Pividal Padrón, Francisco. *El Movimiento 26 de Julio en Venezuela y Quienes lo Apoyaron.* San Nicolás de Hidalgo, Mexico: Universidad Michoacana, 1996.

Rodríguez Loeches, Enrique. *Bajando del Escambray.* Havana: Editorial Letras Cubanas, 1962.

Smith, Earl E. T. *The Fourth Floor: An Account of the Castro Communist Revolution.* New York: Random House, 1962.

Smith, Wayne S. *The Closest of Enemies: A Personal and Diplomatic History of the Castro Years.* New York: W. W. Norton, 1987.

Taber, Robert. *M-26: Biography of a Revolution.* New York: Lyle Stuart, 1961.

Urrutia Lleó, Manuel. *Fidel Castro and Company, Inc.: Communist Tyranny in Cuba.* New York: Praeger, 1964.

Varona, Manuel Antonio de. *El Drama de Cuba o la Revolución Traicionada.* Buenos Aires: Editorial Marymar, 1960.

Ventura Novo, Esteban. *Memorias.* Mexico City: Imprenta León M. Sánchez, 1961.

SECONDARY BOOKS AND ARTICLES

Ameringer, Charles D. "The Auténtico Party and the Political Opposition in Cuba, 1952–1957." *Hispanic American Historical Review* 65 (May 1985): 327–352.

Anderson, Jon Lee. *Che Guevara: A Revolutionary Life.* New York: Grove Press, 1997.

Benjamin, Jules R. *The United States and the Origins of the Cuban Revolution: An Empire for Liberty in an Age of National Liberation.* Princeton, N.J.: Princeton University Press, 1990.

Bethell, Leslie. *Cuba: A Short History.* Cambridge: Cambridge University Press, 1993.

Bonachea, Ramón, and Marta San Martín. *The Cuban Insurrection, 1952–1959.* New Brunswick, N.J.: Transaction, 1974.

Carr, Barry. "Identity, Class, and Nation: Black Immigrant Workers, Cuban Communism, and the Sugar Insurgency, 1925–1934." *Hispanic American Historical Review* 78 (Feb. 1998): 83–116.

Castañeda, Jorge G. *Compañero: The Life and Death of Che Guevara.* New York: Alfred A. Knopf, 1997.

Córdova, Efrén. *Castro and the Cuban Labor Movement: Statecraft and Strategy in a Revolutionary Period, 1959–1961.* Lanham, Md.: University Press of America, 1987.

Darushenkov, Oleg. *Cuba, el Camino de la Revolución,* 3d ed. Moscow: Editorial Progreso, 1984.

Debray, Régis. *Revolution in the Revolution? Armed Struggle and Political Struggle in Latin America.* New York: Monthly Review Press, 1967.

Desnoes, Edmundo, ed. *La Sierra y El Llano.* Havana: Casa de las Americas, 1961.

Domínguez, Jorge I. *Cuba: Order and Revolution.* Cambridge, Mass.: The Belknap Press of Harvard University Press, 1979.

Dorschner, John, and Roberto Fabricio. *The Winds of December: The Cuban Revolution, 1958.* New York: Coward, McCann & Geoghegan, 1980.

Draper, Theodore. *Castroism: Theory and Practice.* New York: Praeger, 1965.

———. *Castro's Revolution: Myths and Realities.* New York: Praeger, 1962.

Farber, Samuel. "The Cuban Communists in the Early Stages of the Cuban Revolution: Revolutionaries or Reformists?" *Latin American Research Review* 18, no. 1 (1983): 59–84.

García Montes, Jorge, and Antonio Avila. *Historia del Partido Comunista de Cuba.* Miami: Ediciones Universal, 1970.

García Pérez, Gladys Marel. *Insurrection and Revolution: Armed Struggle in Cuba, 1952–1959.* Boulder, Colo.: Lynne Rienner, 1998.

Gellman, Irwin F. *Roosevelt and Batista: Good Neighbor Diplomacy in Cuba, 1933–1945.* Albuquerque: University of New Mexico Press, 1973.

González, Edward. *Cuba under Castro: The Limits of Charisma.* Boston: Houghton Mifflin, 1974.

Gosse, Van. *Where the Boys Are: Cuba, Cold War America, and the Making of a New Left.* London: Verso, 1993.

Harnecker, Marta. *Fidel Castro: De Moncada a la Victoria.* Buenos Aires: Editorial Contrapunto, 1985.

Hinckle, Warren, and William W. Turner. *Deadly Secrets: The CIA-Mafia War against Castro and the Assassination of J. F. K.* New York: Thunder's Mouth Press, 1992.

Ignacio Taíbo, Paco, II. *Guevara, Also Known as Che.* New York: St. Martin's, 1997.

Judson, Fred C. *Cuba and the Revolutionary Myth: The Political Education of the Cuban Rebel Army, 1953–1963.* Boulder, Colo.: Westview Press, 1984.

Karol, K. S. *Guerrillas in Power: The Course of the Cuban Revolution.* New York: Hill & Wang, 1970.

Kirkpatrick, Lyman. *The Real CIA.* New York: Macmillan, 1968.

Martin, Lionel. *The Early Fidel: Roots of Castro's Communism.* Secaucus, N.J.: Lyle Stuart, 1978.

Mesa-Lago, Carmelo. "Cuba: The Socialist Model." In his *Market, Socialist, and Mixed Economies: Comparative Policy and Performance, Chile, Cuba and Costa Rica.* Baltimore: Johns Hopkins University Press, 2000.

———. *The Labor Force, Employment, Unemployment, and Underemployment in Cuba, 1899–1970.* Beverly Hills, Calif.: Sage Publications, 1972.

Morley, Morris H. *Imperial State and Revolution: The United States and Cuba, 1952–1986.* New York: Cambridge University Press, 1987.

Nieves, Dolores, and Alina Feijóo, eds. *Semillas de Fuego,* vol. 1: *Compilación Sobre la Lucha Clandestina en la Capital.* Havana: Editorial de Ciencias Sociales, 1989.

————. *Semillas de Fuego,* vol. 2: *Compilación Sobre la Lucha Clandestina en la Capital.* Havana: Editorial de Ciencias Sociales, 1990.

O'Connor, James. *The Origins of Socialism in Cuba.* Ithaca, N.Y.: Cornell University Press, 1970.

Ordoqui, Joaquin. *Elementos para la Historia del Movimiento Obrero en Cuba.* Havana: Editorial CTC-R, 1960.

Padula, Alfred. "Financing Castro's Revolution, 1956–1958," *Revista/Review Interamericana* 8 (Summer 1978): 234–246.

Paterson, Thomas G. *Contesting Castro: The United States and the Triumph of the Cuban Revolution.* New York: Oxford University Press, 1994.

Pérez, Louis A., Jr. *Army Politics in Cuba, 1898–1958.* Pittsburgh: University of Pittsburgh Press, 1976.

————. *Cuba and the United States: Ties of Singular Intimacy.* Athens: University of Georgia Press, 1990.

————. *The Cuban Revolutionary War, 1953–1958: A Bibliography.* Metuchen, N.J.: Scarecrow, 1976.

————. *On Becoming Cuban: Identity, Nationality, and Culture.* Chapel Hill, N.C.: University of North Carolina Press, 1999.

Pérez-Stable, Marifeli. *The Cuban Revolution: Origins, Course, and Legacy.* New York: Oxford University Press, 1993.

————. "Reflections on Political Possibilities: Cuba's Peaceful Transition That Wasn't, 1954–1956." Occasional Paper Series, no. 1, Cuban Research Institute, Florida International University, September 1998.

Quirk, Robert. *Fidel Castro.* New York: Norton, 1993.

Roca, Blas. *The Cuban Revolution: Report to the Eighth National Congress of the PSP of Cuba.* New York: New Century, 1961.

Rodríguez, Renán Ricardo. *El Héroe del Silencio.* Havana: Editora Política, 1986.

Sims, Harold D. "Cuban Labor and the Communist Party, 1937–1958: An Interpretation." *Cuban Studies* 15 (Winter 1985): 43–58.

Smith, Wayne S. *The Closest of Enemies: A Personal and Diplomatic History of the Castro Years.* New York: W. W. Norton, 1987.

Suárez, Andrés. "The Cuban Revolution: The Road to Power." *Latin American Research Review* 7 (Fall 1972): 5–29.

Suchlicki, Jaime. *Cuba: From Columbus to Castro.* McLean, Va.: Brassey's (U.S.), 1990.

————. *University Students and Revolution in Cuba, 1920–1968.* Coral Gables, Fla.: University of Miami Press, 1969.

Szulc, Tad. *Fidel: A Critical Portrait.* New York: William Morrow, 1986.

Thomas, Hugh. *Cuba: The Pursuit of Freedom.* New York: Harper and Row, 1971.

Valdés, Nelson. "Ideological Roots of the Cuban Revolutionary Movement." Occasional Paper no. 15, University of Glasgow Institute of Latin American Studies, 1975.

Welch, Richard E., Jr. *Response to Revolution: The United States and the Cuban Revolution, 1959–1961.* Chapel Hill: University of North Carolina Press, 1985.

Zeitlin, Maurice. *Revolutionary Politics and the Cuban Working Class.* Princeton, N.J.: Princeton University Press, 1967.

DISSERTATIONS AND OTHER UNPUBLISHED MATERIALS

Alvarez Tabío, Pedro. "Frank País," paper delivered in Santiago de Cuba, November 1996, courtesy of author.

García Pérez, Gladys Marel. "Cuba: Identidad y Cultura en la Revolución del '59," Research Paper, September 1995, Latin American Studies Association Nineteenth International Congress, Washington, D.C.

Ibarra Guitart, Jorge Renato. "Sociedad de Amigos de la República: Crisis de los Partidos Políticos en Cuba (1955–1958)," Research Paper, September 1995, Latin American Studies Association Nineteenth International Congress, Washington, D.C.

Jenkins, David Robert. "Initial American Responses to Fidel Castro, 1957–1959." Ph.D. diss., University of Texas at Austin, 1992.

Valdés, Nelson P. "The Cuban Rebellion: Internal Organization and Strategy, 1952–1959," Ph.D. diss., University of New Mexico, 1978.

Index